CHEROKEE DESCENDANTS WEST

AN INDEX TO THE
GUION MILLER APPLICATIONS

VOLUME III (N-Z)

Cherokee Potter Maude French Welch and her
granddaughter "Koodaloo" Joyce Welch Tranter

TRANSCRIBED BY
JEFF BOWEN
NATIVE STUDY
Gallipolis, Ohio
USA

Copyright © 2011
by Jeff Bowen

ALL RIGHTS RESERVED
No part of this publication may be reproduced
or used in any form or manner whatsoever
without previous written permission from the
copyright holder or publisher.

Originally published:
Baltimore, Maryland
2011

Reprinted by:

Native Study LLC
Gallipolis, OH
www.nativestudy.com

Library of Congress Control Number: 2020915858

ISBN: 978-1-64968-037-2

Made in the United States of America.

Other Books and Series by Jeff Bowen

1901-1907 Native American Census Seneca, Eastern Shawnee, Miami, Modoc, Ottawa, Peoria, Quapaw, and Wyandotte Indians (Under Seneca School, Indian Territory)

1932 Census of The Standing Rock Sioux Reservation with Births And Deaths 1924-1932

Census of The Blackfeet, Montana, 1897- 1901 Expanded Edition

Eastern Cherokee by Blood, 1906-1910, Volumes I thru XIII

Choctaw of Mississippi Indian Census 1929-1932 with Births and Deaths 1924-1931 Volume I

Choctaw of Mississippi Indian Census 1933, 1934 & 1937, Supplemental Rolls to 1934 & 1935 with Births and Deaths 1932-1938, and Marriages 1936-1938 Volume II

Eastern Cherokee Census Cherokee, North Carolina 1930-1939 Census 1930-1931 with Births And Deaths 1924-1931 Taken By Agent L. W. Page Volume I

Eastern Cherokee Census Cherokee, North Carolina 1930-1939 Census 1932-1933 with Births And Deaths 1930-1932 Taken By Agent R. L. Spalsbury Volume II

Eastern Cherokee Census Cherokee, North Carolina 1930-1939 Census 1934-1937 with Births and Deaths 1925-1938 and Marriages 1936 & 1938 Taken by Agents R. L. Spalsbury And Harold W. Foght Volume III

Seminole of Florida Indian Census, 1930-1940 with Birth and Death Records, 1930-1938

Texas Cherokees 1820-1839 A Document For Litigation 1921

Choctaw By Blood Enrollment Cards 1898-1914 Volumes I thru XVII

Starr Roll 1894 (Cherokee Payment Rolls) Districts: Canadian, Cooweescoowee, and Delaware Volume One

Starr Roll 1894 (Cherokee Payment Rolls) Districts: Flint, Going Snake, and Illinois Volume Two

Starr Roll 1894 (Cherokee Payment Rolls) Districts: Saline, Sequoyah, and Tahlequah; Including Orphan Roll Volume Three

Other Books and Series by Jeff Bowen

Cherokee Intruder Cases Dockets of Hearings 1901-1909 Volumes I & II

Indian Wills, 1911-1921 Records of the Bureau of Indian Affairs Books One thru Seven;

Native American Wills & Probate Records 1911-1921

Turtle Mountain Reservation Chippewa Indians 1932 Census with Births & Deaths, 1924-1932

Chickasaw By Blood Enrollment Cards 1898-1914 Volume I thru V

Cherokee Descendants East An Index to the Guion Miller Applications Volume I
Cherokee Descendants West An Index to the Guion Miller Applications Volume II (A-M)

Visit our website at **www.nativestudy.com** to learn more about these and other books and series by Jeff Bowen

This book is dedicated to Joyce Welch Tranter (Koo da loo). A very special and dear true-blood Cherokee without whose inspiration and friendship this work would not be so meaningful.

                        Love you and God bless.

NATIONAL ARCHIVES MICROFILM PUBLICATIONS

INTRODUCTION

On the 348 rolls of this microfilm publication are reproduced the applications submitted for shares of the money that was appropriated for the Eastern Cherokee Indians by the Congress on June 30, 1906. The Eastern Cherokee applications, August 29, 1906 - May 26, 1909, are part of the Guion Miller Enrollment Records that are among the records of the U.S. Court of Claims. This publication also includes a general index to Eastern Cherokee applications (two vols.).

History

Before the U.S. Court of Claims was established in 1855 there was no procedure by which claims arising against the U.S. Government could be enforced by suit. Consideration of claims was provided for when the Treasury Department was established in 1789; later acts of the Congress authorized the Department to settle all claims by or against the Government. If a claim was rejected by the Treasury Department, the claimant's only course of action was to appeal directly to the Congress. Petitions to that body for relief had become so numerous by the middle of the 19th century that the Congress was beginning to find it impossible to make the proper and necessary investigations for actions on the claims.

The U.S. Court of Claims was established by an act of February 24, 1855, to hear claims against the United States including those referred to the court by the Congress, based on any law of the Congress, any regulation of an executive department, or any contract with the Government, whether explicit or implied. Under this act the court served only as a fact finding agency, and its conclusions were submitted to the Congress for approval and for the granting of awards. In 1863 the Congress enlarged the court's jurisdiction and gave it authority to render judgments against the Government, with the right of appeal to the Supreme Court. An act of 1925 abolished appeals from the Court of Claims to the Supreme Court and substituted writs of certiorari.

An act approved July 1, 1902 (32 Stat. 726), gave the Court of Claims jurisdiction over any claim arising under treaty stipulations that the Cherokee Tribe, or any band thereof, might have against the United States and over any claims that the United States might have against any Cherokee Tribe or band. Suit for such a claim was to be instituted within 2 years after the act was approved. As a result, three suits were brought before the court concerning grievances arising out of the treaties:

NATIONAL ARCHIVES MICROFILM PUBLICATIONS

(1) *The Cherokee Nation* v. *The United States*, General-Jurisdiction Case No. 23199; (2) *The Eastern and Emigrant Cherokees* v. *The United States*, General-Jurisdiction Case No. 23212; and (3) *The Eastern Cherokees* v. *The United States*, General-Jurisdiction Case No. 23214.

On May 18, 1905, the court decided in favor of the Eastern Cherokees and instructed the Secretary of the Interior to identify the persons entitled to participate in the distribution of funds for payment of the claims. On June 30, 1906, the Congress appropriated more than $1 million for this purpose. The task of compiling a roll of eligible persons was begun by Guion Miller, special agent of the Interior Department. In a decree of April 29, 1908, the court (1) vacated that part of its earlier decision that had given the Secretary of the Interior responsibility for determing[sic] the eligbility[sic] of claimants and (2) appointed Miller as a special commissioner of the Court of Claims.

The same decree also provided that the fund was to be distributed to all Eastern and Western Cherokee Indians who were alive on May 28, 1906, who could establish the fact that at the time of the treaties they were members of the Eastern Cherokee Tribe or were descendants of such persons, and that they had not been affiliated with any tribe of Indians other than the Eastern Cherokee or the Cherokee Nation. The decree further provided that claimants should already have applications on file with the Commissioner of Indian Affairs, or should file such applications with the special commissioner of the Court of Claims on or before August 31, 1907. Additionally, applications for minors and persons of unsound mind were to be filed by their parents or persons having their care and custody, and applications for persons who had died after May 28, 1906, were to be filed by their children or legal representatives.

In his report of May 28, 1909, Miller stated that 45,847 separate applications had been filed, representing a total of about 90,000 individual claimants, 30,254 of whom were enrolled as entitled to share in the fund – 3,203 residing east and 27,051 residing west of the Mississippi River. On June 10, 1909, the court confirmed and approved the roll, submitted by Miller in his report, of Eastern Cherokees who were entitled to a share of the fund except "so much as shall be expected [excepted] to on or before August 30, 1909." After the exceptions had been filed and investigated, Miller submitted a supplemental report and roll to the court on January 5, 1910. In this report he stated that about 11,750 exceptions had been made, that the names of 610 persons [238 east and 372 west if the Mississippi] had been added to the roll, and that the names of 44 persons [5 east and 39 west of the Mississippi] had be stricken from the roll because clerical errors in enrollment had been discovered. Thus the final figure on the total number of persons entitled to share in the fund was 30, 820, of which 3,436

NATIONAL ARCHIVES MICROFILM PUBLICATIONS

persons resided east and 27,384 resided west of the Mississippi River. On March 15, 1910, the court finally decreed that the rolls be approved and that, after certain deductions for expenditures, payments were to be made equally among the Eastern Cherokees who enrolled. The court also authorized the Secretary of the Treasury to issue a warrant in favor of each person.

In certifying the eligibility of the Cherokees, Miller used earlier census lists and rolls that had been made of the Cherokees by Hester, Chapman, Drennen and others between 1835 and 1884. Copies of some of these rolls and the indexes to them are filed with the Miller records [filmed as M685]. Other enrollment records used by Miller are among the classified subject files of the Bureau and are designated as "33931-11-053 Cherokee Nation."

Records

The applications contain sworn evidences of identity and were filed with the Interior Department's Office of Indian Affairs until April 29, 1907 [the last application was No. 22268], after which the applications were filed directly with the court. The application required each claimant to state fully his or her English and Indian names, residence, age, place of birth, name of husband or wife, name of tribe, and names of children. It further required the English and Indian names of the claimant's parents and grandparents, place of their birth, place of their residence in 1851 if they were living at that time, dates of their death, and a statement as to whether any of them had ever before been enrolled as Indians for annuities or other benefits and, if so, with what tribe. Each claimant was also to furnish the names of all brothers and sisters, with their ages and residences, and the names and residences of all uncles and aunts. Applications were required to be made under oath and to be supported by affidavits of two witnesses who were well acquainted with the applicant. With each application is a card showing final action taken and the reasons therefore. Filed with many of the applications are inquiries concerning the status of the cases, requests for further evidence, protests about unfavorable actions, form letters that had been sent by the special commissioner to the applicants as notices of rejection of their applications and returned by the Post Office Department as unclaimed, affidavits and statements of witnesses, powers of attorney, and last wills and testaments. The applications are arranged by the number assigned at the time the application was received. There are some gaps in the application numbers; these are explained on insert sheets at the appropriate places on the film. The index is arranged alphabetically by name [either English or Indian] of claimant.

NATIONAL ARCHIVES MICROFILM PUBLICATIONS

Many of the files contain a cross-reference card to other applications. This cross-reference card often refers to the EX file, the report on exceptions filed by Miller on January 5, 1910.

Related Records

The records reproduced in this microfilm publication are part of the records in the custody of the National Archives and Records Service [NARS] designated as Records of the U.S. Court of Claims, Record Group [RG] 123. Among related records in this record group are additional records relating to Miller's enrollment of the Eastern Cherokees. These include receipts for Treasury warrants and miscellaneous correspondence, 1906 - 11. The original of these records is in RG 123; a copy is in RG 75.

Some related records in Records of the Bureau of Indian Affairs, RG 75, have been reproduced as NARS Microfilm Publication T496, *Census Roll, 1835, of the Cherokee Indians East of the Mississippi and Index to the Roll.* Also in RG 75 are the classified subject files of the Bureau.

Records Relating to Enrollment of Eastern Cherokees by Guion Miller, 1908-10, M685, contains the general index to Eastern Cherokee applications, 2 volumes; the report submitted by Guion Miller, May 28, 1909, 10 volumes; the roll of Eastern Cherokees, May 28, 1909; the report on exceptions filed, January 5, 1910; the supplemental roll of Eastern Cherokees, January 5, 1910; transcripts of testimony, February, 1908 - March, 1909, 10 volumes; various indexes and rolls of Eastern Cherokee Indians, 1851, 1854, and 1884; and miscellaneous notes and drafts.

Additional records relating to the enrollment of Eastern Cherokee Indians are in Records of the Office of the Secretary of the Interior, Record Group 48.

These records were prepared for filming by Jestine Turner and William D. Grover, who also prepared these introductory remarks.

THE EASTERN CHEROKEES

           v.   No. 23,214

THE UNITED STATES

ORDER.

Ordered this 10th day of June, 1909, that the report of Special Commissioner Guion Miller, bearing date the 28th day of May, 1909, together with the exhibits therewith, including the roll of the individual Eastern Cherokees reported by the said Special Commissioner as entitled to participate in the fund arising from Item 2 of the judgment filed in this cause, be received and filed in this cause.

2. It is further ordered that the said Special Commissioner cause the said roll of individual Eastern Cherokees found by him to be entitled to share in said fund, to be printed and distributed.

3. It is further ordered hat the said roll of individual Eastern Cherokees entitled to share in the fund arising from the judgment in this cause, as reported by Special Commissioner Guion Miller on the 28th day of May, 1909, be and the same is hereby approved, ratified and confirmed, except as to so much of the same as shall be specially excepted to on or before the 30th day of August, 1909. All such exceptions shall be forwarded to the Clerk of the Court of Claims, Washington, D.C., and shall be in writing, and shall state fully the grounds upon which such exceptions are based, and shall be supported by an affidavit of a person having knowledge of the facts and shall contain the name, age and post office address of each individual claimed

to have been omitted from said roll, or to have been improperly placed thereon. Said exceptions and affidavits shall be filed in duplicate in each case, but only the originals must be sworn to. In case an exception is filed on behalf of an individual whose name has been omitted from said roll the said exception shall set forth fully the English and Indian name, the ancestor through whom claim is made, who was living in 1835 or 1851, and shall give the age of said ancestor in 1835 or 1851. Such exceptions must further state the number of the claimant's application. All such exceptions shall be set down for hearing on the third Monday in October, 1909.

Sample Application

The following information obtained from Microfilm M1104- Roll # *104*, Cherokee (Eastern & Western) Applications of the U.S. Court of Claims.

Application No. *10258*		**Action:**	*Admitted*	
Name: *Sequichie Squirrel*	and	*X*		children.

Residence: *Cookson, OK*

Reasons: *Appl. was enrolled by Chapman as No. 242. Father of #4855, claims through same source.*
Misc. Test 3327 & 3523

Commissioner of Indian Affairs,   Washington, D.C.

Sir:
  I hereby make application for such share as may be due me of the fund appropriated by the Act of Congress, approved June 30, 1906, in accordance with the Decrees of the Court of Claims of May 18, 1905, and May 28, 1906, in favor of the Eastern Cherokees. The evidence of identity is herewith subjoined.

1. State full name:
   English name: *Sequichie Squirrel*

   Indian name: *Si qui tse   Sa lo li*

2. Residence: *Ills Dict*[sic] *Cherokee Nation Ind. Ty.*

3. Town and post office: *Cookson Ind. Ty*

4. County: *Cherokee Nation*   5. State: *Indian Territory*

6. Date and place of birth: *1840 Cherokee Co, North Carolinia*[sic]

Sample Application

7. By what right do you claim to share? If you claim through more than one relative living in 1851, set forth each claim separately: *By being on the Roll of 1851. My father U-cluh no ta Sa lo li; my mother Ann Da ya ne; my grandfather N tlu no do; my grandfather on mother's side Johnson Gees Kee U li gv da; my aunt Da Gi; my niece Da tle vv sdo; my ½ bro. U lv ne nv; For my grandfather's ½ uncle I tsu la lv.*

8. Are you married? *No*

9. Name and age of wife or husband: *None*

10. Give names of your father and mother, and your mother's name before marriage:

    Father - English name:

        Indian name: *U cluh no ta Sa lo li*

    Mother - English name: *Ann*

        Indian name: *Da ya*

        Maiden name:

11. Where were they born?

    Father: *In Cherokee Co, North Carolinia[sic]*

    Mother: *In Cherokee Co, North Carolinia[sic]*

12. Where did they reside in 1851, if living at that time

    Father: *In Cherokee Co, NC*   Mother: *In Cherokee Co, NC*

Sample Application

13. Date of death of your father and mother:

Father: *1894*   Mother: *died 18??* *(unable to read)*

14. Were they ever enrolled for annuities, land or other benefits? If so, state when and where:

Yes, on Roll of 1851 East. They never did come to the Cherokee N. West but died in North Carolina.

15. Name all your brothers and sisters, giving ages, and if not living, the date of death:

1)   *½ Sister   A-li se ni de nei   D: about 1867*

2)   *½ Bro   U lv ne nv   D: about 1863*

16. State English and Indian names of your grandparents on both father's and mother's side, if possible:

Father's side: *U tlu no da*

Unknown

Mother's side: *Johnson Gees Kee;   U-li gv da*

Unknown

17. Where were they born? *In Cherokee Co. North Carolinia*[sic]

18. Where did they reside in 1851, if living at that time? *In Cherokee Co. North Carolinia*[sic]

Sample Application

19. Give names of all their children, and residence, if living, if not living, give dates of death:

1) *U cluh no ta Sa lo li   my father [dead]*

2) *Ann   Cherokee Da ya ne   my mother [dead]*

3) *Da tle vv sda   killed during Civil War*

4) *Dick Johnson   about 1868*

5) *Da tsv s*

6) *Aunt Da gi   died before Civil War*

20. Have you ever been enrolled for annuities, land or other benefits? If so, state when and where *Yes.*
On Roll of 1851 East on Roll of 1880 and all authenticated rolls since made a Cherokee allottee on Dawes Commission

21. To expedite identification, claimants should given the full English and Indians names, if possible, of their paternal and maternal ancestors back to 1835:

REMARKS
(Under this head the applicant may give any additional information that he believes will assist in proving his claim.)

A full blood Cherokee

Sample Application

I solemnly swear that the foregoing statements made by me re true to the best of my knowledge and belief.

(Signature) *Sequichie* x *Squirrel*
                his ... *mark*

Subscribed and sworn to before me this *8th* day of *Jan.*, 1907.

Notary Public *W. C. Davis*

INTRODUCTION

There are many Native American rolls but most of the time that's exactly what they are, census rolls.

These are the Guion Miller Application numbers both accepted and rejected. They were applying for monies from the annuities that were granted to the Cherokee Nation in the years 1835-6 and 1846 but were never paid out. In this multiple-volume set you will find that over 45,000 applications were processed representing approximately 90,000 people. Many of these applications cross reference to each other time and again. The ability to cross reference alone will possibly bring out family names never before heard.

These applications contain letters from lawyers, relatives, and friends as well as personal statements regarding their background, birth, death dates and references to other Cherokee rolls. You can find this film in the National Archives publication *American Indians*. It is under the 'U.S. Court of Claims (Record Group 123), Eastern Cherokee Applications of the U.S. Court of Claims, 1906 - 1909; M1104; there are 348 rolls of this film.

You will find an index of the Eastern and Western Cherokee Applications and any supplemental lists later provided in this series. A replicated sample of an application form is provided from the actual film in each volume.

This series *Cherokee Descendants* was completed by this author during the mid to late 1990's. Since then I have transcribed a complete series titled *Eastern Cherokee By Blood 1906-1910*, twelve volumes, completed in 2009.

There have been several questions as to what the differences are between the two series. *Cherokee Descendants* is an index that contains the head of household, their Miller Roll number, and their family members with age and relation of each. In *Eastern Cherokee By Blood 1906-1910*, it again has the head of household and Miller Roll number but contains an abstract of each enrollee's case and the disposition (admitted or rejected). These volumes differ in the form of information, *Cherokee Descendants* possibly holds thousands of names as an index that *Eastern Cherokee By Blood* does not because of its form as an abstract and not an index where all family members would be mentioned.

So in actuality the two series complement each other with information from two different sets of archival records.

Jeff Bowen
Gallipolis, Ohio
NativeStudy.com

Roll *of* Eastern Cherokees

ENTITLED TO PARTICIPATE IN THE FUND ARISING FROM THE JUDGMENT OF THE COURT OF CLAIMS OF MAY 28, 1906

AS REPORTED BY

GUION MILLER, SPECIAL COMMISSIONER

May twenty-eight, nineteen hundred and nine

CHEROKEE DESCENDANTS RESIDING WEST OF MISSISSIPPI RIVER.
VOLUME III   (N – Z)

Key: Guion Miller Application Number; Name; Address, Relation (to Head); Age in 1906

[NA, Thompson. See #10587]   *(Note: entry separate from other family groups)*

31789 NADING, Pearl, Hudson, OK, 23; Ethel M, D, 5; Glenn A, S, 3; Irene L, D, 1
8351 NAKEDHEAD, Harlan, Evansville, AR, 50; 5329, Lizzie, W, 47; Tom, S, 18; John, S, 8
8349 NAKEDHEAD, Jack, Evansville, AR, 26
17077 NAKEDHEAD, James, Long, OK, 50; Jinny, D, 4; Rachel, D, 1
8978 NAKEDHEAD, John, Evansville, AR, 26; 5684, Narcissa, W, 26; 5684, James, S, 2 [Died 5-23-1908]
5874 NAKEDHEAD, Lizzie, Tullahassee, OK, D, 16; Sammie, S, 12; By Martha Napier, Gdn.
16763 NAKEDHEAD, Sallie, Long, OK, 32; Eagle Israel, S, 5; Jennie, D, 2
16725 NALL, Sarah, Kinnison, OK, 26; Morris L, S, 6; Mildred E, D, 4; William E, S, 2
1604 NALL, Joella, Pensacola, OK, 42; Dora Ella, D, 13; Josie Esther, D, 11; Georgia A, D, 4; Mary A, D, 1/7
23775 NANCE, Lula M, Fairland, OK, 17
1111 NANCE, Sarah A, Fairland, OK, 44; Walter S, S, 4; William M, S, 6; Mary J, D, 10; James E, S, 12; Claud W, S, 16; John F, S, 19
25966 NASH, Corinne, Ft. Gibson, OK, 21
1165½ NASH, Edwin O, Ft. Gibson, OK, 16;   By Florian H. Nash, Gdn.
25963 NASH, Fanny Elizabeth, Ft. Gibson, OK, 31
25967 Nash, Florian Harradan, Jr, Ft. Gibson, OK, S, 14
25968 NASH, Francis Ayer, Ft. Gibson, OK, 29
25965 NASH, Hilda, Ft. Gibson, OK, 19
1494 NASH, Lewis R, Ft. Gibson, OK, 42; Fairy Fawn, D, 15; Edgar Ross, S, 13; Dorothy M, S, 7; Clarence E, S, 1
25964 NASH, Lucy Morgan, Ft. Gibson, OK, 25
8807 NAVE, Andrews[sic] R, Tahlequah, OK, 53; George, S, 19; Fannie B, D, 16; Myrtle Ida, D, 14; Susie M, D, 8
30267 NAVE, Andrew R, Jr, Tahlequah, OK, 23
17801 NAVE, Charles Robert, McAlester, OK, 30
30264 NAVE, Ella C, Tahlequah, OK, 26
5534 NAVE, Henry D, Tahlequah, OK, 37; John M, S, 1
882 NAVE, Joseph, Tiawah, OK, 49; Alfred, S, 12; Joseph, Jr, S, 17
26171 NAVE, Thomas, Gideon, OK, 28; Louis E, S, 5; Leon S, S, 3; Ruby M, D, 1
102 NAVE, Walter D, Claremore, OK, 47
3162 NAZWORTHY, Hannah, Vinita, OK, 43; Spurlock, Louis, Vinita, OK, S, 14; Spurlock, Harden, S, 16
109 NEAL, James, Sr, McLain, OK, 74
985 NEAL, James, Jr, Inola, OK, 31 [Died 9-'06]; 35481, Richard, Jr, S, 6; 35481, Florence Ethel, D, 2;   By Joe[sic] W. Neal, Wife and Mother.
144 NEAL, Richard, McLain, OK, 22; James Carl, S, 2;   By Bessie L. Neal, Wife and Mother.
27083 NEAL, Samuel Henry, McLain, OK, 30

CHEROKEE DESCENDANTS RESIDING WEST OF MISSISSIPPI RIVER.
VOLUME III (N – Z)

Key: Guion Miller Application Number; Name; Address, Relation (to Head); Age in 1906

[NEBEL, Laura F. See #12558]   *(Note: entry separate from other family groups)*

10952 NED, John, Muldrow, OK, 33
12558 NEBEL, Laura F, San Francisco, CA, 1280 46th Ave, 34; 12556, Bowley, Alton F, S, 16
17022 NEDSON, Leach, Stilwell, OK, 25

[NEE-DA-GAR-GAH. See #6978]   *(Note: entry separate from other family groups)*

28714 NEEDHAM, John S, Dewey, OK, 24
31545 NEEDHAM, Valentine W, Dewey, OK, 24; Alice A, D, 4; Thomas R, S, 2

[NEEDLES, Jug. See #24434]   *(Note: entry separate from other family groups)*

23906 NEEL, Sarah A, Gideon, OK, 19; Ola May, D, ¼
30099 NEELEY, Noley, Oglesby, OK, 21; Iva Florence, D, 1
8350 NEELEY, Smith, Stilwell, OK, 50; 5327, Lucinda, W, 49; James, S, 13
4229 NEFF, Sarah F, Stilwell, OK, 34; Jim, S, 15; Mary, D, 13; Ada, D, 10; Edgar [Thomas E.], S, 7; Watie, D, 3; Jesse E, S, 1
7946 NEIGHBORS, Muta A, Afton, OK, 20
5866 NELEMS, Felix, Chelsea, OK, 53; Mathews, Madaline, GD, 11
8909 NELLIE, Nancy, Cherokee City, AR, 64
9918 NELMS, Adam, Foyil, OK, 27
6469 NELMS, Arch E, Bushyhead, OK, 39
7506 NELMS, Ibby, Foyil, OK, 53; Victoria, D, 19; Ellen, D, 16
7502 NELMS, John, Jr, Foyil, OK, 28
17216 NELMS, Luke, Foyil, OK, 26
16676 NELMS, Rachel A, Foyil, OK, 25

[NELSON, Eddie. See #35564]
[NELSON, Arthur. See #35564]   *(Note: entries separate*
[NELSON, Myrtle. See #35564]   *from other family groups)*
[NELSON, John. See #35564]

4693 NELSON, Effie O. H, Briartown, OK, 32; Jessie U, D, 13; Ethel L, D, 11; Erah B, D, 8; Marion Wesley, D, 5; Watie Zelia, D, 1
1549 NELSON, Esther, Porum, OK, 49; Cramp, Johnson, S, 11
28891 NELSON, Jessie S, Checotah, OK, 30; Denison, S, 6; Sarah Adele, D, 3; Ernest Price, S, 1

[NELSON, Ruby. See #23042]
[NELSON, Pollie A. See #23042]   *(Note: entries separate*
[NELSON, Effie. See #23042]   *from other family groups)*
[NELSON, James. See #23042]

CHEROKEE DESCENDANTS RESIDING WEST OF MISSISSIPPI RIVER.
VOLUME III   (N – Z)

Key: Guion Miller Application Number; Name; Address, Relation (to Head); Age in 1906

28198 NELSON, Sarah B, Long, OK, 25; George D, S, 4; Clara M, D, 2
16862 NELSON, Wesley N, Uniontown, AR, 47; Lewis, S, 10; Henry, S, 8; Jessie, D, 5; Olie, S, W
5229 NETTLES, Ruth, Dora, AR, 51; Charles C, S, 16; Leona H, D, 12; Fred M, S, 8
23549 NEUGIN, Cornelious, Proctor, OK, 23
2447 NEUGIN, Henry, Hulbert, OK, 41; 2443, Rachel, W, 50
1809 NEUGIN, Jack, Proctor, OK, 54; 3545, Emeline, W, 50; Frank, S, 18; Jack, Jr, S, 13
23550 NEUGIN, Willard, Proctor, OK, 22
2455 NEUGIN, Neal, Hadley, OK, 39; 5508, Jennie, W, 36; Susie, D, 9; Joseph, S, 5; Bark, S, 3; Eagle, John, S of W, 20 [Deceased 3-'07]; Eagle, Annie, D of W, 19
33938 NEUGIN, Nelson, Proctor, OK, 20
2448 NEUGIN, Rebecca, Hulbert, OK, 71
6478 NEVILLE, Rosa L, Adair, OK, 27; Helen G, D, 5; James C, S, 4; Crayton, Oliver, S, 2
8030 NEW, Josephine, Fairland, OK, 33; Ezra E, S, 12; Isaac A, S, 10; Nancy A, D, 9; Sarah Dawes, OK, D, 6; William D, S, 4; Jose O, D, 1/12
17225 NEWTON, Saphronia, Oswego, KS, 57
2001 NEWMAN, Nama V, Welch, IT, 30; William T, S, 9; Nora M, D, 7; Virgie K, D, 3; Luther P, S, 6; Earl J, S, 1/6

[NEWMAN, Sallie F. See #29987]   *(Note: entry separate from other family groups)*

25935 NEWTON, Clifford, Tahlequah, OK, 24; John, S, 3; Claude, S, 2/3
1731 NEWTON, Elizabeth, Peggs, OK, 35; Emma D, D, 14; Josie E, D, 7; Mack J, S, 5; Walter L, S, 1
17752 NEWTON, Ida L, Tahlequah, OK, 29; Irvin C, S, 9; Clyde, S, 4; Carl E. B, S, 1; Jesse, S, 1/3
1380 NEWTON, Laura, Tahlequah, OK, 58; Edgar, S, 18
29205 NEWTON, Leola F. W, Maysville, AR, 23; Laura M, D, ¼
24739 NEWTON, Leote, Miami, OK, 27
27417 NEWTON, Oscar F, Collinsville, OK, 21

[NEWTON, Saphronia. See #17225]   *(Note: entry separate from other family groups)*

16047 NEWTON, Theodosia A, Nadill, OK, 22
23418 NEYHARD, Florence L, Bartlesville, OK, 18; Thomas W, S, 19; Claude D, S, 16; Clifford C, D, 14; Maude I, D, 12

[NICHOLS, Frank. See #4520]   *(Note: entry separate from other family groups)*

27342 NICHOLS, Henrietta, Vinita, OK, 38; Robinson, Josie, D, 20; Jessie, D, 18; Nichols, Annie V, D, 2
31748 NICHOLS, James L, Afton, OK, 5;   By Ed. Nichols, Gdn.

CHEROKEE DESCENDANTS RESIDING WEST OF MISSISSIPPI RIVER.
VOLUME III (N – Z)

Key: Guion Miller Application Number; Name; Address, Relation (to Head); Age in 1906

13448 NICHOLS, Josephine, Choteau, OK, 33; Frank L, S, 15; Nettie M, D, 11; Cleo, D, 3
 6522 NICHOLS, Lorena T, Wimer, OK, 18; Glenn, Franklin, S, 2
  590 NICHOLSON, Daniel G, Talala, OK, 26
 3917 NICHOLSON, Edward V R, Chelsea, OK, 36; Leah G, D, 6; Eva E, D, 4; Ralph C, S, 2
  589 NICHOLSON, Henry, Talala, OK, 22
 5006 NICHOLSON, Henry F, Muskogee, OK, 31; 28720, Mittie, W, 20; Willie, S of H, 11; David L, S of H, 9; Cornelia, D of H, 7; Leo B, S of H, 5; Henry, S of H, 3
 4371 NICHOLSON, James P, Chelsea, OK, 24
  587 NICHOLSON, Richard E, Talala, OK, 30; Roy P, S, 5; Edgar R, S, 2
 4505 NICHOLSON, Richard H, Chelsea, OK, 35
 3454 NICHOLSON, Sim, Talala, OK, 17;   By George Bible, Gdn.
 3894 NICHOLSON, Thos K, Chelsea, OK, 31; Gracie L, D, 6; Eva L, D, 4
17907 NICKLES, Mary, Fawn, OK, 22
23463 NIDIFFER, Charley, Afton, OK, 35; Otis E, S, 4
29463 NIDIFFER, Edward O, Sacramento City, CA, 29; Louisa E, D, 6; Roy O, S, 3; Pauline E, D, 1/12
 2719 NIDIFFER, Emma, Fairland, OK, 47
24549 NIDIFFER, Ezekiel, Fairland, OK, 24; Grover V, S, 1
 1814 NIDIFFER, Freeman, Fairland, OK, 57; Robert H, S, 13; Eula M, D, 9; 22607, Mary D, D, 20
 1815 NIDIFFER, George, Vinita, OK, 44; Jesse G, S, 17; Lucile F, D, 8; 42123, Minnie G, D, 19
 5239 NIDIFFER, Henrietta E, Afton, OK, 23
24550 NIDIFFER, Isaac, Fairland, OK, 28; Beulah, D, 7; Doyle, S, 6; Rollin, S, 3

[NIDIFFER, John R. See #1329]
[NIDIFFER, Geo. W. See #1329]   *(Note: entries separate*
[NIDIFFER, Freeman. See #1329]   *from other family groups)*
[NIDIFFER, Mamie L. See #1329]

 5682 NIDIFFER, Nancy, Maysville, AR, 41
 1813 NIDIFFER, Samuel, Fairland, OK, 59; Henry, S, 17; George, S, 13; Rufus, S, 10; Claud, S, 6; Connolly, S, 6
23133 NIDIFFER, Samuel, Jr, Fairland, OK, 27; 27081, Eliza E, W, 20
11544 NICKS [or NIX], Peter, Maysville, AR, 49; 11545, Rachel, W, 36; Luisa, D, 14; Huston, S, 12; Alford, S, 10; Alvy, S, 8; Bessie, D, 2
 8848 NIGHT, Mary, Westville, OK, 21
35654 NIPPER, Robert W, Claremore, OK, 20

[NIVENS, Archibald R. See #31841]   *(Note: entries separate*
[NIVENS, Helen Eliza. See #31841]   *from other family groups)*

[NIX, Chu-nu-lu-hunski. See #10605] *(Note: entry separate from other family groups)*

CHEROKEE DESCENDANTS RESIDING WEST OF MISSISSIPPI RIVER.
VOLUME III   (N – Z)

Key: Guion Miller Application Number; Name; Address, Relation (to Head); Age in 1906

13472 NIX, Ethel M, Sallisaw, OK, 22; Nix, John K, S, 3
28457 NIX, Frank M, Centralia, OK, 22; 28456, Nix, Mariah E, W, 24
27262 NIX, James O, Centralia, OK, 25; 27263, Daisy L, W, 20; Lucile J, D, 1
29185 NIX, John S, Pryor Creek, OK, 30
23128 NIX, Maude E, Centralia, OK, 21
11546 NIX, Nancy, Maysville, AR, 36

[NIX, Rachel. See NICKS.]

30139 NIX, Robert, F, Centralia, OK, 32; 30140, Saphronia E, W, 26; Roger F, S, 2
 5843 NIX, Sabrima[sic], Centralia, OK, 55; William I, S, 19; George F, S, 15
24008 NIX, Sarah E, Centralia, OK, 28
22618 NOAH, Georgia A, Choteau, OK, 31; Elijah, S, 9; Nathaniel, S, 7; Benjamin F. V, S, 2
15072 NOBLETT, Newton A, Okoee, OK, 13; James E, B, 10; By Henry N. Cook, Gdn.
31301 NOEL, Anna E, Tahlequah, OK, 28; Augusta M, D, 2
 9017 NOFIRE, Allen, Wauhillau, OK, 25
 9018 NOFIRE, Jane, Wauhillau, OK, 55
17109 NOFIRE, John, Vian, OK, 17;   By Alex McCoy, Gdn.
17479 NOFIRE, John, Wauhillau, OK, 29; 17573, Margaret, W, 31
11922 NOFIRE, Joshua, Long, OK, 30; Mary, D, 6; Sequoyah, S, 4; Nannie, D, 2
17132 NOISY, Mack, Campbell, OK, 38; 17220, Susie, W, 33; John, S, 12; Taswell, S, 2
17219 NOISY, Tom, Campbell, OK, 32; 17183, Wakie, W, 24; Mary, D, 8; Sissie, D, 2
 1327 NOISYWATER, John, Stilwell, OK, 35; 1410, Jennie, W, 34; Pigeon, S, 10; Nancy, D, 5
26670 NOLEN, Ethel L. T, Casa, AR, 28; Johnie Nelle, D, 3
10717 NOLEN, Henry N, Big Cabin, OK, 14; 10719, James A, Jr, Bro, 19; By James A. Nolen, Gdn.
 2143 NOLEN, Nancy, Big Cabin, OK, 48; Balew, Jennie, D, 13
33474 NORMAN, Albert C, Wagoner, OK, 40; Mary Jett, D, 6; Albert C, Jr, S, 4; Louis Edward, S, 3; Howard Owen, S, 1
32861 NORMAN, Cyrus W, Wagoner, OK, 39; Carlton W, S, 8; Alice M, D, 2
34889 NORMAN, James A, Muskogee, OK, 43
 7515 NORMAN, Martha J, Ft. Gibson, OK, 70
  162 NORMAN, Mary J, Porum, OK, 52; Phillips, Willie L, S, 17; Norman, Rufus [James R], S, 11; Levi, S, 9
 7438 NORRID, Ada Ross, Muldrow, OK, 37;   Myrtle May, D, 8
29991 NORRID, Mahulda E, Brent, OK, 28; Rena [Serena], D, 12; Willie B, S, 9; David, S, 6

[NORRIS, Florence. See #5518]

15050 NORTON, Jeannett, Marble City, OK, 12;   By Geo. E. Norton, Gdn.
26845 NOWLIN, Jessie, Oxnard, CA, 28

CHEROKEE DESCENDANTS RESIDING WEST OF MISSISSIPPI RIVER.
VOLUME III (N – Z)

Key: Guion Miller Application Number; Name; Address, Relation (to Head); Age in 1906

33115 NOYES, Mary Alice, Oolagah, OK, 31; Noyes, Benj. F, Oolagah, OK, S, 13; Edwin, S, 11; Roger L, S, 9; Georgia M, D, 5

35561½ NUCKOLLS, Emma J, Grove, OK, 27; Jennie F, D, 10; Ollie, D, 9; James S, S, 8; Opal, D, 4; Gladys F, D, 2

35562 NUCKOLLS, Lula M, Grove, OK, 4;   By Ira V. Nuckolls, Gdn.

12586 NUGIN [or NEUGIN], Dave, Hulbert, OK, 34; 26855, Nugin [or Neugin], Alice, W, 22; Titus, S, 9

26968 NUSSBAUM, Thursey, Moody, OK, 26; Craig, Coleman, S, 7

6680 OAKBALL, Betsy, Whitmire, OK, 69

6623 OAKBALL, John, Whitmire, OK, 33; 8108, Jennie, W, 37; Dave, S, 11; Annie, D, 9; Coo-wee-seoo-wee, S, 6; Watt, S, 1

16636 OAKBALL, Susie, Whitmire, OK, 30; Walter [Fallingpot], S, 11; Alisa, D, 2

6679 OAKBALL, White, Whitmire, OK, 38

25764 OATMAN, Norma O, Centralia, OK, 21

28704 OBORN, Willye Meek, Vinita, OK, 29

24405 O'BRIEN, Martha, Melvin, OK, 26; Etta, D, 5

575 ODELL, Margaret, Nowata, OK, 50

13959 ODLE, Etta, Kansas, OK, 33; Louisa, D, 14; Margaret M, D, 12; James, S, 11; William, Jr, S, 7; Jack, S, 3; Renia, D, 1

23185 ODLE, Fannie, Chance, OK, 22

26837 ODLE, Sallie, Kansas, OK, 27; Bessie, D, 5; Alvin, S, 5; Cora, D, 4; Ada, D, 1

12568 OER, John, Campbell, OK, 24; Emma May, D, 2

3931 OER, Nannie, Campbell, OK, 18

3981 OER, Nora, Campbell, OK, 11; Sarah, Sis, 8; Eva, Sis, 6; By Angeline Oer, Gdn.

8775 O'FIELD, Charley, Eucha, OK, 51; 8776, Nellie, W, 44; George, S, 19; Pollie, D, 17; Sallie, D, 16; Charlotte [Lizzie], D, 14; Noah, S, 12; Rebecca [Maggie], D, 10; Abel, S, 8

10087 O'FIELD, Eva, Pryor Creek, OK, 47

3055 O'FIELD, Sarah, Southwest City, MO, 21; Janana, D, 3; Jeff, S, 2

1969 O'FIELDS, Austin, Needmore, OK, 47; Rosa F, D, 15; Eldorado, D, 13

15601 O'FIELDS, Charlotte, Oaks, OK, 73

683 O'FIELDS, David, Locust Grove, OK, 57; 5991, Emma, W, 48; James, S, 10

43259 O'FIELDS, Jim, Eucha, OK, 23

33444 O'FIELDS, Lee, Eucha, OK, 21

1248 O'FIELDS, Robert, Southwest City, MO, 42; 2418, Nona, W, 22; Smith, S, 3; Ella May, D, 1

17247 OGDEN, Emma, Texanna, OK, 18

30618 OGLESBY, James M, Collinsville, OK, 36; Ruth C, D, 8; John L, S, 7; Lee May, D, 5; Eldee, D, 5; Gladys, D, 2; Susana, D, 1/12

[OGLESBY, Okla. See #9202]   *(Note: entry separate from other family groups)*

344 OLDFIELD, Ben, Maysville, AR, 48; 340, Annie, W, 56; Bettie, D, 13; Sallie, D, 10

CHEROKEE DESCENDANTS RESIDING WEST OF MISSISSIPPI RIVER.
VOLUME III   (N – Z)

Key: Guion Miller Application Number; Name; Address, Relation (to Head); Age in 1906

  337 OLDFIELD, Elizabeth, Maysville, AR, 71
8161 OLDFIELD, Lillie, Claremore, OK, 6;   By J. C. Goss, Gdn.
4382 OLDFIELD, Mary, Locust Grove, OK, 59
1544 OLDFIELD [or O'FIELD], Moses, Eucha, OK, 47; 421, Jennie, W, 42; James, S, 14; Minnie, D, 8; Cintha, D, 4
9486 OLDFIELD, Samuel, Ketchum, OK, 45
23969 OLDFIELDS, Sam, Kansas, OK, 30; Joe, S, 4; Ina, D, 3; Lillie, D, 1/6
4851 OLD KINGFISHER, Philip, Zena, OK, 41; 4853, Jennie, W, 38; 4851, Mary, D, 18; Joe, S, 16; Lewis, S, 11; Tom, S, 7; Sam, S, 5; Nancy, D, 1
4870 OLD KINGFISHER, Watie, Zena, OK, 64; 4859, Susan O, W, 30

[OLD SACK. See #6978]   *(Note: entry separate from other family groups)*

23402 OLIVER, James M, Talala, OK, 28
23403 OLIVER, Martha J, Talala, OK, 17; Maud L, Sis, 15; Pixie, Sis, 13; Hattie, Sis, 9; By Henry H. Oliver, Gdn.
23401 OLIVER, William F, Talala, OK, 25; Charles L, S, 1
27537 OLSON, Floyd, Afton, OK, 20
27536 OLSON, Lewis A, Afton, OK, 22
 2788 OLSON, Lydia, Afton, OK, 41; Richard F, S, 17; Andrew B, S, 14; James F, S, 10; Oliver R, S, 4
20241 OMSTEAD, Bessie M, Galena, KS, 20
30187 O'NEAL, Lieu A, Dewey, OK, 30; Georgia B, D, 13; William C, S, 12; Robert E, S, 0; James E, S, 7; Lieu A, Jr, D, 4; Sophronia E, D, 2
31538 ONE-LA-SA, Lucy, Uniontown, AR, 14;   By Susanna Fodder, next Friend

[ON-THE-HILL, John. See #31190]   *(Note: entry separate from other family groups)*

 2670 ON-THE-HILL, Steve, Estella, OK, 47
10587 OO-CHI-LA-TA, Thompson, Southwest City, MO, 63; 10586, Oo-squi-ne, W, 64
 5970 OO-DA-LE-DA, John, Maysville, AR, 55; 5988, Jennie, W, 46; Emma, D, 7
11604 OO-DA-LE-DA, Ross, Maysville, AR, 26
27965 OO-DA-LE-DA, Sallie, Maysville, AR, 18
 2504 OO-LOO-LAH, Susie, Vinita, OK, 24
  517 OO-SA-WEE, Annie Harry, Eucha, OK, 32
  519 OO-SA-WEE, Jake, Eucha, OK, 20

[OO-SA-WEE, Ona. See #2416]   *(Note: entry separate from other family groups)*

  518 OO-SA-WEE, Sallie, Eucha, OK, 51
 4861 OO-SA-WEE, Taylor, Eucha, OK, 36
11846 OO-YU-SUT-TAH, Cherry, Oaks, OK, 22
17046 OO-YU-SUT-TAH, Sarah, Leach, OK, 64; Joe, S, 15
11850 OO-YU-SUT-TAH, Rufus, Oaks, OK, 31

CHEROKEE DESCENDANTS RESIDING WEST OF MISSISSIPPI RIVER.
VOLUME III (N – Z)

Key: Guion Miller Application Number; Name; Address, Relation (to Head); Age in 1906

[ORCHARD, Jeremiah. See #1766] *(Note: entry separate from other family groups)*

31343 ORDWAY, Daisy, Riverbank, CA, 35; Walter, S, 18; Gustave, S, 16; Gladys, D, 14; Alma, D, 12; Pearl, D, 9; Guilda, D, 7; Vivian, D, 4; Alvah, S, 2; Elizabeth, D, 1/12
13762 OSAGE, Charles, Cookson, OK, 26
9382 OSAGE, Eben E, Tulsa, OK, 16; Mary E, Sis, 11;   By S. R. Lewis, Gdn.
5603 OSAGE, Jeff, Locust Grove, OK, 30; 31578, Minnie, W, 25; 43489, Susie, D, 2; 31578, Osage, S, 7; Mandy, D, 4
1614 OSAGE, Mary, Westville, OK, 30

[OSAGE, Philip. See #23100] *(Note: entry separate from other family groups)*

5625 OSAGE, Sallie, Hulbert, OK, 19; Vina, Sis, 1
17010 OSAGE, Stephen, Peggs, OK, 27; 23100, Polly, W, 22; Martha, D, 2; Philip, Jr, S, 7; [Mary Osage, Gdn]
23871 OSBORN, Leah, Monett, MO, 18
30373 OSBORN, Ora J, Oxford Junet, IA, 24; Orville O, S, 5; Edwin V, S, 3
22091 OSBORNE, Fannie, Collinsville, OK, 19; Ruby Dale, D, 3; ; Twyla, Child, ¼
1628 OSKISON, Richard, Estella, OK, 29; Sadie Lee, D, 3; Leona May, D, 1
5361 OSKISON, William, LaJunta, CO, 35
13155 OTTERLIFTER, Andy, Bunch, OK, 52; 13209, Susie, W, 48
26558 OTTING, Lola E, Miami, OK, 22; Opal O, D, 2; Vivian L, D, 1/6
31090 OVERLEY, Myrtle B, Miami, OK, 27; Forest W, S, 7; Paul K, S, 5; Fern L, S, 2; Rossie E, D, 1
21637 OVERTAKER, Fannie, McKey, OK, 9; Maggie, Sis, 7; Cornell, Bro, 5;   By Julia McClenathan, Gdn.
27758 OWEN, Caledonia, Campbell, OK, 25; Gertie Mabel, D, 2
6923 OWEN, Charley, Eucha, OK, 43; James, S, 16; Rebecca [Maggie], D, 14; Betsy, D, 12; Jennie, D, 10; Easter, D, 8; Scott [Skaklelawski], S, 6; Judge, S, 4; Jeh-geh-yu-e, S, 2
6924 OWEN, Dave, Eucha, OK, 44; 17199, Kah-nee-yor-eh, W, 26; 22016, Annie, D, 14; 22018, Jesse, S, 12; 6924, Aggie [Akey], D, 5; Allie, D, 3; Ar-ye-li-ky, S, 1
6960 OWEN, Isabell McD, Tulsa, OK, 35; Stella, D, 15; Neliebell[sic], D, 7
6925 OWEN, Lucy, Eucha, OK, 69
22598 OWENS, Eugene, Ft. Gibson, OK, 30; Chester A, S, 1

[OWENS, Florence. See #25009] *(Note: entry separate from other family groups)*

12140 OWENS, Henry, Webbers Falls, OK, 34
28830 OWENS, Laura E, Pryor Creek, OK, 24; Webb, Emmett P, S, 1
7004 OWENS, Lila, Southwest City, MO, 35; Joe, S, 12; Ida, D, 10; Sallie, D, 8; Iva, D, 6; Florence, D, 3
13947 OWENS, Malzerine, Tahlequah, OK, 28; Samuel P, S, 3
17011 OWENS, Martin, Vian, OK, 33

CHEROKEE DESCENDANTS RESIDING WEST OF MISSISSIPPI RIVER.
VOLUME III (N – Z)
Key: Guion Miller Application Number; Name; Address, Relation (to Head); Age in 1906

23903 OWENS, Samantha J, Gideon, OK, 19; Arnold A, S, 1 2/3
13948 OWENS, Samuel, Warner, OK, 30
44311 OWENS, Susie, Cherokee City, AR, 14; Annie, Sis, 12; Mary, Sis, 9; Sarah, Sis, 7; By Nona Wofford, Gdn.
42850 OWL, Charley, Stilwell, OK, 22; 3586, Mollie, W, 24
 5922 OWL, Lewis, Stilwell, OK, 31
11668 OWL, Nancy, Stilwell, OK, 65
 9005 OWL, Nick, Locust Grove, OK, 29; Nannie, D, 8 [Died 4-1907]; Lucy, D, 5; Lizzie, D, 2
10905 OWL, Sam, Wauhillau, OK, 39; 12498, Ella, W, 34; Charles, S, 12; Joseph, S, 9; Cat, S, 7; Daniel, S, 4; Washington, S, 1
 2691 OWNBEY, Mary A, Afton, OK, 14; Margaret E, Sis, 11; James L, Bro, 9; By Aaron L. Owenbey, Gdn.
24956 OYLER, Minnie E, Southwest City, MO, 32; Amos, Pansy Madeline, D, 6

 1844 PACE, Annie L, Welch, OK, 36; Elbert E, S, 7; Hayden A, S, 5; Lewis C, S, 5; Joel S, S, 2; Lorette L, D, 1/3
25010 PACE, Etta E. W, Choteau, OK, 28; M. Gladyce[sic], D, 9; Joseph C, S, 6; Elva M, D, 4
24064 PACE, Minnie, Chelsea, OK, 30; Lora, D, 13; Leonard, S, 10; Rosie L, D, 7; James W, S, 5; Carrie M, D, 2
23387 PACK, Allie Jane, Muldrow, OK, 26
24685 PACK, Laura, Proctor, OK, 31; Fred, S, 12; Ella, D, 10; Clayton, S, 8; Lee, S, 6; Ida, D, 4; Anna, D, 1
26821 PACK, Lila, Blackgum, OK, 5; Lilly, Sis, 3;   By James A. Pack, Gdn.
31300 PACK, Mary A, Bunch, OK, 37; Ezekiel, S, 18; Abraham, S, 11; Charles Wesley, Jr, S, 7; Nelson, S, 4; Emma, D, 3
 1748 PACK, William Shory, Muldrow, OK, 55; 902, Arminta, W, 63
 4731 PADEN, Andrew T, Stilwell, OK, 69; 4042, Martha J, W, 63
 5900 PADEN, Benjamin F, Stilwell, OK, 71; 5989, Lucinda, W, 52; Susan O, D, 10; Lucinda E, D, 14; Benjamin F, S, 12
 2645 PADEN, Bennie, Fairland, OK, 10; Riley, Bro, 11; Kittie, Sis, 15; Russell, Bro, 16; By Lena Goins, Gdn.
 6784 PADEN, Darthula, Tahlequah, OK, 24; Miller, Mary J, D, 7; William J, S, 6; Thomas H, S, 4
23217 PADEN, George W, Stilwell, OK, 32; Charles B, S, 8; Jackson T, S, 6; Mamie B, D, 3; Ina A, D, 1
 2677 PADEN, Howard, Fairland, OK, 25
 8976 PADEN, John B, Stilwell, OK, 45; 8890, Maud A, W, 34; Charles L, S, 15; Lucinda R, D, 13; Colbert H, S, 10; Mamie, D, 5; John B, Jr, S, 2
27716 PADEN, John H, Welch, OK, 37; John E, S, 15; George T, S, 12; Claud Elliott, S, 9; Beuna J, D, 7; Zachariah, S, 6; Gean D, S, 3
 5699 PADEN, Laura J, Stilwell, OK, 41
23569 PADEN, Louis D, Fairland, OK, 37; Louis D, Jr, S, 2; Alex A, S, 4; John B, S, 8

CHEROKEE DESCENDANTS RESIDING WEST OF MISSISSIPPI RIVER.
VOLUME III (N – Z)

Key: Guion Miller Application Number; Name; Address, Relation (to Head); Age in 1906

3808 PADEN, Lucy J, Fairland, OK, 54; 2675, Homer, S, 20; James, S, 18; Coffee W, S, 16; Jesse J, S, 12; Mary, D, 6
2676 PADEN, Maggie, Fairland, OK, 23
55 PADEN, Mark L, Centralia, OK, 40; John H, S, 10
2646 PADEN, Maud J, Doty, WA, 18
26691 PADEN, Nora L, Stilwell, OK, 26; Clifford E, S, 7; Ethel O, D, 4; Arthur H, S, 1
23212 PADEN, Robert E. L, Stilwell, OK, 29; Cora A, D, 2
2648 PADEN, Taylor, Fairland, OK, 22
6786 PADEN, Thomas A, Tahlequah, OK, 52; 27445, Phoebe, W, 23; Mattie, D, 2½; Cloyd, S, ¾
6788 PADEN, Thomas J, Tahlequah, OK, 52; 6787, Vann, S, 20; Nannie E, D, 16; Lucy, D, 10
2647 PADEN, William R, Leavenworth, KS, Gen. Del, 20
23391 PADEN, Zachariah, Stilwell, OK, 35
4590 PADGET, Eliza, Stilwell, OK, 38; Jacob, S, 17; Maria, D, 14; Annie, D, 12; Jesse, S, 11; Robert, S, 9; Luke, S, 7; Perry, S, 5; Taylor, S, 2

[PADGET, George. See #26203]   *(Note: entry separate from other family groups)*

33800 PADGETT, Charlie, Dutch Mills, AR, 22
36503 PADGETT, Ella L, Independence, KS, 201 N 10th St, 23
9959 PADGETT, Rena, Pryor Creek, OK, 20
5100 PALMER, Elizabeth, Sallisaw, OK, 24; Ocie, D, 4; Vella, D, 2; Voda, D, ¼
27056 PALMER, Fannie, Sallisaw, OK, 21
33777 PALMER, Georgie, Coffeyville, KS, 29; Pope, Clem W, S, 12; Robert S, S, 10; Madolyn K, D, 8
26523 PALMER, Luella, Collinsville, OK, 27; Cherry M, D, 4; Elizabeth H, D, 1
3834 PALMOUR, Benjamin A. F, Chelsea, OK, 57; 36417, Mary L, D, 19; Sarah, D, 17; Hugh A, S, 14
36416 PALMOUR, Bessie, Chelsea, OK, 23
3836 PALMOUR, Charles F, Chelsea, OK, 46; Asa, S, 19; Newton, S, 16; Paul A, S, 14; Roe E, S, 11
3835 PALMOUR, David S, Chelsea, OK, 52
Fannie A, D, 16
23636 PALMOUR, Emily E, Chelsea, OK, 24
23635 PALMOUR, Ina, Chelsea, OK, 22
3833 PALMOUR, James A, Chelsea, OK, 55
26152 PALMOUR, John D, Chelsea, OK, 24
23637 PALMOUR, John R, Chelsea, OK, 21
36415 PALMOUR, Robert, Chelsea, OK, 21

[PALONE. See POLONE.]

8109 PALONE, Andy, Oaks, OK, 27
12613 Bill [or Bill Proctor], Chance, OK, S, 4

CHEROKEE DESCENDANTS RESIDING WEST OF MISSISSIPPI RIVER.
VOLUME III   (N – Z)

Key: Guion Miller Application Number; Name; Address, Relation (to Head); Age in 1906

[PALONE, Clarence. See #6444]   *(Note: entry separate from other family groups)*

 4910 PALONE, Frank, Dutch Mills, AR, 49; 4911, Mary, W, 33; Charlie, S, 19; Tom, S, 14; Ruthie, D, 12; Walkingstick, Ezekiel, S of W, 13
 4211 PALONE, Jennie, Vian, OK, 52
26055 PALONE, Jessie, Dutch Mills, AR, 19; Henry Franklin, S, 3; Nancy, D, 1
 4463 PALONE, Lacie R, Lenapah, OK, 33

[PALONE, Nancy. See #2829]   *(Note: entry separate from other family groups)*

[PALONE, Ochelata. See #17202]   *(Note: entry separate from other family groups)*

24695 PALONE, Stephen, Dutch Mills, AR, 27; Gussie F, S, 4; Arvia, D, 2
 5545 PALONE, Tom, Westville, OK, 28; Clara, D, 9; Cleveland, S, 6; Vernon, S, 1/6
10789 PALONE, Wilson, Webbers Falls, OK, 45
  376 PANN, Dick, Hulbert, OK, 70; 2988, Susan, W, 72
 6037 PANN, James, Hulbert, OK, 33; 38723, Nannie, W, 28; Richard, S, 4; Walter, S, 2
 2816 PANN, Robin, Melvin, OK, 59; 1202, Jennie, W, 39; Carey, Frances, D of W, 11
 5352 PANN, Lewis, Locust Grove, OK, 36; 25463, Sarah, W, 30
22946 PANTER, Lula M, Stilwell, OK, 23
 2868 PANTER, Nancy R, Stilwell, OK, 52; George S, S, 17; Tommy, S, 16; Benjamin F, S, 10
22948 PANTER, Susan D, Stilwell, OK, 21
10722 PANTHER, Alice, Marble City, OK, 16;   By Martha Panther, Gdn.
 6038 PANTHER, John, Marble City, OK, 23

[PANTHER, Josiah. See #3642]   *(Note: entries separate*
[PANTHER, Lydia. See #3642]   *from other family groups)*

 4216 PANTHER, Martha, Marble City, OK, 45
 7671 PANTHER, Sequoyah, Sallisaw, OK, 29; James S, S, 7
10721 PANTHER, Tom, Marble City, OK, 13;   By Martha Panther, Gdn.

[PARCHCORN, Nancy. See #8326]
[PARCHCORN, Price. See #8325]
[PARCHCORN, Jers-gar-yo-yih. See #8326]
[PARCHCORN, Si-nar-s-der. See #8326]   *(Note: entries separate*
[PARCHCORN, Gar-do-yo-eh. See #8326]   *from other family groups)*
[PARCHCORN, Yo-neh-qua. See #8326]
[PARCHCORN, Jih-nar-sar. See #8326]

[PARDO. See PERDUE and PURDUE.]

CHEROKEE DESCENDANTS RESIDING WEST OF MISSISSIPPI RIVER.
VOLUME III   (N – Z)

Key: Guion Miller Application Number; Name; Address, Relation (to Head); Age in 1906

[PARHAM, Claud C. See #29202]
[PARHAM, Clarence W. See #29202]   *(Note: entries separate*
[PARHAM, Ada E. See #29202]   *from other family groups)*

23670 PARIS, Archibald, Chelsea, OK, 23; Lamoin, S, 1
29291 PARIS, Cora, Chelsea, OK, 17
11637 PARIS, Frank W, Catale, OK, 20; John C, Bro, 18; Delbert C, Bro, 15; Marion F, Bro, 14; Susie O, Sis, 9;   By Annie E. Paris, Gdn
3639 PARIS, Lemuel, Chelsea, OK, 57
17051 PARIS, William F, Chelsea, OK, 46; Mattie, D, 13; Fay, D, 10; Nina, D, 8; Verna Alice, D, 2
18894 PARKER, David, Chloeta, OK, 17
9625 PARKER, Fred, Gideon, OK, 14; Bertha, Sis, 10; Dewey, Bro, 4; Stella, Sis, 2; By Eli Parker, Gdn
18895 PARKER, Joe, Chloeta, OK 14
4716 PARKER, Laura, Copan, OK, 38; Josephine, D, 20; Emma Jane, D, 13; Minnie, D, 9; John Y, S, 11; William, S, 7
26147 PARKER, Lizzie, Welch, OK, 34; Claud J, S, 12; John M, S, 11; Mack R, S, 11; Grace, D, 9; Edna, D, 8; Benjamin F, S, 7; Robert [Joseph R], S, 6; Walter, S, 4; Omer, S, 3; Lake, S, 2; Annie L, D, 1/6
35808 PARKER, Lizzie, Claremore, OK, 17
35329 PARKER, Ludie S, Vinita, OK, 29
34629 PARKER, Lula M, Welch, OK, 23; Williard, S, 3
2101 PARKER, Mary A. F, Hulbert, OK, 27; Ida O, D, 1
19201 PARKER, Myrtle, Fawn, OK, 16
31384 PARKER, Ruth, McLoud, OK, R.F.D. #2, 20
27456 PARKER, Ruth D, Hulbert, OK, 8;   By James Henry Parker, Father.
2173 PARKHURST, Mary, Grove, OK, 29; John, S, 10; Martha, D, 7; Mary E, D, 4; Rossaulden, D, 1/12
22843 PARKHURST, Mary C, Grove, OK, 28; Maggie, D, 8; Jesse J, S, 6; Mattie J, D, 4; Henry, S, 2
34472 PARKINSON, Addie C, Wagoner, OK, 36; Rachel M, D, 14; Ruth, D, 13; Jo Terry, S, 11; Isabel Jane, D, 10; Addie Florence, D, 6; Bruce C, S, 5; Evaline, D, 4; James, S, 2
23948 PARKS, Annie, Bartlesville, OK, 34; Martha S, D, 5; Mary J, D, 3
27007 PARKS, George B, Centralia, OK, 31; Ruby Lee, D, 3; Margauretta, D, 1
4135 PARKS, James A. T, Durant, OK, 39
29872 PARKS, James G, Chelsea, OK, 41
3799 PARKS, Jeff T, Tahlequah, OK, 44; 42237, Etta, W, 35; Ruth A, D, 11; Mildred J, D, 8; Wahlelle T, D, ¼
28693 PARKS, John C, Chelsea, OK, 33
25164 PARKS, John R. B, Chelsea, OK, 23
2151 PARKS, Johnson C, Cowskin, MO, 55; James W, S, 19; Missouri, D, 16; Luta E, D, 11
29874 PARKS, Maggie M, Chelsea, OK, 38

CHEROKEE DESCENDANTS RESIDING WEST OF MISSISSIPPI RIVER.
VOLUME III   (N – Z)

Key: Guion Miller Application Number; Name; Address, Relation (to Head); Age in 1906

 4011 PARKS, Maud, Adair, OK, 24; Myrtle C, D, 2; Bertha E, D, 1
24674 PARKS, Melvin C, Cowskin, MO, 27; Byron D, S, 4
29873 PARKS, Oscar M, Chelsea, OK, 25
28694 PARKS, Richard B, Chelsea, OK, 42
 2152 PARKS, Richard T, Chelsea, OK, 83
25163 PARKS, Robert C, Chelsea, OK, 25
 1064 PARKS, Robert C, Chelsea, OK, 55; Milton B, S, 16; Alexander B, S, 16
24974 PARKS, Samuel F, Vinita, OK, 35; 10284, Alberta M, W, 26
 5844 PARKS, Sterling P, Adair, OK, 44; Amanda A, D, 16; Johnny C, S, 9; Susie S, D, 6; James W, S, 5; Carra M, D, 3; Elmer A, S, 1
30417 PARKS, Thaddeus T, Chelsea, OK, 27
 2039 PARNELL, Celia, Cookson, OK, 57; Benjamin, S, 20

[PARNELL, Jesse. See #4719]   *(Note: entries separate*
[PARNELL, Floyd. See #4719]   *from other family groups)*

 3014 PARNELL, Mary, Cookson, OK, 36; Annie, D, 18; Grover C, S, 13; Wallace, S, 8; Myrtle E, D, 3
 3013 PARNELL, Ruth, Cookson, OK, 27
28058 PARNELL, Samuel, Cookson, OK, 21
21839 PARRIS, Albion, Tahlequah, OK, 22
 5797 PARRIS, Andy, Rose, OK, 61; John, S, 19; Fannie, D, 17
  855 PARRIS, Betsy, Gideon, OK, 55
 5498 PARRIS, Celia, Chance, OK, 57; Ezekiel, S, 18; Hick, S, 15
24690 PARRIS, Charley R, Rose, OK, 28
10921 PARRIS, Cynthia, Rose, OK, 21?
 8315 PARRIS, Edward, Gideon, OK, 36; 11690, Elvia E, W, 40; Allen R, S, 17; Flossie, D, 15; Robert B, S, 12; Theodore, S, 6; Lee, S, 3; Violet, D, 1
24106 PARRIS, Eliza, Chance, OK, 29
24804 PARRIS, George, Chance, OK, 29; 24802, Ella, W, 20; Green L, S, 2; Elizabeth, D, ¾
28384 PARRIS, Ella M, Long, OK, 18; Unie C, Sis, 17; Moses O, Bro, 15;   By Mary S. Armstrong, Gdn.
23160 PARRIS, Ellen, Chance, OK, 7;   By Ransom Parris, Gdn.
  938 PARRIS, Ezekiel P, Tahlequah, OK, 49
16657 PARRIS, George Bud, Rose, OK, 54; 5766, Johanna, W, 45; Hopper, Martin, S of W, 17; Parris, Richard, S, 13; Nannie, D, 8; George Bud, Jr, S, 6; Bertha L, D, 2
 3504 PARRIS, George W, Tahlequah, OK, 34
21675 PARRIS, Henry C, Tahlequah, OK, 27
33598 PARRIS, Ivie, Adair, OK, 1;   By Annie Parris, Gdn.
23070 PARRIS, Jackson, Gideon, OK, 24
  187 PARRIS, James, Rose, OK, 55
 1977 PARRIS, James E, Gideon, OK, 55; 1978, Margaret, W, 48; Taylor, S, 20; Susan, D, 17; Matilda, D, 13; Samantha, D, 9
22884 PARRIS, James K, Tahlequah, OK, 26; Mabel E, D, 4; Eloise M, D, 1

CHEROKEE DESCENDANTS RESIDING WEST OF MISSISSIPPI RIVER.
VOLUME III (N – Z)

Key: Guion Miller Application Number; Name; Address, Relation (to Head); Age in 1906

22883   PARRIS, Jesse H, Tahlequah, OK, 22
29771   PARRIS, Jesse R, Chance, OK, 35; 11703, Frances, W, 36; Fannie, D, 12; Elizabeth, D, 10; Josie B, D, 6
22882   PARRIS, Johnson, Tahlequah, OK, 26; 30265, Joanna G, W, 19;
23071   PARRIS, Loonie, Gideon, OK, 36

[PARRIS, Loring. See #8316]   *(Note: entry separate from other family groups)*

 5250   PARRIS, Malachi, Westville, OK, 63
23885   PARRIS, Mary, Rose, OK, 19
23068   PARRIS, Mose, Gideon, OK, 32
 1233   PARRIS, Noah, Tahlequah, OK, 59; William B, S, 20
15796   PARRIS, Noah L, Jr, Ramona, OK, 23
  737   PARRIS, Richard J, Bartlesville, OK, 29
 7984   PARRIS, Robert E, Pensacola, OK, 37;   By Mike Mulcare, Gdn.
32273   PARRIS, Sallie, Ahniwake, OK, 22
26283   PARRIS, Taylor, Gideon, OK, 20
23067   PARRIS, Thomas, Gideon, OK, 26
 1662   PARRIS, Thomas J, Tahlequah, OK, 53; Betsy, D, 14; Anna, D, 12; Moses, S, 6; Curtis, S, 4
31888   PARRIS, Wilbern, Siloam Springs, AR, 10;   By Margaret Parris, Gdn.
 9628   PARRIS, Wilkerson, Gideon, OK, 62; 3259, Jane, W, 60; 23069, Charlotte, D, 17; 9628, Rattlinggourd, Morgan, GS, 6
  719   PARRIS, William, Tulsa, OK, 36; Ezekiel, S, 7; Roscoe, S, 4
23884   PARRIS, William, Rose, OK, 29
34157   PARRIS, William, Tahlequah, OK, 32
 4453   PARRISH, Maudie, El Paso, TX, 24; John, S, 1/12
  750   PARSLEY, Nannie, Claremore, OK, 34; Pauline, D, 13; Cora E, D, 12; Fred, S, 9; Sallie, D, 4; Robert, S, 2
 3216   PARSONS, Cicero, Cookson, OK, 24; 27954, Lula, W, 24; Mary H, D, 4; Carl, S, 3; William L, S, 1
 3217   PARSON[sic], Johnson, Braggs, OK, 35; Myrtle, D, 3; Aggie, D, 1
23443   PARSONS, Rebecca A, Keefeton, OK,   25; Mary, D, 5; John, S, 3
31849   PARTAIN, Bonnie, Muldrow, OK, 18; Verell Everett, S, 1/3
 4409   PARTAIN, Lydia, Locust Grove, OK, 26; Wickliff, Sam, S, 9; Partain, Rosa May, D, 6; Charles H. T, S, 3; Millie E, D, 1/3
  264   PARTAIN, Susie, Rush Springs, OK, 21
22838   PASCHAL, George, Tulsa, OK, 28
 6627   PASCHAL, Ridge, Tahlequah, OK, 61   [Died 2-2-1907]
11984   PATHKILLER, John, Proctor, OK, 47; 9609, Fanny, W, 54
13595   PATHKILLER, John, Sallisaw, OK, 18
29369   PATHKILLER, John R, Proctor, OK, 21
 9207   PATHKILLER, Johnson, Proctor, OK, 47; Sarah J, D, 14; Cora L, D, 12; William E, S, 10; J. M, S, 8
23458   PATHKILLER, William, Proctor, OK, 24

CHEROKEE DESCENDANTS RESIDING WEST OF MISSISSIPPI RIVER.
VOLUME III   (N – Z)

Key: Guion Miller Application Number; Name; Address, Relation (to Head); Age in 1906

28193 PATILLO, Willie E, Long, OK, 20; Ernest Andy, S, 3; Eva M, D, 1
22600 PATRICK, Alec, Wann, OK, 20
1597 PATRICK, Florence, Claremore, OK, 24
42964 PATRICK, Cleveland M, Ramona, OK, 17
564 PATRICK, George W, Wann, OK, 56; Rachel, D, 15; Eliza, D, 12; Lucy, D, 10; Fannie, D, 6; David, S, 1
13303 PATRICK, John, Ramona, OK, 43; Flossie, D, 10; Lela E, D, 9; Addie P, D, 6; Mary E, D, 2
4585 PATRICK, John J, Braggs, OK, 63; 4584, Almira, W, 73; Grover, S, 19
22559 PATRICK, Mike, Wann, OK, 43; John J, S, 19; Maggie L, D, 13; Harold B, S, 6; Clara, D, 1
13717 PATRICK, William, Cookson, OK, 15; Mary, Sis, 13;   By Zack Lillard, Gdn.
9678 PATTERSON, Charles W, Wann, OK,   27
31868 PATTERSON, Isabelle, Brent, OK, 30; Grover C, S, 13; Lillie M, D, 10; Lucy M, D, 6; Arthur L, S, 3
12000 PATTERSON, John A, Marble City, OK, 29; Joseph, S, 8; Kinney V, S, 4
21670 PATTERSON, Joseph A, Argenta, AR, C.R.I. & P. Ry. c/o Master Mechanic, 24
9640 PATTERSON, Leonard B, Wann, OK, 30
22543 PATTERSON, Lillian D, Stilwell, OK, 24; Homer L [Died 11-6-1906]; Ada V, D, 4; Flora C, D, 1
8070 PATTERSON, Mary, Collinsville, OK, 36; Chambers, James, S, 20; John Q, S, 17; Clementine, D, 13; Patterson, Frank, S, 8; Edna M, D, 6
8347 PATTERSON, William P, Stilwell, OK, 33; 39392, Mary L, W, 25; Lucy J, D, 8; Annie L, D, 6

[PATTIE. Cora E. See #11958]
[PATTIE. Frederick H. See #11958]   *(Note: entries separate from other family groups)*
[PATTIE, Sophie F. See #11958]

25575 PATTON, Ada, Stilwell, OK, 32; Franklin N, S, 10; Ruth, D, 8; Leola, D, 5; Joseph A, Jr, S, 2
23537 PATTON, Catherine M, Stilwell, OK, 24; George H, S, 6; Clifton B, S, 3; Herbert N, S, 1
1967 PATTON, Charles F, Paw Paw, OK, 35; 33328, Caleb F, S, 9; Minnie M, D, 7; Robert S, S, 3
9309 PATTON, Charlotte, Paw Paw, OK, 52; Robert E, S, 17; Lucy M, D, 11
22801 PATTON, Dumont, Muldrow, OK, 36; William Dumont, S, 8; Lucile Helen, D, 6; Roy Gideon, S, 3
1623 PATTON, Elizabeth, Muldrow, OK, 69
22799 PATTON, Gideon, Muldrow, OK, 32; Marie, D, 7; William M, S, 6; Gideon J, S, 2
2113 PATTON, Jane, Muskogee, OK, 65
9308 PATTON, Turner B, Muldrow, OK, 37; Delta C, D, 8; Robert I, S, 5; Grace L, D, 3
26926 PATTON, William S, Paw Paw, OK, 24

CHEROKEE DESCENDANTS RESIDING WEST OF MISSISSIPPI RIVER.
VOLUME III   (N – Z)

Key: Guion Miller Application Number; Name; Address, Relation (to Head); Age in 1906

39988 PATZOL, Rollin Leon, Bellingham, 912 Harris Ave, WA, 27
11568 PAUL, Ella, Warner, OK, 25; Bertha, D, 2
8852 PAYMASTER, *(No other name given)*, Locust Grove, OK, 39; 26066, Lula, W, 17; William, S, 1/6
31047 PAYNE, Alfred W, Foyil, OK, 20; Claude L, Bro, 17;   By William Payne, Gdn.
1919 PAYNE, Alice, Welch, OK, 59
2126 PAYNE, Amzia M, Blue Jacket, OK, 34; Lewis L, S, 16; Joseph E, S, 13; Glessnor M, D, 11; William C, S, 9
101 PAYNE, Andrew Lane, Foyil, OK, 29
6419 PAYNE, Elizabeth, Humboldt, KS, 60
27203 PAYNE, Florence, Oaks, OK, 21
21641 PAYNE, Floy G, Joplin, MO, 10;   By Catherine Payne, Gdn.
8953 PAYNE, George E, Dutch Mills, AR, 35
4594 PAYNE, Hattie C, Tahlequah, OK, 35
31046 PAYNE, Henry W, Foyil, OK, 24
7492 PAYNE, Isabel D, Ft. Smith, AR, 40; Mabel C, D, 15; Howard A, S, 13; Gerald L, S, 11; Myra L, D, 9; Houston C, S, 5
5276 PAYNE, James M, Tahlequah, OK, 23
29488 PAYNE, James M, Welch, OK, 42; Edna E, D, 16; James E, S, 13; Leonard W, S, 10; Freddie L, S, 8; Floyd W, S, 4; Alice, D, 1
43079 PAYNE, John H, Ft. Smith, AR, 26
248 PAYNE, Jonathan R, Pryor Creek, OK,   47; Mary E, D, 10; Nettie, D, 3
16436 PAYNE, Julius C, Vinita, OK, 35; Julia M, D, 10; Willie W, D, 8; Hallis Eva, D, 5; Luttie A, D, 3
6540 PAYNE, Katie, Vian, OK, 36
2414 PAYNE, Mary E, Tahlequah, OK, 46; Lena E, D, 13; Willie B, S, 11; Beatrice E, D, 6
35345 PAYNE, Robert C, Ft. Smith, AR, 24
29984 PAYNE, Sarah A, Ft. Smith, AR, 51; Claude, S, 18; Harrold[sic], S, 16; Lee R, S, 14
31437 PAYNE, Silas D, Welch, OK, 36; 31438, Annie, W, 21; Silas B, S, 6; Charles C, S, 4; Ellen O, D, 1/6
27440 PAYNE, William H, Welch, OK, 28; Flossy, D, 5; Ruby, D, 1
31045 PAYTON, Charlotte, Narcissa, OK, 26;   Lee, S, 5; Bessie, D, 3; Elizabeth, D, 1
24859 PAYTON, Emma A, Westville, OK, 33; Fred F, S, 15; John M, S, 14; Fannie E, D, 12; Maude F, D, 8; Garland S, S, 5; Horace, S, 1
3059 PAYTON, Ida, Lynch, OK, 30; Ray, S, 9; Rean, S, 8; Coleman, S, 4; Nora M, D, 2
24414 PAYTON, Martha Jane, Dodge, OK, 29
26695 PAYTON, Sarah O, Eucha, OK, 25; Minnie May, D, 7; Robert Francis, S, 1/12
38520 PEACHEATER, Nellie, Welling, OK, 50

[PEAK, Connell. See #175]   *(Note: entry separate from other family groups)*

[PEAK, Lillie M. See #11975]   *(Note: entry separate from other family groups)*

CHEROKEE DESCENDANTS RESIDING WEST OF MISSISSIPPI RIVER.
VOLUME III (N – Z)

Key: Guion Miller Application Number; Name; Address, Relation (to Head); Age in 1906

 5985 PEAK, Stephen W, Maysville, AR, 31; 5940, Maud, W, 20; Charles C, S, 4; Jesse, S, 2
 4206 PEAK, William, Vian, OK, 26
22619 PEARCE, Mary E, Watova, OK, 20; Lewis G, S, 1
32003 PEARCE, Sophronia B, Southwest City, MO, 30; Cooper, Claud D, S, 5; Floyd J, S, 3; John M, S, 1
 1833 PEARSE, Jackson, Coffeyville, KS, 31; Berdie S, D, 5; Louise E, D, 4; John W, S, 1
26299 PECK, Eliza C, Sallisaw, OK, 24; Ben A, S, 5; Lafe B, S, 3; Beulah, D, 2
23235 PECK, Elizabeth, Claremore, OK, 27
 6790 PECK, Mary, Claremore, OK, 50; Charles E, S, 10; Jesse B, S, 6
 3673 PEEBLES, James L, Tahlequah, OK, 45; 5127, Nannie, W, 32; Joseph L, S, 13; James S, S, 11; Lottie M, D, 9; Edgar V, S, 7; George D, S, 4; Vera E, D, 2
16593 PEEK, Edward W, Sulphur City, MO, 22

[PEEK, N. W. See #16593]   *(Note: entry separate from other family groups)*

 6600 PEEK, Susan E, Southwest City, MO 34; Potts, Richard, S, 17; Peek, Russell, S, 3
33759 PEETZ, Ola, Leesville, LA, 26
13256 PEGG, Swimmer, Locust Grove, OK, 26; 23974, Annie, W, 18
  192 PEGG, Thomas, Locust Grove, OK, 47; 179, Nancy, W, 31; Wat, S, 18; Leach, Che-arke, D of W, 13; Amela, D of W, 11

[PELONE. See PALONE.]

24231 PELSUE, Ethel R, Ramona, OK, 24; Sarah I, D, 8; Owen E, S, 5; Florence R, D, 3
25775 PENDERGRAFT, Callie B, Tahlequah, OK, 23; Ira R, S, 2
16364 PENDERGRAFT, Martha M, Doty, WA, 22; Oswald, S, ¼
30095 PENDLETON, Sally G, Tahlequah, OK, 37
 9814 PENINGTON, Lillie, Broken Arrow, OK, 26
14094 PENNEL, Dora, Wagoner, OK, 32; Alice, D, 12; Thomas, S, 10; Charley, S, 8; James, S, 6; Hamilton, S, 4; Bernice, D, 2
27843 PENNINGTON, Rose A, Fairland, OK, 19; Allie Maxim, D, 1
33732 PENNINGTON, William H, Webb City, AR, 25; Melvin, S, 4; Harvie, S, 2; Asa B, S, 1
39729 PENOI, Eloise R, Anadarka, OK, 26; Una Josephine, D, 1

[PERDUE. See PARDO and PURDUE.]

12413 PERDUE, Charles, Cookson, OK, 26; 12401, Susie, W, 36; Deer-in-Water, Star, S of W, 1
  454 PERDUE, James S, Eucha, OK, 29; Dan W, S, 1
11193 PERDUE, Richard, Cookson, OK, 28

CHEROKEE DESCENDANTS RESIDING WEST OF MISSISSIPPI RIVER.
VOLUME III   (N – Z)

Key: Guion Miller Application Number; Name; Address, Relation (to Head); Age in 1906

[PERLONE. See PALONE.]

- 3190 PERRY, Artemus J, Pittsburg, KS, 412 E. 16th St, 27; Orville Lee, S, 3
- 3187 PERRY, Columbus H, Pittsburg, KS, 1621 N. Michigan St, 34; Pearl, D, 10; Kenneth B, S, 6
- 9218 PERRY, Ernest, Vinita, OK, 25
- 893 PERRY, Ernest G, Welch, OK, 26
- 3158 PERRY, Ezekiel H, Dodge, OK, 53; Ezekiel S, S, 17; Stella, D, 14
- 3451 PERRY, Floyd L, Miami, OK, 14; Earl E, Bro, 12; Almeda, Sis, 10;   By Augusta L. Perry, Gdn.
- 27133 PERRY, Irene, Cowskin, MO, 22; Susan M, D, 1
- 892 PERRY, Mary G, Saline, OK, 15;   By Fannie D. Perry, Gdn.
- 3188 PERRY, Myrtle, Vinita, OK, 19
- 3160 PERRY, Nathan M, Grove, OK, 52; Elizabeth K, D, 13; James R, S, 12; Lewis L, S, 10; Robert L, S, 8; Morris G, S, 5; Vinita, D, 10/12
- 3186 PERRY, Oliver H, Vinita, OK, 17;   By Stacy E. Perry, Gdn.
- 694 PETERS, Annie A, Sallisaw, OK, 42; Lorenzo M, S, 19; Minnie S, D, 17; Nora A, D, 14; Iantha S, D, 12; Plumie, D, 9
- 25337 PETERS, Bessie E, Sallisaw, OK, 21
- 10753 PETERS, Cynthia, Porum, OK, 39 [Dead]; Ratliff, Henry, S, 15
- 26442 PETERS, Florence W, Braggs, OK, 17
- 25336 PETERS, Thomas L, Sallisaw, OK, 24; Flora Annie, D, 3; Teddy Wesley, S, 5/12
- 8746 PETERS, John, Locust Grove, OK, 41; 8866, Nellie, W, 38; Joe, S, 14; James [or Jno, Jr,], S, 11

[PETERS, Losie. See #14180]   *(Note: entry separate from other family groups)*

- 3691 PETERS, William, Locust Grove, OK, 19
- 25833 PETERSON, Emma, Warner, OK, 29; Emma, D, 3; Lizzie, D, 1
- 25291 PETERSON, Mary, Warner, OK, 24; Gibson, James, S, 7; Satterwhite, Elizabeth, D, 4; Hereford, Blanche M, D, 2

[PETIETT, Andrew. See #1058]   *(Note: entry separate from other family groups)*

[PETITT. See PETTIT.]

- 30016 PETITT, Charles P, Cookson, OK, 27
- 35444 PETITT, Dick, Edna, OK, 15; Emma, Sis, 14;   By Dollie Petitt, Gdn.
- 18429 PETITT, Edward, Braggs, OK, 54; Eliza, D, 17; Mack, S, 15; Lizzie, D, 8; Beulah, D, 6
- 25009 PETITT, Eliza, Cookson, OK, 29; Owens, Florence, D, 3
- 29635 PETITT, Elsie, Cookson, OK, 23
- 1859 PETTIT[sic], Frank, Edna, KS, 71; Watie, GS, 17
- 2119 PETITT, George W, Cookson, OK, 55; Frank, S, 17; Susie, D, 16; Adna, D, 14; Mart, S, 12; Jennie, D, 10; Sadie E, D, 7

CHEROKEE DESCENDANTS RESIDING WEST OF MISSISSIPPI RIVER.
VOLUME III (N – Z)
Key: Guion Miller Application Number; Name; Address, Relation (to Head); Age in 1906

13271 PETITT, Jack, Sallisaw, OK, 26
13754 PETITT, John, Sallisaw, OK, 14; Cora, Sis, 1; By Annie Petitt, Gdn.
2169 PETITT, John R, Cookson, OK, 50
11825 PETITT, Lizzie, Braggs, OK, 63; Jenny, D, 15; Susie, D, 10
6263 PETITT, Richard M, Cookson, OK, 24
9132 PETITT, Rufus, Ft. Duchesne, UT, 26
2165 PETITT, Thomas J, Cookson, OK, 53; 2903, Nancy, W, 63
17256 PETITT, Timothy, Warner, OK, 29; 31599, Rachel, W, 29; Lola, D, 6; Hansel, S, 1; Hood, Susie, D, 9
17554 PETITT, Tom, Sallisaw, OK, 24

[PETITT, Watie. See #14798]   *(Note: entry separate from other family groups)*

4197 PETITT, William, Inola, OK, 39; 4196, Mary Jane, W, 32; Pearl O, D, 11; Bertha, D, 8; Floyd H, S, 6; William P, S, 4; Mazie O, D, 1
13196 PETITT, William, Marble City, OK, 29

[PETTIT. See PETITT.]

30190 PETTIT, Cynthia, Edna, KS, 15; Guy, Bro, 11; Robert B, Bro, 9; Mary, Sis, 7; Roberta, Sis, 5;   By Jane Pettit, Gdn.
8766 PETTIT, Jake, Sallisaw, OK, 59
35533 PETTITT, Jennie, Braggs, OK, 10; Susan, Sis, 16;   By Lizzie Pettit, Gdn.
2114 PETTIT, Joseph, Edna, KS, 44; Frank J, S, 15; Alvin D, S, 12; Marie, D, 9; Lizzie, D, 7; Joseph, Jr, S, 3; Amelia, D, 1
7660 PETTIT, Joseph C, Braggs, OK, 46
434 PETTIT, Lourinda H, Pawhuska, OK, 62
3986 PETTIT, Oscar D, Muldrow, OK, 47; 3985, Emma, W, 47; Marion J, S, 16; Floyd E, S, 13
24676 PETTY, Charlotte E, Cove, OK, 33; Michael G, S, 13; James Scott, S, 10; William C, S, 8; Carl Clifton, S, 6; Sarah M, D, 2
28175 PETTY, Clarence, Cove, OK, 16; George R, Bro, 15;   By James F. Petty. Gdn.
3453 PETTY, John T, Warner, OK, 34; George W, S, 7; Rachel M, D, 4; Jewel E. J, D, 2; John C, S, 1
8952 PETTY, Vetoria, Dutch Mills, AR, 29; Sarah L, D, 8; Ida M, D, 6; Rosella C, D, 4; Leona, D, 2; Roy Lee, S, 1/6
28335 PEVEHOUSE, Prudence E, Collinsville, OK, 37
847 PEVEHOUSE, Sonora A, Collinsville, OK, 47; William A, S, 15; Sarah E, D, 13

[PEYTON, Nancy. See #2452]   *(Note: entry separate from other family groups)*

2480 PFANNKCHE, Agnes, Vinita, OK, 64
22745 PFANNKCHE, Charles C, Vinita, OK, 22; 6722, Martha, W, 23
24932 PFOFF, Amelia E, Sallisaw, OK, 17
29320 PHAGAN, Eliza, Siloam Springs, AR, 26

CHEROKEE DESCENDANTS RESIDING WEST OF MISSISSIPPI RIVER.
VOLUME III   (N – Z)

Key: Guion Miller Application Number; Name; Address, Relation (to Head); Age in 1906

   279 PHARISS, Agga, Choteau, OK, 79
26036 PHARISS, Farle, Choteau, OK, 56; Allen, S, 14; Amy A, D, 12
26037 PHARISS, Jackson L, Choteau, OK, 43; Clinton L, S, 6
26035 PHARISS, John B, Choteau, OK, 53
26040 PHARISS, Pleasant H, Choteau, OK, 37; Selvert, S, 11; Ada B, D, 5; Elmus Gertrude, D, 2
16654 PHEASANT, Abraham, Westville, OK, 20
12615 PHEASANT, Alex, Westville, OK, 23; 16580, Susan, W, 28; Ratcliff, Nannie, D of W, 3; Wat, S of W, 2
16463 PHEASANT, Charley, Christie, OK, 35
  8961 PHEASANT, Dick, Rose, OK, 68; 10270, Annie, W, 50
  1840 PHEASANT, Eliza, Stilwell, OK, 73
16556 PHEASANT, George, Porum, OK, 41; Tams [Tims], S, 4
15622 PHEASANT, James, Christie, OK, 32; 8242, Lula, W, 28; Jenanna, D, 9; Bell, Charlotte, D of W, 13

[PHEASANT, Lizzie. See #26516]   *(Note: entry separate from other family groups)*

[PHEASANT, Lucy. See #7656]   *(Note: entry separate from other family groups)*

[PHILLIPS, Arch. See #14780]
[PHILLIPS, Johnson. See #14780]
[PHILLIPS, John. See #14780]
[PHILLIPS, Jim. See #14780]
[PHILLIPS, Jim. See #14780]
[PHILLIPS, Ahama. See #14780]
[PHILLIPS, Lucy. See #14780]
[PHILLIPS, Aggie. See #14780]
[PHILLIPS, George. See #14780]
[PHILLIPS, Sinda. See #14780]
[PHILLIPS, Ollie. See #14780]

(Note: entries separate from other family groups)

  9226   PHILLIPS, Bettie, Texanna, OK, 49; Ida, D, 16; Sarah, D, 14; Rachel, D, 10; Walter Lee, S, 6

[PHILLIPS, Caroline. See #38556]   *(Note: entry separate from other family groups)*

22895 PHILLIPS, Charlie, Porum, OK, 25; Clintie, D, 6; Virgia, D, 3
12569 PHILLIPS, Eliza, Braggs, OK, 22; Steve, S, 4
31357 PHILLIPS, Frank, Skiatook, OK, 39; Spencer O, S, 8; Ewell, S, 6; Ula Maud, D, 4; Ola May, D, 1
38753 PHILLIPS, Grace, Nowata, OK, 25
26401 PHILLIPS, Harvey, Porum, OK, 32; Delia, D, 10; Elvia E, D, 8; Lizzie, D, 3
17419 PHILLIPS, Henry, Hoffman, OK, 33; George W, S, 5

CHEROKEE DESCENDANTS RESIDING WEST OF MISSISSIPPI RIVER.
VOLUME III   (N – Z)

Key: Guion Miller Application Number; Name; Address, Relation (to Head); Age in 1906

11189 PHILLIPS, James, Braggs, OK, 40; 11481, Lizzie, W, 47; Nellie, D, 16; Joseph, S, 12; Thomas, S, 6
22894 PHILLIPS, James H, Porum, OK, 30; John, S, 2; Clarence, S, 1
10179 PHILLIPS, Jane A, Vinita, OK, 33
24055 PHILLIPS, Jessie J, Texanna, OK, 23
28474 PHILLIPS, John M, Lowrey, OK, 38; John R, S, 12; Mary M, D, 9
8023½ PHILLIPS, Josephine V, Nowata, OK, 60; Josephine, D, 18
32527 PHILLIPS, Julius, Porum, OK, 27; 35984, Florence, W, 29; Zoe, D, 2
11178 PHILLIPS, Lucy, Vian, OK, 22; Daniel J, S, 4; Henry, S, 3
4713   PHILLIPS, Martha L, Westville, OK, 59
22671 PHILLIPS, Mary Etta, Alluwee, OK, 27; Cecil, S, 2; Othal, S, 1/6
43348 PHILLIPS, Maude A, Eureka, OK, 22; Senora M. B, D, 2
33823 PHILLIPS, Maud H, Chelsea, OK, 21; Joel A, S, ¼
29191 PHILLIPS, Nancy J, Park Hill, OK, 32; Bud H, S, 10; Mamie L, D, 8; Andy J, S, 5; Craig, Julie M, D, 1
24054 PHILLIPS, Nancy J, Texanna, OK, 21
43266 PHILLIPS, Robert A, Spavinaw, OK, 34
31908 PHILLIPS, Roberts S, Cess, KS, 23
24582 PHILLIPS, Rufus, Chance, OK, 32; Mary, D, 10; Harvie, S, 8; Barney, S, 6; Jesse, S, 4
27023 PHILLIPS, Tommie I, Tahlequah, OK, 24; Fred, S, 1
22893 PHILLIPS, Walter, Porum, OK, 34; William Levi, S, 11; Cordelia, D, 9; Calvin Cecil, S, 5; Alice, D, 2; Roy, S, ½
25794 PHILLIPS, William, Leavenworth, KS, 33; 1846, Betsey, W, 32; Walter E, S, 6
28474 PHILLIPS, William, Lowrey, OK, 36; Martha, D, 18; Lizzie, D, 13; Ada B, D, 9; Laura A, D, 6; James W, S, 1

[PHILLIPS, Willie L. See #162]   *(Note: entry separate from other family groups)*

15599½ PHIPPS, Amanda, Ft. Gibson, OK, 45; Joe, S, 17; Beulah M, D, 13; Lulu P, D, 11; Ella B, D, 8; Alberta, D, 5
27400 PHIPPS, John, Rex, OK, 22
10614 PICAMAN, Clara M, Claremore, OK, 18; Clarenca M, Bro, 18; Jennie, Sis, 16; August C, Bro, 14; Julius W, Bro, 11; Dewey M, Bro, 8; Caroline S, Sis, 6;   By John Picaman, Gdn.
26168 PICKARD, Sarah C, Proctor, OK, 30; Warnetta, D, 3; Onie J, S, 1
26389 PICKNEY, Mattie E, Dallas, TX, 22
2819   PICKUP, Dick, Locust Grove, OK, 50; 24698, Jennie, W, 28; 2819, Sallie, D, 12; Joe, S, 10; 24698, Falling, Car-na-noo-lis-kie, S of W, 8; Pickup, Ah-nee, D of W, 4; Lucy, D, 2 [Dead]
2968   PICKUP, Emma, Spavinaw, OK, 36; Tagg, Soggie, D, 18; Ida, D, 15; Hully, Webster [Jalum], S, 10; Pickup, Sogie, S, 3; John, S, 5/12
14205 PICKUP, George, Locust Grove, OK, 20; 23826, Maggie, W, 19; Jennie, D, 1
31571 PICKUP, Jim, Wagoner, OK, 21; Gordon J, S, 1/3
23972 PICKUP, Mose, Locust Grove, OK, 32

CHEROKEE DESCENDANTS RESIDING WEST OF MISSISSIPPI RIVER.
VOLUME III (N – Z)

Key: Guion Miller Application Number; Name; Address, Relation (to Head); Age in 1906

12672 PICKUP, Ned, Leach, OK, 33; 26530, Susie, W, 33; Johnson, S, 5
11525 PICKUP, Simon, Locust Grove, OK, 25

[PIERCE, Charles P. See #4864]
[PIERCE, Claud. See #4864]   *(Note: entries separate*
[PIERCE, Ruth. See #4864]   *from other family groups)*
[PIERCE, Edna. See #4864]

[PIERCE, Stella. See #16396]   *(Note: entry separate from other family groups)*

[PIERCE, May. See #25740]   *(Note: entry separate from other family groups)*

30422 PIERCE, Cornelius, Braggs, OK, 23
26027 PIERCE, Effie, Braggs, OK, 19
　338 PIERCE, Helen E, Nowata, OK, 26; Mary E, D, 10; Athefstan Roger, S, 7
17488 PIERCE, Jessie B, Watova, OK, 29; Herbert E, S, 3
　2200 PIERCE, John William, Nowata, OK, 18
31391 PIERCE, Nancy J, Ft. Gibson, OK, 23; Gertie, D, 9; Mark, S, 8; James C, S, 4; Earl B, S, 2
26026 PIERCE, Susan, Braggs, OK, 21
22061 PIGEON, Charles, Wauhillau, OK, 27; 43362, Lizzie, W, 24; Katie, D, 4; Tail, Henry, S of W, 9; Sallie, D of W, 8
　4383 PIGEON, Coo-wee, [John R], Spavinaw, OK, 37; 4384, Nannie, W, 30; Dave, S, 9; Oo-kel-ly, D, 5; Char-noh, you-ka, D, 1; Arl-san [Olsie], D, 1
　8666　PIGEON, George, Cookson, OK, 44; 41508, Nannie, W, 26; Maggie, D, 7; Charlotte, D, 5; George, S, 3
16438 PIGEON, James, Zena, OK, 10;　By Albert Starr, Gdn.
17448 PIGEON, Jesse, Wauhillu, OK, 52
11235 PIGEON, John, Oaks, OK, 68　[Died 5-1907]
35448 PIGEON, Lillie, Chelsea, OK, 8; Vann, Bro, 3;　By Emma Stelle, Gdn.
28742 PIGEON, Lulu, Wauhillau, OK, 26; Lugenia, D, 10; Tom, S, 3; Robert, S, 5
10792 PIGEON, Milie[sic], Wauhillau, OK, 56

[PIGEON, Sam. See #43358]   *(Note: entry separate from other family groups)*

17443 PIGEON, Thomas, Wauhillau, OK, 30; 17444, Nannie, W, 20
　　89 PIGEON, Woluke [Wasa-lou-kee], Locust Grove, OK, 60; 912, Susie, W, 44; George, S, 16
　6473 PIGEON, William, Rose, OK, 66
40697 PIKE, Lillie A, Moody, OK, 37; Crain, Mary May, D, 9; Pike, Effey, D, 4; Joe Elbert, S, 1
10901 PITCH, Janie Ellen, Leach, OK, over 56
24125 PITTS, Callie, Muskogee, OK, 107½ N. Cherokee St, 24; Elizabeth, D, 3; William V, S, 7/ 12
　9265 PITTS, Cora C, Sallisaw, OK, 23; Clarence, S, 5; Gladys, D, 3; Pauline, D, 1/12

CHEROKEE DESCENDANTS RESIDING WEST OF MISSISSIPPI RIVER.
VOLUME III (N – Z)
Key: Guion Miller Application Number; Name; Address, Relation (to Head); Age in 1906

24607 PITTS, Frances F, Tahlequah, OK, 24; Alma E, D, 2
1131 PLANK, Marsella M, Bartlesville, OK, 32; Russell W, S, 15; Norris B, S, 13; Bertha I, D, 10; Uziel S, S, 5; Garnett, D, 2

[PLEASANT, Lizzie. See #26516]   *(Note: entry separate from other family groups)*

23283 POGUE, Nancy, Muskogee, OK, 29; Jesse, S, 7; Jimmie, S, 4
5548 POINDEXTER, Maggie, Sleeper, OK, 42; William, S, 19; Benjamin, S, 16; Parlee, S, 12; Elen[sic], D, 10; Lucinda, D, 6; Louisa, D, 4
4818 POINTER, Patsy, Sallisaw, OK, 31; Samuel J, S, 5

[POLAN, Ochelata. See #17202]   *(Note: entry separate from other family groups)*

2826 POLECAT, Andrew, Long, OK, 56; William, S, 7; Sela [Celey], D, 5; John, S, 2
19202 POLECAT, Walter, Long, OK, 36; 17053, Lucy, W, 34; Betsey, D, 13; Isaac, S, 22; Levi, S, 9; Sarah Ann, D, 6; Bethel, S, 2

[POLOGNE, Nancy. See #9692]   *(Note: entry separate from other family groups)*

[POLONE. See PALONE.]

5249 POLONE, Fred, Westville, OK, 31; John D, S, 8; Richard, S, 7; Fred E, S, 5; Cora, D, 3; Grover, S, 2; Ora M, D, 1
7485 POLONE, James M, Lenapah, OK, 37; 7484, Lizzie, W, 37; 25646, Dovey, D, 18; Lovie, D, 14; Mary, D, 12; P. V, S, 7; Ray, S, 5; Tiff, S, 3; Lillie May, D, 1
5247 POLONE, John, Westville, OK, 24; Mary E, D, 3; Floyd, S, 1
5246 POLONE, Mary A, Westville, OK, 65
24976 POLSON, Freddie, Welch, OK, 30; Jasper L, S, 12; James D, S, 10; William R, S, 5; Cornelius V, S, 2
11931 POLSON, Lou, Oologah, OK, 29; John M, S, 9; Eddie, S, 7; Willie E, S, 3; Jewell, D, 1
4028 POLSON, Margarette F, Southwest City, MO, 4;   By Mary A. Hardy, Gdn.
3455 POLSON, Nellie, Coffeyville, KS, 31
3698 POLSON, William D, Southwest City, MO, 31; Ridge, S, 6; Marie A, D, 4; Marjorie, D, 1
35709 POLSTON, Ida C, Oologah, OK, 16
23781 POOL, Bertha E, Welch, OK, 24
14315 POOLE, Charles W, Chelsea, OK, 47; Walton C, S, 17; Carlisle A, S, 12; Scott O, S, 7; Gladys C, D, 5
6280 POORBEAR, Hunter, Bunch, OK, 57; 13230, Aggy, W, 57
1388 POORBEAR, Uphaney [Famy], Ft. Gibson, OK, 56
8774 POORBIRD, *(No other name given)*, Oaks, OK, 48
26516 POORBIRD, Mattie, Dragger, OK, 22; Pleasant [or Fodder], D, 6
18856 POORBOY, Israel, Tahlequah, OK, 34; Jeff, S, 12
16628 POORBOY, Jack, Oaks, OK, 31; 17670, Peggie, W, 22; Dave, S, 1

CHEROKEE DESCENDANTS RESIDING WEST OF MISSISSIPPI RIVER.
VOLUME III (N – Z)

Key: Guion Miller Application Number; Name; Address, Relation (to Head); Age in 1906

[POORBOY, Sallie. See #11238]   *(Note: entry separate from other family groups)*

 3284 POORBOY, Thomas, Hulbert, OK, 32; Willie, S, 3
36042 POORBOY, Waitie, Hulbert, OK, 16

[POPE, Clem W. See #33777]   *(Note: entries separate*
[POPE, Robert S. See #33777]   *from other family groups)*
[POPE, Madolyn K. See #33777]

13067 POPEJOY, Clara, St. Louis, MO, 2112 Pine St, 24
 4205 PORTER, Dick, Marble City, OK, 65; 10906, William, S, 19; Wolfe, S, 17; Sarah, D, 14

[PORTER, Edward. See #41227]   *(Note: entry separate from other family groups)*

 4932 PORTER, Emma, Marble City, OK, 34; Spaniard, Lizzie, D, 11; Lydia, D, 7; Sanders, Nellie, D, 4; Bird, Eloise, D, 1
10902 PORTER, James, Marble City, OK, 29
 5903 PORTER, James M, Sallisaw, OK, 33; Myrtle, D, 4; J. George, S, 2
12514 PORTER, Mary, Rose, OK, 25; Mildred M, D, 5
11566 PORTER, Sarah, Texanna, OK, 17
38863 POSEY, Henry R, Neck City, MO, 23
14186 POTATO, George, Locust Grove, OK, 51; 8739, Lucinda, W, 40
 9698 POTATO, Ned, Catoosa, OK, 30
 4200 POTTER, Eliza, Row, OK, 34; Ed, S, 15; Joe, S, 13; Laura, D, 10; Susie, D, 8; Green, S, 6; Mary, D, 1
 8905 POTTER, Hester, Row, OK, 34; George W, S, 14; Florence E, D, 12; Mollie L, D, 10; Robert L, S, 8; John W, S, 6; Jessie J, D, 4; Chloe E, D, 2
31319 POTTER, Ray, Salina, OK, 10;   By John Potter, Gdn.
32380 POTTER, Susie, Row, OK, 20
14716 POTTS, Anna, Melvin, OK, 22
 8804 POTTS, Annie, Gideon, OK, 16
13835 POTTS, Arphy N, Hulbert, OK, 21
   87 POTTS, Betsey, Locust Grove, OK, 86 [Dead]
16713 POTTS, Carrie, Hulbert, OK, 17
 8901 POTTS, Lou Ella, Choteau, OK, 24
 9809 POTTS, Lydia A, Melvin, OK, 35; Hughey E, S, 17; Mont E, S, 15; Virgie L, D, 12; Amy T, D, 7; Campbell, S, 5; Barnard, S, 3; Earnest M, S, 1/6

[POTTS, Richard. See #6600]   *(Note: entry separate from other family groups)*

[POTTS, Samuel. See #4498]
[POTTS, John. See #4498]   *(Note: entries separate*
[POTTS, Sallie. See #4498]   *from other family groups)*
[POTTS, Mary, See #4498]

CHEROKEE DESCENDANTS RESIDING WEST OF MISSISSIPPI RIVER.
VOLUME III   (N – Z)

Key: Guion Miller Application Number; Name; Address, Relation (to Head); Age in 1906

8854 POTTS, William, Rose, OK, 22
3734 POWELL, Cornella, Chelsea, OK, 67
23149 POWELL, Ivy A, Big Cabin, OK, 55
16714 POWELL, James F, Salina, OK, 14;   By Sarah Kinslow, Gdn.
5068 POWELL, James W, Big Cabin, OK, 24
9166 POWELL, Joseph, Sallisaw, OK, 53; 3889, Sarah L, W, 36
7585 POWELL, Mary E, Vinita, OK, 58
24396 POWELL, Minnie J, Oologah, OK, 27; Fannie, D, 9; Sam, S, 5; Ochelata, S, 3; Mary May, D, 1
5070 POWELL, Richard W, Big Cabin, OK, 23
5069 POWELL, Robert L, Big Cabin, OK, 20
16742 POWELL, William H, Salina, OK, 18;   By Sarah Kinslow, Gdn.
136 POWHATTAN, Cordelia, Evansville, AR, 15; Sarah L, Sis, 14; By Sarah L. Price, Gdn
26091 POWHATAN, Norma P, Evansville, AR, 17
24165 PRATHER, Eva L, Foyil, OK, 26; James L, S, 4; Flora M, D, 3
25759 PRATHER, Frances P, Grove, OK, 38; Minnie O, D, 17; Charilla C, D, 15; Fannie D, D, 13; Martha E, D, 11; James F, S, 9; Alvie M, S, 7; Bertha R, D, 5; Robert D, S, 2

[PRATHER, Richard L. See #25076]   *(Note: entry separate from other family groups)*

25298 PRESTON, Rose E, Needmore, OK, 36; Foust, Thomas J, S, 18; James M, S, 11; Preston, Halle E, D, 4; Dixie Ione, D, 1

[PRESTON, Willie M. See #22565]   *(Note: entry separate from other family groups)*

22566 PRESTON, Zachariah, Oglesby, OK, 33; Goldie A, D, 3; Herman J. D, S, 1
22892 PRICE, Addie E, Texanna, OK, 35; Maggie J, D, 15; Clarence McK, S, 13; Henry P, S, 10; Mary K, D, 9; Ila I, D, 7; Essa L, D, 5
28469 PRICE, Bertha A, Estella, OK, 26
11500 PRICE, Charles C, Inola, OK, 36; 11501, Daisy E, W, 27; Charles B, S, 7; Clarence T, S, 4
32400 PRICE, Charles E, Brushy, OK, 13;   By Reece B. Price, Gdn.
26561 PRICE, Clara, Sallisaw, OK, 4;   By W. R. Sloan, Gdn.
16193½ PRICE, David W, Durant, OK, 1215 W. Ark. St, 32
8992 PRICE, Ella M, Texana, OK, 7; Florence L, Sis, 3;   By Joseph Price, Gdn.
32399 PRICE, George W, Cookson, OK, 19;   By Reece B. Price, Gdn.
16192 PRICE, Ida Leona, Madill, OK, 27
23224 PRICE, James H, Evansville, AR, 37; Joseph W, S, 6; Arley G, S, 4; Mira L, D, 2; Emma E, D, 1/6
13461 PRICE, James S, Tiawah, OK, 40; 13462, Ida, W, 23; 13461, Ruthie E, D, 13; Ailsie Ann, D, 5; John J, S, ½
30666 PRICE, James S, Tahlequah, OK, 37; Ross A, S, 3; Samuel W, S, 1
16180 PRICE, Jasper P, Durant, OK, 25; William E, S, 4; Emmett T, S, 1

CHEROKEE DESCENDANTS RESIDING WEST OF MISSISSIPPI RIVER.
VOLUME III (N – Z)

Key: Guion Miller Application Number; Name; Address, Relation (to Head); Age in 1906

27961 PRICE, Joe S, Evansville, AR, 25; Ottus, S, 4; Veda O, D, 2
 4592 PRICE, John R, Tahlequah, OK, 60; 967, Katy, W, 60; 23914, Lotto Edith, D, 19
12110 PRICE, Mack E, Sallisaw, OK, 23
22943 PRICE, Mary, Ramona, OK, 26; Cecil D, S, 5
13674 PRICE, Mary L, Sallisaw, OK, 17;   By Martha J. Griffith, Gdn.
32384 PRICE, Reece B, Brushy, OK, 28
26669 PRICE, Samuel, Tahlequah, OK, 26
11463 PRICE, Sarah, Metory, OK, 50
23041 PRICE, Shorey A, Peggs, OK, 28; Cordelia M, D, 3; Samuel F, S, 2
 2117 PRICE, Susie, Sallisaw, OK, 41; John W, Jr, S, 14; Annie, D, 12; Sarah L, D, 10; Charley T, S, 7; Eddie, S, 6; Lena, D, 2
25563 PRICE, William, Vian, OK, 20
32385 PRICE, William T, Brushy, OK, 9;   By Reece B. Price, Gdn.
12894 PRIM, Annie E, Miami, OK, 30; Lawrence D, S, 1
 5336 PRITCHETT, Blackbird, Stilwell, OK, 57
 1123 PRITCHETT, Ed, Welling, OK, 17;   By William A. Evans, Gdn.
15949 PRITCHETT, Eliza, Welling, OK, 26
13791 PRITCHETT, George, Long, OK, 33; 16379, Bettie, W, 42; Curtis, S, 7; Isaac, S, 4; Lillie, D, 1
 8290 PRITCHETT, Henry, Welling, OK, 20 [Dead]
 2712 PRITCHETT, Hyane, Bunch, OK, 70
 5537 PRITCHETT, Jennie, Tahlequah, OK, 60; Proctor, Mike, GS, 15; Pritchett, Lizzie, GD, 2
 9379 PRITCHETT, Jesse, Stilwell, OK, 22
 8371 PRITCHETT, Jesse Fiction, Stilwell, OK, 16;   By Wilson Blackbird, Gdn.
 6672 PRITCHETT, Laura, Tahlequah, OK, 46
29909 PRITCHETT, Lila, Welling, OK, 16 [Died 9-15-1906];   (By) Sallie Manus, Grandmother
 6233 PRITCHETT, Lucy, Bunch, OK, 52; Swimmer, Lizzie, D, 11
 8298 PRITCHETT, Nannie F, Tahlequah, OK, 18;   By Wilson Blackbird, Gdn.
12689 PRITCHETT, Red, Stilwell, OK, 30; 12692, Fannie, W, 29; Nannie, D, 13; Philip, S, 10; Jesse, S, 7; Stephen, S, 3
13755 PRITCHETT, Tom, Long, OK, 40; 12693, Jennie, W, 33; Nannie, D, 13; Philip, S, 10; Jesse, S, 7; Stephen, S, 3
13755 PRITCHETT, Tom, Long, OK, 40; 12693, Jennie, W, 33; 42187, Annie, D, 15; Eliza, D, 16; John, S, 10; Narcissa, D, 5; Ollie, D, 2

[PRITCHETT, Tom Fixin. See #3674] *(Note: entry separate from other family groups)*

 6671   PRITCHETT, Toney, Proctor, OK, 19; Bird, Bro, 15; Janeanna, Sis, 12; Rufus, Bro, 8; By Charley Pritchett, Gdn
27854 PRITCHETT, Will, Proctor, OK, 22
13753 PRITCHETT, William, Long, OK, 34; 16380, Allie, W, 18; Nancy, D of H, 9; Katie, D of H, 3; Sallie, D, 1/3

CHEROKEE DESCENDANTS RESIDING WEST OF MISSISSIPPI RIVER.
VOLUME III (N – Z)

Key: Guion Miller Application Number; Name; Address, Relation (to Head); Age in 1906

[PRITCHETT, Wilson. See #28160] *(Note: entry separate from other family groups)*

  331 PRIVAT, Louisa, Grove, OK, 61
1272 PROCTOR, Adam, Pryor Creek, OK, 13; By A. L. Brown, Gdn.
  445 PROCTOR, Alex, Spavinaw, OK, 65; 469, Toowarte, W, 56; Betsy, D, 18; Thomas, S, 12
23848 PROCTOR, Alex, Jr, Spavinaw, OK, 31; 453, Sarah, W, 35; Eliza, D, 11; Columbus, S, 8

[PROCTOR, Bill. See #12613] *(Note: entry separate from other family groups)*

43251 PROCTOR, Charlie, Stilwell, OK, 25
 1606 PROCTOR, Crawler, Stilwell, OK, 67; 1602, Nancy, W, 49
23847 PROCTOR, Cumming, Spavinaw, OK, 29; 443, Nellie, W, 28; Sallie [Charlotte], S, 9; Willie, S, 7; Aggie, D, 3
23846 PROCTOR, Bird, Spavinaw, OK, 34; 458, Lola, W, 35; Wiley, S, 12; Daggie, D, 10; Cornsilk, D, 8; Nancy, D, 6; Eddie, S, 5; Mollie, D, 3; Abraham, S, 1
13379 PROCTOR, Daniel, Cookson, OK, 32; 12419, Akey, W, 22; 13379, Charley, S, 2
 3752 PROCTOR, Ezekiel, Ballard, OK, 72
32849 PROCTOR, Ezekiel, Jr, Proctor, OK, 40; 3912, Sallie, W, 44; Sam M, S, 19; Eli, S, 17; Charley J, S, 15; William C, S, 13; Walter, S, 10; Mary J, D, 8
26801 PROCTOR, Ezekiel P, Tahlequah, OK, 20
 2297 PROCTOR, George, Stilwell, OK, 34; 7468, Sallie, W, 27; Isaac, S, 6; Feather, S, 3
23842 PROCTOR, Hunter, Spavinaw, OK, 23; Euch, Child, 3
30189 PROCTOR, Joe, Remy, OK, 18; By Money Daugherty, Gdn.
42571 PROCTOR, Joe, Stilwell, OK, 21; 16584, Lucy, W, 17
12609 PROCTOR, John, Chance, OK, 5; By Betsy Snake, Gdn.
 5705 PROCTOR, Joseph, Baron, OK, 32

[PROCTOR, Linnie. See #16448] *(Note: entry separate from other family groups)*

  176 PROCTOR, Lucy, Rose, OK, 80

[PROCTOR, Lucy. See #23844] *(Note: entry separate from other family groups)*

[PROCTOR, Mike. See #5537] *(Note: entry separate from other family groups)*

 1167 PROCTOR, Nelson, Stilwell, OK, 52; 1168, Lydia, W, 55
 6686 PROCTOR, Sallie, Kansas, OK, 31; 6684, Nancy, D, 13
15636 PROCTOR, Sallie, Baron, OK, 9; By Joseph Proctor, Gdn.
16441 PROCTOR, Sallie, Zena, OK, 54
 8859 PROCTOR, Tom [or Black Fox], Muldrow, OK, 57; 8858, Sallie, W, 57
23849 PROCTOR, Walker, Spavinaw, OK, 27
23210 PROCTOR, Watt, Stilwell, OK, 23

CHEROKEE DESCENDANTS RESIDING WEST OF MISSISSIPPI RIVER.
VOLUME III (N – Z)

Key: Guion Miller Application Number; Name; Address, Relation (to Head); Age in 1906

11013 PROCTOR, William R, Ballard, OK, 34; 32292, Bell, W, 23; Willie Bell, D, 4
26963 PROPP, Mary E, Adair, OK, 39
11788 PRUETT, Jesse T, Terrell, TX, 39; I. Mabel, D, 11; J. Lillian, D, 5; C. Glenn, S, 4
 5351 PULLER, Leach, Locust Grove, OK, 25 [Insane]; By Robbin Puller, Father
 2949 PULLER, Robin, Locust Grove, OK, 66; 5322, Lizzie, W, 60
10696 PUMPKIN, Annie, Tahlequah, OK, 18; Hogshooter, Charlotte, D 1

[PUMPKIN, Charley. See#41784](Died 7-1906)
(Note: entry separate from other family groups)

 9246 PUMPKIN, Eli, Whitmire, OK, 30; 12968, Jennie, W, 20
16098 PUMPKIN, George, Whitmire, OK, 26
16395 PUMPKIN, George, Baron, OK, 26
10598 PUMPKIN, James, Moodys, OK, 33; 10697, Mary, W, 27
16085 Pumpkin, Richard, Whitmire, OK, S, 12; By George Pumpkin, Gdn.

[PUMPKIN, Johny[sic]. See #12619]
(Note: entry separate from other family groups)

 8259 PUMPKIN, Tom, Whitmire, OK, 61; 6482, Nellie, W, 56
 2805 PUMPKINPILE, Frank, Choteau, OK, 23; Ada, D, 1
 2804 PUMPKINPILE, George, Lometa, OK, 67
 9388 PUPPY, Sally, Evansville, OK, 59; Ned, S, 20; Dollie, D, 15

[PURDUE. See PERDEW and PERDUE.]

[PURKEY, Effie. See #27789]   *(Note: entry separate from other family groups)*

30815 PURYEAR, Gean, Tahlequah, OK, 34
31443 PUTNAM, Florence Elizabeth, Sapulpa, OK, 28; Cox, William Jerome, S, 9; Lena Leota, D, 7
 3733 PUTNAM, Josephine J, Pryor Creek, OK, 33; Jessie V, D, 12
29875 PUTNAM, Katie, Ft. Gibson, OK, 26; Samuel Owen, S, 9
29087 PYATT, Rosa C, Pawnee, OK, 17
 8140 PYEATT, Cherrie L, Hulbert, OK, 18

[QUALLATE, John. See #4923]   *(Note: entry separate from other family groups)*

13801 QUALLS, Maggie F, Tahlequah, OK, 33; Romulus A, S, 14; James F, S, 12; William R, S, 8; Dudley A, S, 6; Leona, D, 4; Mary J, D, 2
 7640 QUARLES, Caroline E, Baptist, OK, 72
27477 QUILLIAN, Norma W, Vinita, OK, 44; Allie, D, 14; Douglas, S, 11; Whitcomb, S, 7
30167 QUINTON, Cornelius, Dewey, OK, 23
12204 QUINTON, David, Sallisaw, OK, 31; 12206, Emma L, D, 9

CHEROKEE DESCENDANTS RESIDING WEST OF MISSISSIPPI RIVER.
VOLUME III   (N – Z)

Key: Guion Miller Application Number; Name; Address, Relation (to Head); Age in 1906

10465 QUINTON, Ethel M, Texanna, OK, 17; Isaac S, Bro, 15; Nancy E, Sis, 13; Mary E, Sis, 11;   By Roxie Haney, Gdn.
6980 QUINTON, Frank, Brushy, OK, 28
16378 QUINTON, George, Bunch, OK, 36; 769, Lydia, W, 39; Laura, D, 9; Sequoyah, S, 7
16904 QUINTON, Jack, Hoffman, OK, 45; Jesse, S, 16
16703 QUINTON, Jeff, Brushy, OK, 41
11172 QUINTON, Johnson, Brushy, OK, 18;   By Letha Quinton, Gdn.

[QUINTON, Lewis. See #7035]   *(Note: entry separate from other family groups)*

4814 QUINTON, Lila, Locust Grove, OK, 34; Noah, S, 11; Nannie M, D, 10
37501 QUINTON, Lonnie, Sequoyah, OK, 16;   By Dave Quinton, Gdn.
6982 QUINTON, Mack, Hanson, OK, 34; 13667, Emily, W, 35; Jackoline A, D, 10; Joseph, S, 5; Zelma, D, 3; Winona, D, 1
3485 QUINTON, Maggie, Stilwell, OK, 27; Fogg, Dick, S, 10; Becca, D, 6; Quinton, Lizzie, D, 1/12

[QUINTON, Myrtle C. See #12497]   *(Note: entry separate from other family groups)*

8853 RABBIT, Arch, Locust Grove, OK, 40

[RABBIT, Carrie. See #9412]   *(Note: entry separate from other family groups)*

6582 RABBIT, Nelly, Bunch, OK, 40
359 RABBIT, Thomas, Southwest City, MO, 51
16607 RACKLIFF, George, Tahlequah, OK, 13; 16608, John, Bro, 7;   By Edward W. Rackliff, Gdn.
2445 RACKLIFF, Katie, Hulbert, OK, 39; Cochran, Silas, S, 4 [Died 12-1907]
6808 RAGGIO, Emily Jane, Angels Camp, CA, 47; Rolstoro, S, 20; Leland C, S, 16
38853 RAGGIO, Joseph B, San Andres, CA, 23; Ardis B, S, 4; Alberta L, D, 1
31367 RAGSDALE, Alice, Tahlequah, OK, 23
27253 RAGSDALE, Benjamin, Metory, OK, 29
4381 RAGSDALE, David W, Rose, OK, 75; 16520, Ruthie, W, 48; Maggie, D, 16; David, S, 14; Nancy, D, 11; Claude, S, 9; Muggie, S, 5; Raper, Sam, S of W, 28 [Died 11-1906]
26834 RAGSDALE, George II, Chance, OK, 31; 2215, Maggie, W, 25; Rease, S, 2
835 RAGSDALE, Jack, Metory, OK, 55
25271 RAGSDALE, Joe, Muldrow, OK, 25
23389 RAGSDALE, John, Muldrow, OK, 24
1035 RAGSDALE, Johnsanna, Owasso, OK, 52; Charles O, S, 19; John A, S, 16; Robert, S, 13
204 RAGSDALE, Riley, Baron, OK, 54
3790 RAGSDALE, Thomas, Warner, OK, 33; Willie A, S, 5; Vera, D, 3; Cherokee, D, 1/3

CHEROKEE DESCENDANTS RESIDING WEST OF MISSISSIPPI RIVER.
VOLUME III (N – Z)

Key: Guion Miller Application Number; Name; Address, Relation (to Head); Age in 1906

23388 RAGSDALE, Wilburn, Muldrow, OK, 45; 3309, Ellen, W, 38; May, D, 17; Sadie, D, 15; Willard, S, 6; Ezekiel, S, 4
4720 RAINCROW, Charles, Cookson, OK, 25; 26149, Mary J, W, 20
28019 RAINCROW, Cornelius, Cookson, OK, 21
5800 RAINCROW, Jess, Dragger, OK, 28
4722 RAINCROW, Joe, Cookson, OK, 51; 5209, Mary E, W, 55; 2808, Elsie, D, 19; 5209, Kate, D, 16; Rachel, D, 13
4721 RAINCROW, Rachel, Cookson, OK, 82
25112 RAINCROW, Sallie, Locust Grove, OK, 30; Rowe, Felix, S, 9

[RAINCROW, Susie. See #1721]   *(Note: entry separate from other family groups)*

25075 RAINES, George M, Vinita, OK, 21
43908 RAINES, William H, Vinita, OK, 19; Gordon B, Bro, 7; By William B. Raines, Gdn.
4029 RALEY, Mary L, Muldrow, OK, 55

[RALL, Ella May. See #5496]   *(Note: entry separate from other family groups)*

2490 RALSTON, Beulah, Needmore, OK, 23
5380 RALSTON, James D, Lenapah, OK, 55
2491 RALSTON, John, Needmore, OK, 26; Vera B, D, 2
1060 RALSTON, John T, Needmore, OK, 80
1411 RALSTON, Robert L, Cleora, OK, 19
24406 RAMEY, Mary Evaline, Westville, OK, 25; Maurice Earl, S, 1
36594 RAMEY, Ora D, St. Joe, ID, 26; Allen A, S, 5

[RAMMING, Susan. See #25310]   *(Note: entry separate from other family groups)*

23605 RAMSEY, Ella N, Adair, OK, 32; James W, S, 4; Rufus E, S, 1
36414 RAMSEY, Jannette, Catoosa, OK, 17
29409 RAMSOUR, Irene, Tyler, TX, 27; Coy D, S, ½
4235 RANDEL, Cinderilla, Manard, OK, 64
8127 RANDOLPH, Eliza, Hanson, OK, 27; Pinkey M, S, 5; James H, S, 3; Tim G, S, 3; Robert C, S, 1

[RANDOLPH, Joel. See #1843]   *(Note: entry separate from other family groups)*

1034 RANSON, Nancy C, Needmore, OK, 71
3649 RAPER, Berry, Durant, OK, 47; Oscar, S, 16; Dona, D, 14; Pearley, D, 12; Bertha, D, 10; Robert, S, 8; Rosie, D, 6; Freddie, S, 3; Loney, S, 1
227 RAPER, Charles, Oologah, OK, 51; John, S, 19; Mary Edith, D, 5
6520 RAPER, George W, Eucha, OK, 60; 2107, Nellie, W, 55; Smith, Samuel, S of W, 18; Joseph, S of W, 16
24357 RAPER, James, Melvin, OK, 45; 8321, Martha J, D, 18

CHEROKEE DESCENDANTS RESIDING WEST OF MISSISSIPPI RIVER.
VOLUME III (N – Z)

Key: Guion Miller Application Number; Name; Address, Relation (to Head); Age in 1906

9000 RAPER, James W, School, MO, 44; Asa, S, 20; Dovie, D, 17; Maud, D, 12; Katie, D, 8; Bonnie, D, 6; Arthur, D, 6
212 RAPER, John A, Choteau, OK, 70
23564 RAPER, John A, Jr, Choteau, OK, 11;   By Ora Raper, Gdn.
25869 RAPER, John Henry, Chloeta, OK, 37; 25870, Sarah E, W, 33; 25869, Sarah Jane, D, 16; Willie, S, 14; George G, S, 11; Rosie G, D, 8; Essie M, D, 6
37086 RAPER, Joseph, Chloeta, OK, 24; David W, S, 4; Mary Jane, D, 7/12
13117 RAPER, Laura, Rose, OK, 22

[RAPER, Luella. See #38484]   *(Note: entry separate from other family groups)*

976 RAPER, Martin J, Chance, OK, 98
2749 RAPER, Nancy, Melvin, OK, 55?
27862 RAPER, Ross, Ft. Gibson, OK, 7; Jennie, Sis, 4;   By Mose Raper, Gdn.

[RAPER, Sam. See #16520] (Died 11-1906)
   (Note: entry separate from other family groups)

211 RAPER, William Lewis, Choteau, OK, 28
22596 RAPER, William P, Choteau, OK, 38; Alvin F, S, 13; Jess M, S, 8
25471 RAPER, Young, Oologah, OK, 21
4439 RASMUS, Buena V, Muskogee, OK, 29; Nannie E, D, 7; Norma E, D, 4; Josephine F, D, 1
1654 RASMUS, Josephine C, Tahlequah, OK, 66
43091 RATT, Ahlee, Welling, OK, 5;   By Sarah Ratt, Gdn.
31015 RAT, Jennie, Stilwell, OK, 19
13750 RAT, Jim, Stilwell, OK, 22
7874 RAT, John, Welling, OK, 40; 7887, Jennie, W, 35; Tom, S, 12; Lewis, S, 9
14274 RAT, Mary, Bunch, OK, 17
13136 RAT, Peggy, Stilwell, OK, 24

[RAT, Polly. See #604]   *(Note: entry separate from other family groups)*

[RAT, Susani[sic]. See #12630]
[RAT, Polly. See #12630]   *(Note: entries separate*
[RAT, John. See #12630]   *from other family groups)*

17212 RATCLIFF, Eva E, Vinita, OK, 48; Finnie R, S, 17; Mary E, D, 15; Norville, S, 13
32430 RATCLIFF, Fred F, Vinita, OK, 23
24051 RATCLIFF, James W, Vinita, OK, 21

[RATCLIFF, Nannie. See #16580]   *(Note: entries separate*
[RATCLIFF, Wat. See #16580]   *from other family groups)*

CHEROKEE DESCENDANTS RESIDING WEST OF MISSISSIPPI RIVER.
VOLUME III (N – Z)

Key: Guion Miller Application Number; Name; Address, Relation (to Head); Age in 1906

20248 RATLEY, Charley, Sallisaw, OK, 19
28040 RATLEY, Lona M, Checotah, OK, 14; Pearl, Sis, 12; By Jane Winkelpleck, Gdn.
 5761 RATLEY, Moses J, Muskogee, OK, 45; Lawrence, S, 13; Beulah, D, 9
18491 RATLEY, Nettie, Sallisaw, OK, 22
 6736 RATLEY, Wallace, Campbell, OK, 67
 1078 RATLIFF, Daniel, Cookson, OK, 73; 27949, Eliza, D, 19

[RATLIFF, Henry. See #10753]   *(Note: entry separate from other family groups)*

27944 RATLIFF, Houston, Cookson, OK, 25; Robbin S, S, 5; Kale, S, 2 [Died 6-1906]; Van, S, 1
27950 RATLIFF, Richard, Cookson, OK, 30; 27941, Lizzie M, W, 30; Mary A, D, 9; John, S, 6; Maggie, D, 1
 1898 RATTLER, Nancy, Uniontown, AR, 12

[RATTLER, Nannie. See #16580]   *(Note: entries separate*
[RATTLER, Wat. See #16580]   *from other family groups)*

  345 RATTLER, Rider, Porum, OK, 44; 1580, Lizie, W, 31; 345, Lillie, D, 13; Nora, D, 4; Timothy, S, 3; Luke, S, ¼

[RATTLER, Sar-da-gah. See #2275]   *(Note: entry separate from other family groups)*

13101 RATTLER, William, Stilwell, OK, 38; Lizzie, D, 8; Gehena, D, 6; Josie, D, 3; Charley, S, ¼
11773 RATTLINGGOURD, Alexander, Claremore. OK, 43; Artemiss, D, 20; Susie, D, 17; Andrew, S, 12
 5384 RATTLINGGOURD, Artemiss, Claremore, OK, 49; Gertrude, D, 16

[RATTLINGGOURD, Bertha. See #13686]
                (Note: entry separate from other family groups)

16087 RATTLINGGOURD, Callie, Tahlequah, OK, 26; Nick, (S?), 3; Martin, (S?), 1
 5624 RATTLINGGOURD, Charley, Tahlequah, OK, 39
12210 RATTLINGGOURD, Charley, Braggs, OK, 25
23829 RATTLINGGOURD, Charles A, Claremore, OK, 25
 5027 RATTLINGGOURD, Dan, Southwest City, MO, 38; 4852, Lulu, W, 36; Katie, D, 10; Lewis B, S, 12; Terry, S, 8; Mary Jane, D, 7; May, D, 5; Lee, S, 1/12
15619 RATTLINGGOURD, Daniel, Claremore, OK, 22
40693 RATTLINGGOURD, Dave, Moodys, OK, 25
 9917 RATTLINGGOURD, David, Caney, KS, 22; 33730, Matilda, W, 20; Anderson, S, 1/12
 1980 RATTLINGGOURD, Elias, Tahlequah, OK, 36; Sallie, D, 8; Allen E, S, 6; Roy E, S, 1
40695 RATTLINGGOURD, Eliza, Moodys, OK, 21

CHEROKEE DESCENDANTS RESIDING WEST OF MISSISSIPPI RIVER.
VOLUME III   (N – Z)

Key: Guion Miller Application Number; Name; Address, Relation (to Head); Age in 1906

1976 RATTLINGGOURD, Ellis, Tahlequah, OK, 42; 16609, Mattie, W, 41; John E, S, 17; William P, S, 15; Lucinda R, D, 6; Dobson, Bonnie L, D of W, 10

28531 RATTLINGGOURD, Frank, Alluwe, OK, 34; 8787, Cynthia, W, 34; 28531, Ethel R, D, 15; Harry R, S, 13; Charles R, S, 5; Lee R, S, 3; Clarence R, S, 1/12

16705 RATTLINGGOURD, George, Tahlequah, OK, 41

31612 RATTLINGGOURD, George, Moodys, OK, 33; 31613, Columbia, W, 29

3885 RATTLINGGOURD, Henry, Claremore, OK, 29; Jesse H, S, 8; James E, S, 5; Beta M, D, 3; Cherokee A, D, 1

41201 RATTLINGGOURD, Henry, Moodys, OK, 30; Nick, S, 4; Martin, S, 2

10299 RATTLINGGOURD, Jack, Melvin, OK, 54; 10470, Nellie, W, 59

[RATTLINGGOURD, Jack. See #11651]
[RATTLINGGOURD, George. See #11651]   *(Note: entries separate*
[RATTLINGGOURD, Calvin. See #11651]   *from other family groups)*
[RATTLINGGOURD, Sister. See #11651]

328 RATTLINGGOURD, James, Alluwe, OK, 31
3629 RATTLINGGOURD, James, Claremore, OK, 33
5527 RATTLINGGOURD, James, Tahlequah, OK, 71
26135 RATTLINGGOURD, James, Moodys, OK, 21

[RATTLINGGOURD, Jennie. See #6363]
        (Note: entry separate from other family groups)

[RATTLINGGOURD, John, See #17061]
        (Note: entry separate from other family groups)

1984 RATTLINGGOURD, Jesse, Moodys, OK, 61; 1982, Susan, W, 61; 1984, Samuel, S, 18

[RATTLINGGOURD, Katharine. See #27727]
        (Note: entry separate from other family groups)

3204 RATTLINGGOURD, Katie, Gideon, OK, 18;   By Looney R. Gourd, Gdn.
26137 RATTLINGGOURD, Lila, Tahlequah, OK, 27; Susie Ann, D, 6; Kenepick, S, 4
5357 RATTLINGOURD[sic], Looney, Gideon, OK, 24
6076 RATTLINGGOURD, Looney, Gideon, OK, 78
4337 RATTLINGGOURD, Lorin C, Vinita, OK, 12; 4336, Vera, Sis, 15; By J. W. Orr. Gdn.

[RATTLINGGOURD, Morgan. See #9628]
        (Note: entry separate from other family groups)

26136 RATTLINGGOURD, Ose, Tahlequah, OK, 24
19078 RATTLINGGOURD, Sarah, Sageeyah,   OK, 26

CHEROKEE DESCENDANTS RESIDING WEST OF MISSISSIPPI RIVER.
VOLUME III   (N – Z)

Key: Guion Miller Application Number; Name; Address, Relation (to Head); Age in 1906

40696 RATTLINGGOURD, Sarah, Moodys, OK, 23
10386 RATTLINGGOURD, Thomas, Moodys, OK, 54; 3144, Maria, W, 53; Thomas, Jr, S, 19; Carrie, D, 14; Susie, D, 11; Nancy, D, 9
33393 RATTLINGGOURD, Thomas, Tahlequah, OK, 40; Nancy, D, 15; James, S, 12; Esther, D, 10; Thomas, S, 7; Carl, S, 1
16097 RATTLINGGOURD, Walter, Tahlequah, OK, 27; 38506, Maggie, W, 18
40664 RATTLINGGOURD, William, Moodys, OK, 35; 5742, Mollie, W, 26; Eli, S, 8; Joe, S, 4; Rufus, S, 2 [Died 7-1906]
21148 RAVEN, Albert, Warner, OK, 25
9445 RAVEN, George, Oaks, OK, 50; 9944, Mary, W, 35; Joe, S, 2
355 RAVEN, Joe [Fox], Southwest City, MO, 24
373 RAVEN, John L, Southwest City, MO,   18

[RAVEN, Mary. See #16919]   *(Note: entry separate from other family groups)*

3705 RAVENS, Boney, Southwest City, MO, 66; 5983, Wam-si-ni, W, 60; 3705, Darkey, GD, 10
32736 RAVENS, Jelmier, Zena, OK, 22
7017 RAVENS, Nancy, Southwest City, MO, 26
2791 RAY, Clorinda S, Fairland, OK, 45
27796 RAY, Jennie A, Miami, OK, 23; Cassonia E, D, 6; Bertha Z, D, 4
22592 RAYMOND, Ada V, Webbers Falls, OK, 11; Sus N, Sis, 7; By Carrie Burns, Gdn.
2905 RAYMOND, Amanda J, Vinita, OK, 66
27193 RAYMUS, Annie T, Rio Vista, CA, 21
27720 REAGAN, Arthur G, Tahlequah, OK, 23
3825 REAGAN, Lydia A, Tahlequah, OK, 62; Austin G, S, 18
18526 REAVES, Angie, Warner, OK, 54; Lettie, D, 11
13946 RECTOR, Rosa J, Claremore, OK, 25; Kelly, Edna, D, 7
3798 REDBIRD, Anna, Peggs, OK, 60
4701 REDBIRD, Betsy, Stilwell, OK, 62
14317 REDBIRD George W, Stilwell, OK, 47; 4605, Peggie, W, 48

[REDBIRD, Hoolie. See #26359]   *(Note: entry separate from other family groups)*

9690 REDBIRD, Jackson, Christie, OK, 59; 6745, Nancy, W, 64; Jim, S, 13

[REDBIRD, Johnson. See #16076]   *(Note: entry separate from other family groups)*

4044 REDBIRD, Nathaniel J, Stilwell, OK, 48; 2392, Mary, W, 46; 26358, Lizzie, D, 17; 26358, John L, S, 10; 4044, Mary, D, 8
6685 REDBIRD, Sallie, Kansas, OK, 66

[REDBIRD, Sam. See #10616]   *(Note: entry separate from other family groups)*

CHEROKEE DESCENDANTS RESIDING WEST OF MISSISSIPPI RIVER.
VOLUME III   (N – Z)

Key: Guion Miller Application Number; Name; Address, Relation (to Head); Age in 1906

15965 REDBIRD, Sarah, Welling, OK, 18
9691 REDBIRD, White, Christie, OK, 56; 11217, Quetie, W, 60
29106 REDDELL, Arizona, Mount Judea, AR, 26; James M, S, 6; Effie J, D, 4; Bessie T, D, 1
29105 REDDELL, Easter J, Mount Judea, AR, 21; Osmar T, S, 3
28317 REDDEN, James Z, Long, OK, 22; 6044, Myrtle, W, 17
28316 REDDEN, Lou E, Long, OK, 40; Moses O, S, 20; John, S, 18; William H, S, 15; Nealy M, S, 13; Hugh M, S, 10; Charles O, S, 8; Sarah A, D, 5; Maudie M, D, 2
2703 REDINGER, Mary, Chetopa, KS, 24; Henry F, S, 6; Lawrence B, S, 4
3839 REDMAN, Malinda, Chelsea, OK, 86
23447 REECE, Annie, Hadley, OK, 30
23202 REECE, Eliza, Gritts, OK, 22; George W, S, 1
3911 REECE, Nancy J, Proctor, OK, 53
4423 REECE, Thomas J, Proctor, OK, 31; Levi, S, 5; Roy, S, 3
12803 REED, Andrew, Bartlesville, OK, 48; Linnie I, D, 16; Nancy A, D, 14; Philatus L. A, S, 12; Alice L. V, D, 8; Alee M, D, 10; David A, S, 4; Cleo F, S, 2; Rena B, D, 7/12
5905 REED, Annie, Maysville, AR, 41; Freeman, Peggy, D, 15; Reed, Cillie, D, 3
4393 REED, Emily J, Spavinaw, OK, 45; Rufus Guy, S, 12
1627 REED, Galuga, Clarksville, AR, 20
25198 REED, Joe H, Spavinaw, OK, 23
28886 REED, Lizzie, Chelsea, OK, 30; John R, S, 10; Samuel, S, 8; Anna F, D, 4
22879 REED, Luna, Zena, OK, 23; Harley M, S, 5; Tressie, D, 3; Vernia, D, 2
13140 REED, Molly E, McKey, OK, 38; Walter S, S, 18; Jennie M, D, 16; 25279, Myrtle B, D, 20
1998 REED, Nancy M, Zena, OK, 43; John, S, 18; Pearl, D, 16
11651 REED, Paralee, Claremore, OK, 47; Rattlinggourd, Jack, S, 19; George, S, 15; Calvin, S, 13; Sister, D, 11; Reed, Johnnie, S, 4
23295 REED, Sarah Bell, Checotah, OK, 34; Case, Maud, D, 14; Emma, D, 12; Robert, S, 10; May, D, 8; Reed, John, S, 3
2846 REESE, Charles, Muskogee, OK, 54; President, S, 15; Charles Tony, S, 12
28524 REESE, Charles, Manard, OK, 23
6935 REESE, Charley, Baron, OK, 45; 6965, Ahli, W, 57
3795 REESE, Ellis, Proctor, OK, 26
26268 REESE, Felix, Muskogee, OK, 21
32439 REESE, Henry D, Manard, OK, 32
24573 REESE, Inez, Ft. Gibson, OK, 27; Wolf, Ethel May, D, 2
35543 REESE, James G, Porum, OK, 30
4424 REESE, John, Proctor, OK, 22
1052 REESE, Joseph, Chance, OK, 45; 24671, Ida, W, 33; Charley, S, 15; Andy, S, 13; Jesse, S, 11; Ellis, S, 9; Ada, D, 3
1642 REESE, Joseph, Hulbert, OK, 44; Whittie, S, 15; Lizzie, D, 11; Annie, D, 8; Maggie, D, 5
3797 REESE, Richard, Proctor, OK, 32; 3796, Annie, W, 30; Betsy, D, 8; Emma, D, 5; Johnson, S, 3

CHEROKEE DESCENDANTS RESIDING WEST OF MISSISSIPPI RIVER.
VOLUME III   (N – Z)

Key: Guion Miller Application Number; Name; Address, Relation (to Head); Age in 1906

- 170 REESE, Roddy A, Manard, OK, 65
- 34994 REESE, Rora, Manard, OK: 21
- 4426 REESE, Susan E, Proctor, OK, 28
- 24689 REESE, Tuxie O, Oglesby, OK, 29; Noah, S, 6; Stand B, S, 5; William R, S, 2; Chief H, S, 5/12
- 14267 REEVE, Arlie, Webbers Falls, OK, 35; Nettie, D, 15; Bertha, D, 13; Edward, S, 6; Ida, D, 5
- 16980 REEVES, Hogan T, Pryor Creek, OK, 6; Jesse W, Bro, 3;   By John R. Reeves, Gdn.
- 5756 REEVES, Martha E, Stilwell, OK, 53; John, S, 14; Lawson, S, 9; Theodore, S, 5
- 26094 REEVES, Mary E, Kansas, OK, 33; Edmond Harry, S, 2
- 10372 REEVES, Nancy M, Adair, OK, 56
- 24880 REEVES, Stella, Stilwell, OK, 19; Lowe, Sada, D, 2
- 26162 REID, Cleo T, Tahlequah, OK, 30; Thompson, S, 5; Mary Cleo, D, 3
- 5153 REID, Eva M, Checotah, OK, 26
- 12532 REID, Minnie, Muskogee, OK, 19
- 23941 REINHARDT, Fannie, Wann, OK, 22; Earl, S, 3; Vernon, S, 2
- 8215 REINHARDT, Charles H, Coodys Bluff, OK, 11; Sarah, Sis, 15; Lambert, John, Bro, 17;   By Chas. H, Reinhardt, Gdn.
- 4951 REMSON, Julia E, Grove, OK, 48
- 23158 RENNECKAR, Sarah, Chance, OK, 28; Robert R, S, 9; Andrew J, S, 7; Bettie J, D, 5
- 24517 RENO, Alma E, Ketchum, OK, 18
- 24232 REVARD, Myrtle M, Pawhuska, OK, 21
- 3490 REX, Alfred C, Locust Grove, OK, 18
- 8697 REYNOLDS, Annie P, Afton, OK, 42; Cromwell, Zeddie, S, 17
- 16618 REYNOLDS, Ellen, Texanna, OK, 51; George, S, 16

[REYNOLDS, Eva A. See #16103]   *(Note: entry separate from other family groups)*

- 37133 REYNOLDS, Jesse, Texanna, OK, 51; Jessie M, D, 2; George W, S, 1
- 780 REYNOLDS, Lulu E, Westville, OK, 25; Louis Thelma, D, 6; Vera, D, 1; Gertrude, D, 1
- 17237 RHEA, Sallie, Oo-la-gah, OK, 27; Simmons, George, S, 8; Rhea, Cecal May, D, 2
- 24174 RHOADS, Margaret E. A, Stilwell, OK, 31; Nettie M, D, 3; Watie, S, 1/6

[RHODES, Edward. See #36467]   *(Note: entry separate from other family groups)*

- 31856 RHODES, Ella, Hulbert, OK, 22; John, S, ¼
- 22865 RHODES, Grace, Grove, OK, 25; Ladd, Delmar, S, 7; Clifford, S, 3; Rhodes, Minnie E, D, ¼
- 11227 RHOMER, May, Webbers Falls, OK, 34; Emma N, D, 17; May F, D, 14; Maggie B, D, 13; Fannie C, D, 11
- 10150 RIBBON, Jack, Locust Grove, OK, 50; 7693, Lucy, W, 32
- 8436 RICE, Emma, Chelsea, OK, 25; Dorothy, D, 6; Della, D, 4

CHEROKEE DESCENDANTS RESIDING WEST OF MISSISSIPPI RIVER.
VOLUME III (N – Z)

Key: Guion Miller Application Number; Name; Address, Relation (to Head); Age in 1906

23287 RICE, Fannie, Summit, OK, 27; Mamie, D, 6; Viola May, D, 2
30056 RICE, James A, Minden Mines, MO, 24
2383 RICE, Ruby, Muskogee, OK, 17;   By Isabella Rush, Gdn.
13394 RICE, Viola, Muskogee, OK, 14;   By Isabella Rush, Gdn.
753 RICH, Mae, Prairie Grove, AR, 35; Russell E, S, 8; Beuna M, D, 7; Dona C, D, 4; Onie T, D, 4
26286 RICH, Minnie B, Sallisaw, OK, 35; Vera V, D, 13
4840 RICHARDS, Mary, Tahlequah, OK, 49;   Ella Q, D, 17; Mary W, D, 8
23644 RICHARDS, Roddie, Tahlequah, OK, 22
23645 RICHARDS, Sim B, Tahlequah, OK, 24; 26826, Mable H, W, 19
13966 RICHARDS, Susan M, Wauhillau, OK, 35; Millie, D, 14; Joe, S, 12; Mary, D, 10; Kanzada, D, 1
23466 RICHARDSON, Ida M, Ruby, OK, 20
9461 RICHARDSON, Malinda A. E, Sallisaw, OK, 25; John Elmer, S, 2; Viola Mattie, D, 1; Clercy May, D, 1/6
26090 RICHARDSON, Nancy E, Evansville, AR, 28; Zora I, D, 4; William R, S, 2
5615 RICHARDSON, Nannie V, Pryor Creek, OK, 9; Alma E, Sis, 8;   By Chas. G. Richardson, Gdn.
1986 RICHEY, Anderson, Metory, OK, 26; Gracey L, D, 3
28921 RICHTER, Charles H, Dawson, OK, 7;   By Susan Cook, Gdn.
6274 RIDDLE, Fannie J, Claremore, OK, 36; Ida, D, 17; Fred F, S, 14; Fannie M, D, 10; Dewey L, S, 8; Lillian R, D, 6; Grace T, D, 4; Mabel F, D, ¼
1215 RIDDLE, Leona, Ramona, OK, 17
5644 RIDDLE, Louisa E, Vinita, OK, 29; Giles H, S, 11; Lula M, D, 8; Edna L, D, 4
23211 RIDENHOUR, Margaret A, Stilwell, OK, 27; Woodall, Beuna V, D, 7
38651 RIDER, Ada, Stilwell, OK, 23
4702 RIDER, Austin, Talala, OK, 35; 4703, Flora E, W, 30
7927 RIDER, Benjamin F, Sallisaw, OK, 19;   By J. B. Rider, Gdn.
11805 RIDER, Charles, Talala, OK, 41
17606 RIDER, Charles M, Talala, OK, 19; Susanna, Sis, 12; Stand U, Bro, 7; Abraham, Bro, 2;   By Charles Rider, Gdn.

[RIDER, Emily. See #9404]
[RIDER, Caroline. See #9404]   *(Note: entries separate*
[RIDER, Stan W. See #9404]   *from other family groups)*

7926 RIDER, Jack B, Sallisaw, OK, 23; 26376, Sarah Z, W, 21; L. Dee, D, 1
3756 RIDER, James H, Talala, OK, 29
15953 RIDER, Joe, Stilwell, OK, 38; 7210, Sarah, W, 33
8693 RIDER, John, Baron Forks, OK, 37
4586 RIDER, John G, Oglesby, OK, 32; Jessie G, D, 1
5892 RIDER, John W, Sallisaw, OK, 46; Austin W, S, 14; Tip P, S, 10; Chas. A, S,8; Thomas R, S, 5; Jack C, S, 2
5846 RIDER, Josephine, Bartlesville, OK, 58 [Insane];   By William P. Ross, Gdn.
5305 RIDER, Mary, Evansville, AR, 26; Weta, D, 5

CHEROKEE DESCENDANTS RESIDING WEST OF MISSISSIPPI RIVER.
VOLUME III   (N – Z)

Key: Guion Miller Application Number; Name; Address, Relation (to Head); Age in 1906

25958 RIDER, Mary A, Evansville, AR, 22
28748 RIDER, Ola, Lenapah, OK, 26; French, Dory V, D, 7; Cortise C, S, 4

[RIDER, Oo-squin-ni. See #11964]   *(Note: entry separate from other family groups)*

25028 RIDER, Sadie, Ruby, OK, 23; Violet, D, 3; Jennie May, D, 2; John Elliott, S, 1/12
 7925 RIDER, Samuel D, Sallisaw, OK, 21
27781 RIDER, Thomas, Manard, OK, 29; Wilson, S, ¼
 6503 RIDER, Thomas L, Evansville, AR, 50; 27446, Mittie E, D, 18; Roscoe C, S, 15; Milton, S, 13; Ivey J, D, 11; Cherokee A, D, 9; Anna, D, 1
 5845 RIDER, Wilson, Tahlequah, OK, 68
  526 RIDGE, Adam, Eucha, OK, 34; 527, Alsey, W, 29; 526, Grape, S, 11; Cull, S, 7; Starr, Cora, D, 6; Ridge, Daniel, S, 3; Lucy, D, 1/12 [Died 6-1906]; Tildon, S, 1/12 [Died 8-1906]
 5768 RIDGE, Ben, Kansas, OK, 45; 5769, Malissa J, W, 50; Ose, S, 16
 1492 RIDGE, Callie, Rose, OK, 43; 5311, Fannie, D, 20; Joe, S, 18; Jesse, S, 17; Nannie, D, 14; Myrtle, D, 7; Beveart, Lucie, D, 4
 9816 RIDGE, Darsie R, Grass Valley, CA, 44
 5884 RIDGE, Frank B, San Francisco, CA, 720 Schraeder St, 34
15946 RIDGE, George McLean, San Francisco, 536 Clayton St. CA, 19
15947 RIDGE, Helen Francis, San Francisco, 536 Clayton St. CA, 17
 3704 RIDGE, Jeremiah, Chloeta, OK, 33; 27245, Nellie, W, 18; Peter, S, 8
 3703 RIDGE, John, Chloeta, OK, 40
14197 RIDGE, John, Sallisaw, OK, 20

[RIDGE, John P. See #11278]   *(Note: entry separate from other family groups)*

  366 RIDGE, Moses, Chloeta, OK, 66; 626, Ave, W, 61

[RIDGE, Nellie. See #1711]   *(Note: entry separate from other family groups)*

15945 RIDGE, Nobel John, San Francisco, CA, 536 Clayton St. 21
25484 RIDGE, Polly, Afton, OK, 26; Peter, S, 8
 1712 RIDGE, Susan, Spavinaw, OK, 70
 1574 RIDGE, Young Beaver, Kansas, OK, 56; 5606, Annie, W, 49
13690 RIDGEWAY, Minnie V, McKey, OK, 17; Beulah, D, 1
14141 RIEDEL, Ella, Angels Camp, CA, 29; Thisba Nadine, D, 3
 2975 RIGGS, Eliza, Chelsea, OK, 50
23268 RIGGS, Juliette S, Claremore, OK, 33
11656 RIGSBY, John Hannah, Sallisaw, OK, 31; James F, S, 9; Jessie, D, 7; Tiny, D, 5; Mary L, D, 2; Joe, S, 1/6
34215 RILEY, Cherrie, Chapel, OK, 24
 1276 RILEY, Downing, Locust Grove, OK, 26; 3171, Lizzie, W, 34; Bark, Loonie, S of W, 16; Cornelius Peter, S of W, 5
 3164 RILEY, James T, Fairland, OK, 44; Francis M, S, 20; William I, S, 15; Charles R, S, 11; Joseph H, S, 8

CHEROKEE DESCENDANTS RESIDING WEST OF MISSISSIPPI RIVER.
VOLUME III (N – Z)

Key: Guion Miller Application Number; Name; Address, Relation (to Head); Age in 1906

32387 RILEY, John H, Vera, OK, 41; Ruth P, D, 10; Mamie A, D, 6; Mable, D, 4; Prentice, S, 1

12681 RILEY, John M, Chapel, OK, 55; 12682, Nannie E, W, 46; Welder, S, 16; Owen, S, 13; Mayme, D, 11; Jack, S, 9

35714 RILEY, John M, Ardmore, OK, 27

1692 RILEY, Mary, Gans, OK, 76

29600 RILEY, Mary E, Nowata, OK, 25; Rufus R, S, 4; George W, S, 1

23162 RILEY, Minnie, Nowata, OK, 31; Elizabeth, D, 15; Celia L, D, 6; Helen, D, 3

30106 RILEY, Richard, Vera, OK, 72

28542 RINGO, Charles C, Nowata, OK, 23

28541 RINGO, George G, Nowata, OK, 21

17275 RINGO, Lucy P, Nowata, OK, 45; Nona F, D, 17; William P, S, 15; Libby M, D, 13; Ethel D, D, 8; Alfred V, S, 6; Robert B, S, 3

26566 RIPPETOE, Rebecca, Afton, OK, 35; Bessie May, D, 13; Lee, S, 14; Laura P, D, 4; Beulah, D, 1

4047 RISINGFAWN, Joseph, Needmore, OK, 43; Joseph T, S, 9; Stella M, D, 7; Ada Lee, D, 5; Myrtle E, D, 2

2918 RITTER, Editha[sic] A, Bartlesville, OK, 19

2668 RITTER, Howell W, Fairland, OK, 20; Ada E, Sis, 18; Willie C, Bro, 16; By N. C. Gallomore, Gdn.

34257 RITTER, Martha E, Blackgum, OK, 31; Bessie M, D, 9

72 RIVET, Lurena, Owasso, OK, 58

23450 ROACH, Charley, Hadley, OK, 25

1474 ROACH, George, Tahlequah, OK, 62; Thomas, S, 14

23452 ROACH, James, Hadley, OK, 21

26163 ROACH, Jesse, Proctor, OK, 23

2741 ROACH, John, Hadley, OK, 60; 2970, Nellie, W, 50; Tandy, S, 16; Annie, D, 14; Elmira, D, 12; 23450, Polly, D, 20

4425 ROACH, Mary E, Proctor, OK, 25

3470 ROACH, Mattie, Vinita, OK, 48; Thomas N, S, 16

4991 ROACH, Nancy, Welling, OK, 66

[ROACH, Robert George. See #12805]
(Note: entry separate from other family groups)

23451 ROACH, Sarah, Hadley, OK, 23; 23255, Sarah E, W, 32; Joshua W, S, 16; Nancy, D, 13; Thomas E, S, 4

34563 ROASTINGEAR, Charlotte, Uniontown, AR, 23

34562 ROASTINGEAR, Joe, Uniontown, AR, 35; 34564, Mary, W, 25; Dora, D, 4; Arthur, S, 3

1889 ROASTINGEAR, John, Uniontown, AR, 63; 1995, Katie, W, 55; Jennie, D, 17; Willie, S, 10

6479 ROBARDS, Christopher C, Hillside, OK, 59; Amy, D, 14; Herbert E, S, 12; Cree, S, 9; Tarvis, S, 5

CHEROKEE DESCENDANTS RESIDING WEST OF MISSISSIPPI RIVER.
VOLUME III (N – Z)

Key: Guion Miller Application Number; Name; Address, Relation (to Head); Age in 1906

[ROBBER, Leona. See #8098] ⎤   *(Note: entries separate*
[ROBBER, Lizzie. See #8098] ⎦   *from other family groups)*

43183 ROBBER, Lucy A, Uniontown, AR, 25; Georgie, S, 2
  701 ROBBINS, Nancy Jane, Oaks, OK, 60
16500 ROBBINS, Sallie, Oaks, OK, 16;   By Sarah Chewie, Gdn.
  781 ROBBINS, Susan, Ramona, OK, 20; Goldie C, D, 3; Viola V, D, 1
  700 ROBBINS, William, Oaks, OK, 10;   By N. L. Neilson, Gdn.
16501 ROBBINS, William, Oaks, OK, 13;   By Sarah Chewie, Gdn.
 2917 ROBBS, Mary E, Porum, OK, 53; Lucinda, D, 16
 1874 ROBERSON, Evans, Tahlequah, OK, 26; 27673, Wanonah, W, 21; Ralph Raymond, S, 3; Bertie L, S, 1
10724 ROBERSON, Lutitia, Muldrow, OK, 20
 3671 ROBERSON, Pickens, Pryor Creek, OK, 39; Caleb S, S, 15; Paralee A, D, 11; Beulah I, D, 9; Susie G, D, 6; Minnie J, D, 2
17963 ROBERT, Thomas, Moodys, OK, 39; 8136, Rachel, W, 39; Standingdeer, Nannie, Niece, 7
  482 ROBERTS, Agnes, Southwest City, MO, 25; May, D, 8; Johnnie, S, 6; Orvil, S, 4

[ROBERTS, Alex L. See #2348] ⎤   *(Note: entries separate*
[ROBERTS, Paul W. See #2348] ⎦   *from other family groups)*

 4685 ROBERTS, Anna C, Chelsea, OK, 49; Erle L, S, 17; Arthur S, S, 16; Mary L, D, 12; Lenoir, S, 10
22597 ROBERTS, Callie, Choteau, OK, 34
25868 ROBERTS, Cora B, Fairland, OK, 21; Verna M, D, 3; Zelma A, D, 2
22540 ROBERTS, Edith, Zena, OK, 16
 5381 ROBERTS, Esther S, Dutch Mills, AR, 62
25475 ROBERTS, George W, Oklahoma City, 711 W. Reno Ave. OK, 27
 4190 ROBERTS, Henry Gordon, Chelsea, OK, 38; Fanny Ruth, D, 6; Harry Gilmore, S, 3
27524 ROBERTS, Hubert A, Dutch Mills, AR,   40; Laura E, D, 10
30250 ROBERT[sic], John H, Chelsea, OK, 21
31542 ROBERTS, Joseph, Porum, OK, 26
27167 ROBERTS, Lucy, Rex, OK, 17
27762 ROBERTS, Lulia[sic] J, Orr, OK, 22; Cordelia P, D, 1/6
  214 ROBERTS, Lydia, Oologah, OK, 48
31781 ROBERTS, Marion, Jr, Chelsea, OK, 23
26108 ROBERTS, Martha E, Dutch Mills, AR,   22
16105 ROBERTS, Murry E, Claremore, OK, 25
13169 ROBERTS, Sadie B, Marble City, OK,   27
24156 ROBERTS, Samuel W, Stilwell, OK, 36; Ruby, D, 9; Roy, S 6; Frank, S 3; Mamie, D, 1
27525 ROBERTS, Stephen, Dutch Mills, AR, 26; 5231, Joanna, W, 26

CHEROKEE DESCENDANTS RESIDING WEST OF MISSISSIPPI RIVER.
VOLUME III (N – Z)

Key: Guion Miller Application Number; Name; Address, Relation (to Head); Age in 1906

4155 ROBERTSON, Evans P, Melvin, OK, 50; 2800, Sarah E, W, 51; Arthur E, S, 18; Albion L, S, 16; Lella E, D, 14; William C, S, 6
29931 ROBERTSON, Honor L, Porum, OK, 19; Clem, S, 2
27130 ROBERTSON, Watie E, Melvin, OK, 22
6524 ROBIN, Eli, Hulbert, OK, 40; 26077, Ollie, W, 25; Eli, Jr, S, 8; Prince, S, 6
9657 ROBIN, Sparrow, Peggs, OK, 60; 9730, Lydia, W, 57; George, S, 18
8110 ROBINS, Henry, Oaks, OK, 23
5335 ROBINS, Henry, Jr, Parkhill, OK, 24
24920 ROBINSON, Arthur, Coffeyville, KS, 28
27719 ROBINSON, Elizabeth M, Ramona, OK, 33; Willis, Leander, S, 16; Robinson, Charles, S, 13; Fannie E, D, 11
8704 ROBINSON, Ella F, Muskogee, OK, 409 Callahan St, 59
33136 ROBINSON, Ella M, Muskogee, OK, 34
24895 ROBINSON, Fred, Lenapah, OK, 23
29307 ROBINSON, John C, Muskogee, OK, 38; Joseph F, S 9; Ross L, S, 3; Elizabeth F, D, ¼

[ROBINSON, Josie. See #27342]   *(Note: entries separate*
[ROBINSON, Jessie. See #27342]   *from other family groups)*

13470 ROBINSON, Juliette M, Claremore, OK, 28; Herbert Spencer, S, 3; Lula Eliza, D, 1/6
2910 ROBINSON, Laura, Keefeton, OK, 39; Richard, S, 17; Elizabeth, D, 14; Pearl E, D, 11; Walter S, S, 9; William H, S, 5; Edgar D, S, 1
9613 ROBINSON, Lelia, Locust Grove, OK, 24; William E, S, 4; Margaret, D, 3; Cornelius, S, 1/4
23232 ROBINSON, Lizzie, Lenapah, OK, 44; Lola, D, 16; Tolly, S, 8; Della, D, 11; Hannah, D, 6; Parine, D, 4; Opel, D, 2
29110 ROBINSON, Lizzie, Thurber, TX, 37; William E, S, 13; John B, S, 11; Jess J, S, 9; Katie A, D, 6; Tempie J, D, 1
23312 ROBINSON, Rachel, Muskogee, OK, 23; Johnnie, S, 7; Dora, D, 5; Wadie, S, 3
24842 ROBINSON, Sarah F, Chelsea, OK, 36; Nellie F, D, 16; Annie, D, 13; Samuel R, S, 10; Thelma M, D, 7; Joseph N, S, 5; Thomas C, S, 3
28347 ROBISON, Annie, Roland, OK, 37; Lizzie M, D, 16; William H, S, 13; Emma R, D, 8; Annie J, D, 6; R. T. S, 2

[ROBINSON, Della Edna. See #4300] *(Note: entry separate from other family groups)*

24498 ROBISON, Elzina, Chelsea, OK, 24; Mary Jane, D, 3; Andy, S, 1
5867 ROBISON, Minerva, Bushyhead, OK, 48; Samuel L, S, 18; Charles W, S, 13; George W, S, 6; Clara O'Dean, D, 1
27078 ROCK, Catcher, Locust Grove, OK, 29
5143 RODDEN, Lillie, Claremore, OK, 17; Beulah Lee, D, 1
8001 RODDY, John L, Chelsea, OK, 54; Samuel J, S, 18; Rosa A, D, 16; Alfred C, S, 14; Martha B, D, 12; Francis H, D, 4

CHEROKEE DESCENDANTS RESIDING WEST OF MISSISSIPPI RIVER.
VOLUME III (N – Z)

Key: Guion Miller Application Number; Name; Address, Relation (to Head); Age in 1906

34457 RODDY, Lelia J, Chelsea, OK, 22
34455 RODDY, Oscar T, Chelsea, OK, 24; Newton, S, 2; James, S, ¾
34458 RODDY, Sidney I, Chelsea, OK, 21
30871 RODECKER, Emma, Oglesby, OK, 31; Brant L, S, 7; Lulu M, D, 5; Adda M, D, 3
  323 RODGERS, Bettie, Nowata, OK, 24
6530 RODGERS, Joel, Melvin, OK, 19; Peggy May, Sis, 13;   By Gobe Rodgers, Gdn.
26808 RODGERS, Lizzie, Tahlequah, OK, 41; Charlie, S, 15; Lily Ann, D, 12; William D, S, 10; James V, S, 3
24990 RODGERS, Lydia, Melvin, OK, 48
16182 RODGERS, Willie, Campbell, OK, 38; 14734, Nancy, W, 26
24148 ROE, Polly, Watova, OK, 29; James Fred, S, 9; Grace A, D, 7; Minnie M, D, 5; Dorris Ellen, D, 1
10950 ROGERS, Andrew J, Leach, OK, 40; Henry B, S, 19; Levi H, S, 17; Nannie, D, 15; John, S, 13; George L, S, 7; Andrew, S, 4
1990 ROGERS, Andrew J, Uniontown, AR, 40; 1894, Caroline, W, 48; Lula, D, 14; Winnie D, D, 7
27567 ROGERS, Andrew Lewis, Ft. Gibson, OK, 46

[ROGERS, Annie. See #12592]   *(Note: entry separate from other family groups)*

8098 ROGERS, Athelstan, Aurora, MO, 39; Roy, S, 20; Homer, S, 17; Edric, S, 14; Nannie I, D, 9
24062 ROGERS, Belle, Okoee, OK, 29; Ella K, D, 6; Gilbert L, S, 5; Cleint[sic] D, S, 3; Annie B, S, 2
1045 ROGERS, Berrilla, Fairland, OK, 65
8891 ROGERS, Beulah E, Stilwell, OK, 14;   By Howe L. Rogers, Gdn.
5763 ROGERS, Charles A, Bartlesville, OK, 29
16872 ROGERS, Charles H, Claremore, OK, 27
1165 ROGERS, Cherokee A, Ft. Gibson, OK, 6
27570 ROGERS, Clifford, Ft. Gibson, OK, 33
1051 ROGERS, Connell, Ft. Gibson, OK, 55; 26934, Kate, W, 35; 1051, Marion Sevier, S, 14; Lewis Byres, S, 11; Howard Cunningham, S, 7
10968 ROGERS, David, Oaks, OK, 36; 10966, Lucinda, W, 40; Galcatcher, Emma, D of W, 14
  755 ROGERS, David McN, Adair, OK, 71
38524 ROGERS, Ed, Lenapah, OK, 46; Frank W, S, 15; Nora M, D, 13; Flora S, D, 11; Duby, D, 9; Belle B, D, 8; Ed, Jr, S, 3; Joel M, S, 2; Robbia M, D, 1
26936 ROGERS, Ella C, Ft. Gibson, OK, 23
12697 ROGERS, Emma, Blackgum, OK, 9; James, Bro, 14;   By Levi Rogers, Gdn.
13269 ROGERS, George L, Claremore, OK, 29
24426 ROGERS, George W, Fairland, OK, 26; Gertrude, D, 7; 45506, Leona, D, 1/6 [Leona , by Carrie Rogers, Mother]
26935 ROGERS, Gertrude W, Ft. Gibson, OK, 27
27568 ROGERS, Hugh Morgan, Ft. Gibson, OK, 43

CHEROKEE DESCENDANTS RESIDING WEST OF MISSISSIPPI RIVER.
VOLUME III (N – Z)
Key: Guion Miller Application Number; Name; Address, Relation (to Head); Age in 1906

[ROGERS, Jack. See #1996]   *(Note: entry separate from other family groups)*

16747 ROGERS, Jackson T, Nowata, OK, 54; Pearl Ethel, D, 8
8278 ROGERS, James F, Pensacola, OK, 37; Flora E, D, 13; James F, S, 8; Nellie B, D, 7; Mary J, D, 5; Annie L, D, 3
26113 ROGERS, Jennette, Keefeton, OK, 19; Edmond, S, 2
2408 ROGERS, Jennie H, Greenbrier, OK, 59
13267 ROGERS, John L, Vian, OK, 44; 13266, Annie, W, 36; Artemus, S, 14; Sadie, D, 10; John L, Jr, S, 5; Romona, D, 3
27569 ROGERS, John Otto, Ft. Gibson, OK, 37; 241, Cora, W, 37
9916 ROGERS, Joseph R, Nowata, OK, 48; 1501, Victoria R, W, 41; Gabriel M, S, 18; Guy R, S, 16; Joseph R, Jr, S, 7; Ruth Alice, D, 4
12527 ROGERS, Lewis, Bluejacket, OK, 23
6933 ROGERS, Lewis H, Collinsville, OK, 35; 27936, John K, S, 10; Nettie E, D, 6; Jessie D, D, 5; Edith E, D, 1
23436 ROGERS, Love, Adair, OK, 38; Eula C, D, 8; Nicholas R, S, 6; Mary N, D, 2
9494 ROGERS, Lucy, Vian, OK, 26; Mary, D, 3
9191 ROGERS, Mary, Webbers Falls, OK, 56
11041 ROGERS, Mary K, Chelsea, OK, 54
23652 ROGERS, Mary M, Greenbrier, OK, 19
13956 ROGERS, Mary V, Ramona, OK, 22; Clem H, S, 4
7433 ROGERS, Mattie, Campbell, OK, 18

[ROGERS, Maud E. See #2839]   *(Note: entry separate from other family groups)*

12718 ROGERS, Missouri Emeline, Braggs, OK, 47
6472 ROGERS, Nancy E, Adair, OK, 39; Catharine, D, 14; Knox, S, 13; Eva, D, 11
11191 ROGERS, Ollie, Braggs, OK, 35; Jim, S, 14; Lovely, S, 6; Bessie, D, 1
42932 ROGERS, Oscar L, Nowata, OK, 24
1886 ROGERS, Peter, Locust Grove, OK, 30; 5642, Sarah W, 33; Bear, S, 1; Cabbagehead, Jennie, D of W, 16
23774 ROGERS, Robert L, Fairland, OK, 33; 4922, Minnie V, W, 33; Robert W, S, 4; Wynona, D, 1
31544 ROGERS, Robert R, Nowata, OK, 21
274?1 ROGERS, Rollie E, Dodge, OK, 26
6516 ROGERS, Sallie, Choteau, OK, 37; Pearl, D, 17; Frank, S, 14; Hugh, S, 12; Terry, S, 9; Ethel, D, 7; Eula M, D, 5
43702 ROGERS, Sampson, Rose, OK, 39; 27147*, Lizzie, W, 29; Frank, S, 5; William Penn, S, 3
3456 ROGERS, Sarah, Chelsea, OK, 85
4106 ROGERS, Sirrisia I, Ft. Gibson, OK, 50; Eliza, D, 17; Georgia A, D, 14; Sirrissie, D, 12; William, S, 10; Charley, S, 8
4004 ROGERS, Stonewall J, Chelsea, OK, 44; Fannie L, D, 13; Robert R, S, 11; Morris L, S, 7; Henry C, S, 4; Rebecca Mc, D, 2
11864 ROGERS, Susam[sic], Braggs, OK, 24; George, S, 7; Hoke, S, 3

CHEROKEE DESCENDANTS RESIDING WEST OF MISSISSIPPI RIVER.
VOLUME III   (N – Z)

Key: Guion Miller Application Number; Name; Address, Relation (to Head); Age in 1906

26685 ROGERS, Susan E, Warner, OK, 20
 1912 ROGERS, Thomas J, Kinnison, OK, 43; Lewis D, S, 17; Mary E, D, 13; Ira Thomas, S, 8; Opel, D, 4
26125 ROGERS, Thomas J, Grove, OK, 28
  251 ROGERS, Thomas T, Cowskin, MO, 50; William E, S, 17

[ROGERS, Tipton. See #26124]   *(Note: entry separate from other family groups)*

16389 ROGERS, Walter S, Eaton, OK, 47; Walter P, S, 20; John H, S, 18; Philip O, S, 12; Charley C, S, 8
  616 ROGERS, William G, Dewey, OK, 41; Lula M, D, 15; William E, S, 13; Rilla B, D, 11; Eliza J, D, 9; Arthur M, S, 5; Joseph E, S, 3
 5859 ROGERS, William Henry, Chelsea, OK, 45
24971 ROGERS, William O, Fairland, OK, 31
 9735 ROGERS, William P, Claremore, OK, 27
43800 ROGERS, William P, Keefeton, OK, 15; Charlie H, Bro, 13; George W, Bro, 11; By William T. Rogers, Gdn.
 6743 ROGERS, William R, Chelsea, OK, 52; 6731, Lucie P, W, 50
10640 ROGERS, Wilson, Locust Grove, OK, 53; 14062, Susie, W, 48; Jesse, S, 11; Cullus, S, 6
 1350 ROHR, Lula, Claremore, OK, 33; Viola A, D, 7; Walter H, S, 5; Otis D, S, 3; Roxie T, D, 1
12559 ROHRER, Annie Laura, San Francisco, 204 Utah St. CA, 26
17413 ROLLAND, Martha J, Braggs, OK, 29;   Emma L, D, 14; John E, S, 12; Suseta, D, 10; Maud E, D, 8; Elijah, S, 5; Mary A, D, 3; Elmer, S, 1
 9156 ROLLEN, Annie E, Claremore, OK, 40; William P, S, 18; Joseph M, S, 16; Rufus M, S, 13; Emma D, D, 12; Jerry, Jr, S, 10; Antomeo, S, 8; John C, S, 6; Beulah, D, 4; Paralee, D, 3; Verona, D, 1
 3863 ROLLEN, Elmina, Claremore, OK, 55
25039 ROLSTON, Stella E, Miami, OK, 15
25310 ROMMING, Susan A, Afton, OK, 25; McMullens, Minnie M, D, 8
 6751 ROOSTER, Lizzie, Campbell, OK, 46

[ROOSTER, Maggie. See #17062]   *(Note: entries separate*
[ROOSTER, Dirt Dobber. See #17062]   *from other family groups)*

 7928 ROSE, George, Siloam Springs, AR, 27; George, Jr, S, 2
12570 ROSE, Jennie, Braggs, OK, 30; Pearl, D, 13; Joseph, S, 11; Henrietta, D, 8; J. Warren, S, 3
10431 ROSEBOROUGH, Lucy G, Afton, OK, 45; Jesse F, S, 18; Claude, S, 16; 23330, Sarah L, D, 20
  751 ROSENTHAL, Nannie H, Claremore, OK, 19
 8175 ROSENWINKEL, Anna C, McAlester, OK, 33
16589 ROSIN, Comingdeer, Marble City, OK, 23
16903 ROSIN, Swimmer, Porum, OK, 23; 16902, Annie, D, 16

CHEROKEE DESCENDANTS RESIDING WEST OF MISSISSIPPI RIVER.
VOLUME III (N – Z)

Key: Guion Miller Application Number; Name; Address, Relation (to Head); Age in 1906

 4725 ROSS, Albert, Stilwell, OK, 27
35035 ROSS, Allen C, Chelsea, OK, 24
10629 ROSS, Andrew, Locust Grove, OK, 34
19308 ROSS, Annie, Porum, OK, 14;   By Francis M. Ross, Gdn.
26034 ROSS, Annie Chelsea, OK, 6;   By Hiram Ross, Gdn.
 7678 ROSS, Arlie F, Claremore, OK, 17
   92 ROSS, Belle, Ft. Gibson, OK, 47

[ROSS, Bettie. See #1951]   *(Note: entry separate from other family groups)*

18580 ROSS, Bullet, Sallisaw, OK, 20; Nelson, S, 2
12598 ROSS, Celia, Wauhillau, OK, 51
31985 ROSS, Charles N, Tahlequah, OK, 39 [Died 1908]; 31986, Susie E, W, 28; Edwin Blake, S, 12; Susie Helen, D, 7
41136 ROSS, Clarence, Solomonville, AZ, 17;   Ray, Bro, 15; Mary E, Sis, 12;   By William Ross, Gdn.
40712 ROSS, Commodore, Locust Grove, OK, 20
12484 ROSS, Cucumber, Braggs, OK, 49; Minerva, D, 17; Annie, D, 14; John, S, 11; Rachel, D, 8
 4583 ROSS, Daniel, Rose, OK, 59; 1368, Rutha C, W, 55; Cornelious, S, 18; Carrie E, D, 16; Daniel W, S, 6
16119 ROSS, Daniel H, Tahlequah, OK, 24
10468 ROSS, Eck, Locust Grove, OK, 47; Neoma, D, 4; Henry Pigeon, S, 1
 4330 ROSS, Edward G, Bartlesville, OK, 49
16121 ROSS, Eliza, Tahlequah, OK, 34
  403 ROSS, Eliza J, Lenapah, OK, 26
 1365 ROSS, Emma L, Ft. Gibson, OK, 52
14099 ROSS, Emma T, Tahlequah, OK, 33; 43203, Ray, S, 8
33419 ROSS, Fannie V, Tahlequah, OK, 27
 4107 ROSS, Flora J, Vian, OK, 46
13240 ROSS, Flora L, Sapulpa, OK, 25
34497 ROSS, Florence E, Rose, OK, 26
19310 ROSS, Francis M, Porum, OK, 22
 5015 ROSS, Frank, Choteau, OK, 38; 5017, Ella, W, 30; Allie N. C, D, 8; Cherry, D, 6; Joseph E, S, ¼
 2870 ROSS, George, Locust Grove, OK, 56
19307 ROSS, George, Porum, OK, 16;   By Francis M, Ross, Gdn.
  930 ROSS, Gilbert R, Vera, OK, 57; Robert J, S, 19; Rufus G, S, 16; James Russell, S, 5
41796 ROSS, Henry, Tahlequah, OK, 25
 1362 ROSS, Hubbard, Ft. Gibson, OK, 39; Marjorie, D, 6; Mamie E, D, 3; Jennie P, D, 2
 8742 ROSS, Jack Spears, Locust Grove, OK, 58
 4696 ROSS, Jackson, Locust Grove, OK, 35; 3289, Jessie, W, 30; Susie, D, 7; Jack, S, 5; Adam, S, 2; Alsie, D, 1

CHEROKEE DESCENDANTS RESIDING WEST OF MISSISSIPPI RIVER.
VOLUME III (N – Z)

Key: Guion Miller Application Number; Name; Address, Relation (to Head); Age in 1906

9612 ROSS, James L, Muskogee, OK, 58; Jennie P, D, 14; Susie, D, 4
41783 ROSS, Jennie, Tahlequah, OK, 23
3627 ROSS, Joanna, Lynch, OK, 27; Willie, S, 4; Lucille, D, 2
4695 ROSS, John, Locust Grove, OK, 27; 28741, Anna, W, 20; Field, S, 1
13719 ROSS, John H, Inola, OK, 37; Ray R, S, 11; Daisy M, D, 10; Mildred F, D, 3
4497 ROSS, Joseph M, Locust Grove, OK, 26
2142 ROSS, Josephine, Locust Grove, OK, 47; Felix H, S, 19; Mary J, D, 16
145 ROSS, Joshua, Muskogee, OK, 73
18581 ROSS, Kye, Sallisaw, OK, 18;   By James Wool, Gdn.
35822 ROSS, Lee, Chelsea, OK, 21
8213 ROSS, Leonard, Inola, OK, 47; James, S, 18
7439 ROSS, Leonidas C, Tahlequah, OK, 34
3582 ROSS, Lewis, Salina, OK, 29; Jody, D, 11; Annie, D, 9; Joseph, S, 5; Nancy, D, 1
13285 ROSS, Lewis, Bunch, OK, 38
16122 ROSS, Lewis A, Tahlequah, OK, 29
183 ROSS, Lewis W, Locust Grove, OK, 37
13195 ROSS, Lizzie, Bunch, OK, D of 13285, 9;   By Lewis Ross, Gdn.
44172 ROSS, Lizzie V, Chelsea, OK, 22
827 ROSS, Lucinda, Stilwell, OK, 63

[ROSS, Lugie. See #4916]   *(Note: entries separate*
[ROSS, Ora I. See #4916]   *from other family groups)*

11679 ROSS, McDuff, Texanna, OK, 51; Dot, D, 15; Kit, S, 14; Lola, D, 11; McKinley, S, 8
30007 ROSS, Maggie, Chelsea, OK, 30; David W, S, 14; Daisy M, D, 12; Midget, S, 8; Annie L, D, 5
41784 ROSS, Maggie, Tahlequah, OK, 21 [Died 1-1907]; By Silas D. Ross; Charley, S, 5/12   [Died 7-1906]
34498 ROSS, Maggie M, Rose, OK, 23
44927 ROSS, Malissa, Claremore, OK, 57
19309 ROSS, Margaret V, Porum, OK, 11;   By Francis M. Ross, Gdn.
1364 ROSS, Mary Jane, Ft. Gibson, OK, 79
18582 ROSS, Maud, Sallisaw, OK, 16;   By James Wool, Gdn.
37492 ROSS, Minnie, Lenapah, OK, 14;   By Ella Rushen, Gdn.
4694 ROSS, Nancy, Locust Grove, OK, 25
9977 ROSS, Nannie, Foyil, OK, 22
13194 ROSS, Nannie, Bunch, OK, D of #13285, 7;   By Lewis Ross, Gdn
14321 ROSS, NELLIE N, Claremore, OK, 34; 14322, Wayne M, S, 13; Roy V, S, 12
9632 ROSS, Okla, Sallisaw, OK, 25
13284 ROSS, Ollie, Bunch, OK, D of #13285, 5;   By Lewis Ross, Gdn.
947 ROSS, Perry, Claremore, OK, 57
15845 ROSS, Robert B, Tahlequah, OK, 61; Robert B, Jr, S, 18; Anna P, D, 14
18636 ROSS, Rufus, Stilwell, OK, 33; McKinley, S, 9; Lulu Carmen, D, 3

CHEROKEE DESCENDANTS RESIDING WEST OF MISSISSIPPI RIVER.
VOLUME III (N – Z)

Key: Guion Miller Application Number; Name; Address, Relation (to Head); Age in 1906

34214 ROSS, Rufus D, Tahlequah, OK, 33; 8316, Samantha, W, 38; Loring, S, 5; Margaret M, D, ¼
4726 ROSS, Samuel, Evansville, AR, 35
41798 ROSS, Sarah, Tahlequah, OK, 28
16118 ROSS, Shorey, Tahlequah, OK, 35
1300 ROSS, Silas D, Tahlequah, OK, 47; Charley, S, 19; George W, S, 13; Ione, D, 6; Silas M, S, 3
33420 ROSS, Susan M, Tahlequah, OK, 22
26033 ROSS, Susie, Chelsea, OK, 19
25335 ROSS, Viola E, Sallisaw, OK, 22
9751 ROSS, William, Stilwell, OK, 24; 9939, Lillie, W, 21; Frank, S, 2
13160 ROSS, William, Welling, OK, 47; 13159, Polly, W, 48
1361 ROSS, William D, Ft. Gibson, OK, 58
17632 ROSS, William H, Tulsa, OK, 44
4329 ROSS, William P, Bartlesville, OK, 47; 45405, Sadie B, D, 13; 45404, Gunter, S, 5
16127 ROSS, William P, Roswell, NM, 31
4360 ROSS, William W, Chelsea, OK, 55; 4101, Lila J, W, 49; 26173, Janie J, D, 20; Wallace C, S, 14
33416 ROSS, William W, Jr, Tahlequah, OK, 35; 33417, Mary H, W, 25; Francis Carter, S, ¼
4698 ROSS, Willie, Evansville, AR, 27; 4698½, Martha, W, 23; John, S, 8; Tom, S, 6; Joe, S, 3; Lucindy, D, 1
16120 ROSS, Wirt, Tahlequah, OK, 26
7008 ROSSER, Minnie, Tahlequah, OK, 33; Kippling, S, 10; Ada, D, 5; Effie, S, 3; Charles, Jr, S, 1
10379 ROUND, Jack, Maysville, AR, 49; 5973, Annie, W, 64

[ROWDON, Amon. See #3973]   *(Note: entries separate*
[ROWDEN[sic], Emer. See #3973]   *from other family groups)*

2138 ROWE, Betsy, Rose, OK, 20
14142 ROWE, Charlie, Locust Grove, OK, 24; 180, Ida, W, 38
25220 ROWE, Clem V, Pryor Creek, OK, 21
186 ROWE, Dick, Locust Grove, OK, 29
3579 ROWE, Eliza Ellen, Rose, OK, 47; 25222, Maggie E, D, 17; 22994, Lydia, D, 15; Etta May, D, 13; Benjamin B, S, 10; Loreen, D, 7

[ROWE, Felix. See #25112]   *(Note: entry separate from other family groups)*

8270 ROWE, Frank, Choteau, OK, 30; 15594, Sadie, W, 23; Hazie, D, 5
19011 ROWE, Hayward, Talala, OK, 47; Perry, S, 18; Louis, S, 15; Albert, S, 13; Rachel, D, 6; Aggie, D, 4
2986 ROWE, Jack, Locust Grove, OK, 25; 8864, Jennie, W, 17
196 ROWE, James, Locust Grove, OK, 53

CHEROKEE DESCENDANTS RESIDING WEST OF MISSISSIPPI RIVER.
VOLUME III (N – Z)

Key: Guion Miller Application Number; Name; Address, Relation (to Head); Age in 1906

42540 ROWE, Joseph D, Jr, Rose, OK, 26; 5807, Lula, W, 24; Ruby, D, 4; Watt Maysville, S, 2
14208 ROWE, Josiah, Locust Grove, OK, 22
5808 ROWE, Letha, Rose, OK, 55; David, S, 13
25221 ROWE, Martin M, Muskogee, OK, 30; 40060, May B, W, 26; David V, S, 5
26082 ROWE, Mattie M, Locust Grove, OK, 21
25114 ROWE, Mollie, Chapel, OK, 34; Lydia, D, 10

[ROWE, Nelson. See #33145]   *(Note: entry separate from other family groups)*

5640 ROWE, Taylor, Locust Grove, OK, 28; 2503, Nellie, W, 30; Neda, D, 5; Joe, S, 3
12660 ROWE, Thomas, Stilwell, OK, 28; 12661, Katie, W, 25
23619 ROWLAND, Emily, Kilgore, TX, 41
11222 ROWLAND, Mittie, Webbers Falls, OK, 20; Mary, D, 2
22659 ROWSEY, Paul E, Muskogee, OK, 10;   By William E. Rowsey, Gdn.
4624 RUCKER, Clemmie R, Grove, OK, 22
6543 RUCKER, Ethel M, Miles, OK, 20; Franklin O, S, 1/6
30655 RUCKER, Josie, Locust Grove, OK, 16
3020 RUCKER, May Dora, Claremore, OK, 40; Ernest L, S, 18; Mable M, D, 16; Frank M, Jr, S, 11; John M, S, 4
28527 RUDD, Mary F, V, Chetopa, KS, R.F.D. #4, 19; Louis G, S, 1
2108 RUDDLES, Norris, Catoosa, OK, 26
5543 RUNABOUT, Blue, Southwest City, MO, 27; 24003, Myrtle, W, 18
5556 RUNABOUT, Charlotte, Maysville, AR, 43
5736 RUNABOUT, James, Southwest City, MO, 21
647 RUNABOUT, Nancy, Eucha, OK, 70
11199 RUNABOUT, Susie, Braggs, OK, 60
5444 RUNABOUT, White, Southwest City, MO, 18
10938 RUNABOUT, William, Maysville, AR, 12;   By Annie Reed, Gdn.
4236 RUNELS, John, Manard, AR, 53; Anderson, S, 18; Floyd, S, 14; Lizzie, D, 12; Kizzie, D, 10; John, Jr, S, 9; China, D, 7; Wirt, S, 4; Evelyne, D, 1
4055 RUNYON, Robert, Ft. Gibson, OK, 30
33104 RUNYON, Thomas J, Ft. Gibson, OK, 27
17001 RUNYON, William W, Manard, OK, 47
8034 RUSH, Ida, Haworth, OK, 26; Maud S, D, 9; Benjamin, S, 5; Mary A, D, 4
2384 RUSH, Isabell, Muskogee, OK, 58
35594 RUSH, Sibley, Porum, OK, 9;   By William Rush, Gdn.
2045 RUSK, Ella, Oaks, OK, 38; Ned, S, 19; Roscoe, S, 16; Ada, D, 8
13027 RUSK, Joe, Hominy, OK, 6;   By Mary J. Spears, Gdn.
12444 RUSSELL, Alonzo, Kansas, OK, 4;   By Louis C. Horner, Gdn.

[RUSSELL, Annie. See #2213]   *(Note: entry separate from other family groups)*

15596 RUSSELL, Charles, Cookson, OK, 19

CHEROKEE DESCENDANTS RESIDING WEST OF MISSISSIPPI RIVER.
VOLUME III (N – Z)

Key: Guion Miller Application Number; Name; Address, Relation (to Head); Age in 1906

5932 RUSSELL, Connie, Warner, OK, 16; Carl, Bro, 14; Christopher, Bro, 13; By Campbell Russell, Gdn.
2162 RUSSELL, Daniel, Oaks, OK, 24; Lucy, D, 1/3
11237 RUSSELL, David, Kansas, OK, 23; 32383, Sallie, W, 24
34443 RUSSELL, Edward W, Owasso, OK, 21
386 RUSSELL, Francis, E, Ballard, OK, 74
23639 RUSSELL, Froniz E. K, Chelsea, OK, 26; Ollie, D, 5 [Died 8-1906]; David Lee, S, 3; Alice Ola, D, 1/3
1252 RUSSELL, George, Sallisaw, OK, 26
30214 RUSSELL, George, Stilwell, OK, 27
11236 RUSSELL, Jack, Kansas, OK, 29; 16932, Ella, W, 23; Dave, S, 9; Emma, D, 2; Rosco, S, 1; 16931, Young Duck, Mollie, D of W, 6
30213 RUSSELL, James, Stilwell, OK, 30; Jesse, S, 10; Vivian, D, 5; Ellis B, S, 3
23143 RUSSELL, James B, Ballard, OK, 40; Joe M, S, 12; Alice I, D, 11; Ollie M, D, 8; Pearl F, D, 6; Paul H, S, 2
6601 RUSSELL, Jim, Oaks, OK, 49; Davis, S, 20; 2161, Joe, S, 18; Lydia, D, 14; John, S, 12
23144 RUSSELL, Joseph L, Ballard, OK, 34; Charles F, S, 10; Berry A, S, 8; Clara M, D, 6; Ellen I, D, 5; John D, S, 2; Jennie, D, 1/6
27860 RUSSELL, Katie, Gum Log, AR, 21; Flossie May, D, ½

[RUSSELL, Lila. See #1190]   *(Note: entry separate from other family groups)*

4644 RUSSELL, Lizzie, Kansas, OK, 34
24495 RUSSELL, Lucinda, Centralia, OK, 28; Lucy C, D, 10; Frank, S, 6; Flossie, D, 2
3557 RUSSELL, Maggie M, Allen, NM, 24; Cornelius W, S, 6; Mark R, S, 5; Ruby P, D, 3
703 RUSSELL, Ollie, Oaks, OK, 57
23142 RUSSELL, Paul, Ballad, OK, 45
10397 RUSSELL, Polly, Sallisaw, OK, 53
1906 RUSSELL, Richard, Oaks, OK, 21; Girtie L, D, 1
9720 RUSSELL, Robert, Campbell, OK, 30; Ethel May, D, 6; Clem, S, 4
2073 RUSSELL, Robert L, Claremore, OK, 38; Maud, W, 32; Gus, S, 15; Inola, D, 12; Floyd, S, 9; Ada, D, 6; Lela, D, 3
1425 RUSSELL, Watt, Oaks, OK, 29
2075 RUSSELL, William H, Owasso, OK, 58
24375 RUSSELL, William L, Stilwell, OK, 24
1450 RUSSELL, William T, Stilwell, OK, 65; 5605, Lucy, W, 68
10398 RUTHERFORD, Betsy, Wauhillau, OK, 40
16519 RUTHERFORD, Edna, Nowata, OK, 26; Susie E, D, 9; Mary Pearl, D, 5; Samuel E, S, 1
26126 RYALS, Mary J, Gideon, OK, 32; Charlie L, S, 14; Lottie M, D, 11; Melven[sic], S, 9; Simmie[sic] I, D, 7; William Mck[sic], S, 5; Sadie C, D, 2

CHEROKEE DESCENDANTS RESIDING WEST OF MISSISSIPPI RIVER.
VOLUME III (N – Z)

Key: Guion Miller Application Number; Name; Address, Relation (to Head); Age in 1906

[RYAN, Emmett. See #3793]
[RYAN, Calvin. See #3793]   *(Note: entries separate*
[RYAN, William H. See #3793]   *from other family groups)*

6595 RYAN, John, Proctor, OK, 37; 40048, Alice, W, 25; Emmett, S, 10; Calvin, S, 8; William H, S, 5
6705 RYE, Mary A, Porter, OK, 35; Robert Lee, S, 1

43321 SACK, Jack, Locust Grove, OK, 30; Ammu-gar-woo-go, S, 3
6978 SACK, Old or Nee-da-gur-gah, Locust Grove, OK, 68

[SACK, Rachel. See #2499]   *(Note: entries separate*
[SACK, Welling. See #2499]   *from other family groups)*

6976 SACK, Sallie [Ga-ta-yah], Locust Grove, OK, 68
26441 SAGER, Eliza, Braggs, OK, 25 [Died 3-11-1907]; By Henry P. Sager, Husband.
25754 SAGER, Sarah J, Needmore, OK, 26; Lucile, D, 8; L. D, S, 4
2894 ST. JERMAIN, N. Isabella, Lac Du Flambeau, WI, 36
30103 SALLEE, Callie A, Claremore, OK, 26; Minnie V, D, 5; William or Wilmars J, S, 3; Leo Eldridge, S, 2
5278 SAM, Alex, Stilwell, OK, 43; Jacob, S, 14; 16108, Betsy, D, 4
17221 SAM, Charlie, Campbell, OK, 35; Martin, S, 12; Nannie, D, 11; Menser, S, 9; Susan, D, 6; Emma, D, 4
6973 SAM, John, Stilwell, OK, 21
8323 SAM, Nancy, Stilwell, OK, 20
5277 SAM, Sul-tee-skee, Stilwell, OK, 40; 7479, Levi, S, 17; 7479, Joseph [Josiah], S, 15; Annie, D, 8
13423 SAM, Watt, Braggs, OK, 30; 13380, Mary, W, 27; Katie, D, 1
27751 SAM, White Tobacco, Campbell, OK, 22; Eli White Tobacco, S, 3; Polly, D, 1/6
31567 SAMER, Myrtle E, Vinita, OK, 16
32328 SAMSON, Mary, Artesia, NM, 23; Ruth E, D, 2

[SAMUEL, Chas. F. See #44034]   *(Note: entry separate from other family groups)*

15604 SAMUEL, Florence W, Tahlequah, OK, 33; Maurine, D, 3½
1877 SAMUELS, Emma J, Collyer, KS, 48
4821 SAMUELS, Geo. P, Gans, OK, 35; Nannie, D, 4; Florence, D, 3; May, D, 1
10723 SAMUELS, Jessie C, Muldrow, OK, 22
5717 SAND, (No other name given), Oaks, OK, 64

[SAND, Charley. See #11238]   *(Note: entry separate from other family groups)*

5664 SAND, John, Oaks, OK, 31
5722 SAND, Steve, Oaks, OK, 40; 16987½, Maria, W, 24; 5722, James, S, 11; Charlotte, D, 8; William, D, 3; Annie, S, 3; 16987½, Snell, Youngbird, S, 3

CHEROKEE DESCENDANTS RESIDING WEST OF MISSISSIPPI RIVER.
VOLUME III   (N – Z)

Key: Guion Miller Application Number; Name; Address, Relation (to Head); Age in 1906

5663 SAND, Will, Oaks, OK, 34; 16465, Jennie, W, 19
1440 SANDERS, Aggie, Bunch, OK, 53; 2709, Heaven, Steve, S, 14; 2708, Lucy, D, 10; 2707, Jim, S, 17
8792 SANDERS, Andrew, Braggs, OK, 26
11672 SANDERS, Annie Bat, Dragger, OK, 52

[SANDERS, Benjamin. See #1328] *(Note: entry separate from other family groups)*

11497 SANDERS, Carl L, Claremore, OK, 5; By Annie Ward, Gdn.
9453 SANDERS, Carrie, Pryor Creek, OK, 23
6701 SANDERS, Catherine Moore, Sallisaw,   OK, 63
9714 SANDERS, Charlie, Bunch, OK, 26
16578 SANDERS, Charles, Baron, OK, 18; 8951, Jessie, W, 17
12658 SANDERS, Charlotte A, Marble City, OK, 24
27415 SANDERS, Clem, Oolagah, OK, 27; Walter Lee, S, 4; Lizzie Ruth, D, 2
8964 SANDERS, Cornelius, Wimer, OK, 34; 35914, Maude, W, 33; 8964, Clyde, S, 13; Corene, D, 11; Nannie, D, 9; Eddie, S, 4; Jessie C, S, 1
2711 SANDERS, Dave, Bunch, OK, 56; 2710, Betsy, W, 46; Robert, S, 16; Pigeon, S, 14; Jennie, D, 12; Slick, S, 10
6535 SANDERS, Dave, Jr, Coweta, OK, 31; Maude, S, 9; Cena, D, 7; Jessie, D, 5; Lester, S, 3
4602 SANDERS, David E, Braggs, OK, 49
1849 SANDERS, Delilah, Baron, OK, 55
6733 SANDERS, Dexter, Sallisaw, OK, 30; John D, S, 11; Tee Zhee, D, 9; Jenkins, S, 5; Marie, D, 2
1172 SANDERS, Eli, Stilwell, OK, 51; 13961, Ada, W, 34; 16369, Johnson, John, S of W, 14; 1172, Sanders, Florence [Laura], D, 7; Emma, D, 4
5126 SANDERS, Elisabeth, Christie, OK, 33
3199 SANDERS, Eliza, Stilwell, OK, 68
21636 SANDERS, Eliza, Campbell, OK, 12; By Lewis Crapoe, Gdn.
6810 SANDERS, Ellen M, Chelsea, OK, 34; DeWitt, S, 15; Jane Anna, D, 14; Frankie, D, 12
39168 SANDERS, Ellis, Bunch, OK, 20
16423 SANDERS, Fannie, Ft. Gibson, OK, 27
31573 SANDERS, Fannie, Brent, OK, 23
16424 SANDERS, Florence, Ft. Gibson, OK, 29
9184 SANDERS, Frank, Long, OK, 29; 12906, Celia, W, 25; Sam, S, 4; George, S, 2
31952 SANDERS, Franklin L, Stilwell, OK, 10;   By Allie E. Ferguson, Gdn.
407   SANDERS, George [or Soggy], Locust Grove, OK, 65
2928 SANDERS, George, Baron, OK, 40; 1922, Caroline, W, 35
42198 SANDERS, George, Bunch, OK, 34; Daniel, S, 10; Ellis, S, 7
2067 SANDERS, Geo. O, Wauhillau, OK, 69; 6485, Elizabeth, W, 54
8994 SANDERS, Geo. O, Sallisaw, OK, 11;   By Dexter Sanders, Gdn.
9154 SANDERS, Henry H, McKey, OK, 54; 9167, Charlotte E, W, 49; Brown, Marvin, S of W, 14; Sanders, Sam M, S, 11

CHEROKEE DESCENDANTS RESIDING WEST OF MISSISSIPPI RIVER.
VOLUME III (N – Z)

Key: Guion Miller Application Number; Name; Address, Relation (to Head); Age in 1906

6706 SANDERS, Isaac, Bunch, OK, 64
1174 SANDERS, James, Long, OK, 55; Lila, D, 16; Jesse, S, 6; Mollie, D, 2; Mary, D, ¼
1781 SANDERS, James, Baron, OK, 30; 28289, Ada, W, 21; Florence M, D, 4
10399 SANDERS, James, Wauhillau, OK, 34; 16892, Rachel, W, 28; Charles E, S, 10; May, D, 4; Lucinda J, D, 2
25717 SANDERS, James, Tahlequah,. OK, 26

[SANDERS, James. See #30828]   *(Note: entry separate from other family groups)*

28284 SANDERS, James P, Wauhillau, OK, 25
2992 SANDERS, Jas. R, Adair, OK, 50; 885, Mollie, W, 40; Ose O, S, 15
1441 SANDERS, Jennie, Bunch, OK, 56

[SANDERS, Jennie. See #30177]   *(Note: entry separate from other family groups)*

39174 SANDERS, Jennie, Bunch, OK, 31
2935 SANDERS, Jesse, Locust Grove, OK, 29; 1338, Charlotte M, W, 50; Downing, Will, S of W, 15; Wilson, John, S of W, 11; Huston, Ola, D of W, 10; Fisher. Steve, D[sic] of W, 5
38732 SANDERS, Jess, Proctor, OK, 18   [Died 1908]

[SANDERS, Jesse. See #25392]   *(Note: entry separate from other family groups)*

5583 SANDERS, Jesse, Inola, OK, 17; Lucinda, Sis, 13; Arthur, Bro, 11;   By Wm. W. Haver, Gdn
25714 SANDERS, Jesse, Tahlequah, OK, 27; Floyd, S, 4; Matt, S, 3; Jewell, S, 1/12
2131 SANDERS, Jim, Locust Grove, OK, 26; 28760, Susan, W, 24; Abraham, S, 2
10469 SANDERS, Joe, Lometa, OK, 50; 9425, Frances, W, 57; 10469, Berry, S, 17
10658 SANDERS, Joe, Edna, KS, 14;   By Joanna Cooper, Mother and Gdn.
91 SANDERS, John, Claremore, OK, 53; Clem F, S, 5
991 SANDERS, John, Claremore, OK, 56; Clara, D, 20; Frank, S, 17; Ed, S, 14; Linn, S, 11; Eli B, S, 7; Leva, D, 4; Henry T, S, 2
1279 SANDERS, John, Locust Grove, OK, 41; 2129, Mary, W, 40; 1279, Nick, S, 13; Annie, D, 11; Jennie, D, 7; 1279, Sarah, D, 4; Joe, S, 2
16406 SANDERS, John, Proctor, OK, 30; 8135, Ida, W, 38
3153 SANDERS, John, Proctor, OK, 44; Wm, S, 20; Polly, D, 12; Mahala, D, 10; Nick, S, 7; Watt, S, 4; Eli, S, 1
9138 SANDERS, John, Sallisaw, OK, 34
1117 SANDERS, John C, Wauhillau, OK, 40; 5123, Sallie, W, 40; James M, S, 18; Robert L, S, 16; George, S, 14; William A, S, 12; Eddie R, S, 10; John Wesley, S, 7; Caroline May, D, 4; Maurice Etta, D, 1
862 SANDERS, John M, Wauhillau, OK, 52; 28285, Florence C, D, 19; 862, George M, S, 18
1439 SANDERS, Jolly, Bunch, OK, 61; 1436, Mary, W, 58

CHEROKEE DESCENDANTS RESIDING WEST OF MISSISSIPPI RIVER.
VOLUME III (N – Z)

Key: Guion Miller Application Number; Name; Address, Relation (to Head); Age in 1906

42191 SANDERS, Katie, Stilwell, OK, 21; Hass, S, 1
9237 SANDERS, Laura W, Collinsville, OK, 58; 22185, Jas. Allen, S, 15; 22184, Sadie, D, 12

[SANDERS, Lena. See #23048]   *(Note: entry separate from other family groups)*

9463 SANDERS, Lewis, Braggs, OK, 34; 3213, Mary, W, 32; Thomas G, S, 12; Charlotte M, D, 8; Nancy J, D, 3; Allen G, S, 1
1438 SANDERS, Lizzie, Bunch, OK, 57
28286 SANDERS, Lizzie, Wauhillau, OK, 21
28287 SANDERS, Lucinda, Wauhillau, OK, 24
25831 SANDERS, Lulu B, Douglas, AZ, 23
1121 SANDERS, Madison, Tahlequah, OK, 58; 25713, Louisa, W, 47; 25716, Lizzie, D, 20; John H, S, 19; Geneva, D, 17; Carl, S, 13; Maggie D, D, 4
30796 SANDERS, Maggie A, Christie, OK, 25
25121 SANDERS, Margaret C, Stilwell, OK, 26; Flora M, D, 7; John B, S, 5; Mamie H, D, 4; Hazel C, D, 2
8899 SANDERS, Martha A, Pinehill, TX, 51
874 SANDERS, Martha J, Miles, OK, 38; Martha L, D, 16
10273 SANDERS, Mary, Wauhillau, OK, 30
13416 SANDERS, Mary, Marble City, OK, 58; 12695, Edward W, S, 19
31951 SANDERS, Minnie E, Stilwell, OK, 7;   By Allie E. Ferguson, Gdn.
26393 SANDERS, Minnie L, Tahlequah, OK, 21
42179 SANDERS, Mose, Bunch, OK, 24; 10672, Minnie, W, 22
12400 SANDERS, Moses F, Sallisaw, OK, 40; Mary L, D, 2
14735 SANDERS, Myrtle, Porum, OK, 25; Hughie L, D(?), 5; Allen, S, 2
1437 SANDERS, Nakie, Bunch, OK, 64
13092 SANDERS, Nancy, Bunch, OK, 60

[SANDERS, Nannie. See #3151]   *(Note: entry separate from other family groups)*

[SANDERS, Nannie. Wee #8136]   *(Note: entry separate from other family groups)*

[SANDERS, Nellie. See #4932]   *(Note: entry separate from other family groups)*

9454 SANDERS, Nicklas, Pryor Creek, OK, 21
11258 SANDERS, Nicholas S, Pryor Creek, OK, 46; Irene, D, 16

[SANDERS, Peggy. See #7729]   *(Note: entry separate from other family groups)*

10657 SANDERS, Pigeon, Edna, KS, 16;   By Joanna Cooper, Mother and Gdn.
1278 SANDERS, Rat, Choteau, OK, 53; 2500, Annie, W, 60
12883 SANDERS, Richard B, Marble City, OK, 22
9141 SANDERS, Robert, Vian, OK, 41; Claud, S, 18; Clifford, S, 15; Clide, S, 10; Edward B, S, 7; Vera, D, 4; Daisey[sic], D, 19

CHEROKEE DESCENDANTS RESIDING WEST OF MISSISSIPPI RIVER.
VOLUME III (N – Z)

Key: Guion Miller Application Number; Name; Address, Relation (to Head); Age in 1906

- **5503** SANDERS, Sam, Proctor, OK, 35; 26380, Jessie B, W, 33; Charles D, S, 9; Pearl E, D, 7; Thomas, S, 2
- **6585** SANDERS, Samuel, Wauhillau, OK, 63
- **19061** SANDERS, Samuel, Ft. Gibson, OK, 21
- **2996** SANDERS, Samuel L, Melvin, OK, 38
- **14786** SANDERS, Samuel S, Braggs, OK, 34; 14785, Elizabeth, W, 38; Katie A, D, 6; Samuel S, Jr, S, 3
- **10659** SANDERS, Sequoyah, Edna, KS, 18;   By Joanna Cooper, Mother and Gdn.
- **5135** SANDERS, Susie, Leach, OK, 34; Della M, D, 15; John L, S, 11; William A, S, 8; Josey E, D, 5
- **5135** SANDERS, Samuel O, Leach, OK, S, 2
- **9681** SANDERS, Susie, Bunch, OK, 29
- **203** SANDERS, Thomas, Stilwell, OK, 59; 578, Bettie, W, 41; 203, Lydia, D, 17; Lula, D, 15; Felix, S, 11; French, S, 8; Leona [Maggie L], D, 4
- **17563** SANDERS, Thomas, Proctor, OK, 27
- **39396** SANDERS, Thos. J, Stilwell, OK, 28; 39397, Rachel, W, 30; Walter Levi, S, 4; Sarah, D, 1
- **39167** SANDERS, Tim, Bunch, OK, 32; 6704, Lydia, W, (?); Jim, S, (?)
- **21705** SANDERS, Walter, Vian, OK: 24; Adaline, D, 3; John Hulbert, S, ¼
- **39169** SANDERS, Washington, Bunch, OK, 25; 6230, Peggie [Ahnawake], W, 20
- **5906** SANDERS, Watson, Southwest City, MO, 84
- **42199** SANDERS, Watt, Bunch, OK, 27
- **10274** SANDERS, William, Wauhillau, OK, 35
- **5299** SANDERS, William E, Claremore, OK,   47; 5298, Etta J, W, 35; John G, S, 15; William E, S, 10; Dewitt C, S, 8; Henry K, S, 4
- **17674** SANDERS, Wylie, Sallisaw, OK, 8; Bessie, S, 2;   By Alma Sanders, Gdn.
- **27964** SANDIFER, Celie M, Claremore, OK, 24; William F, S, 3; Robert L, S, 1
- **10922** SANGSTER, Kate, Claremore, OK, 43
- **2283** SANTAFEE, Lydia, Oaks, OK, 54
- **25632** SAPSUCKER, David W, Kansas, OK, 21; 16692, Susie, W, 24; Cu-cu-mer [Cochran], S, 6; Johnny, S, 1/12
- **25631** SAPSUCKER, Henry, Kansas, OK, 23; 33438, Lila, W, 21
- **723** SAPSUCKER, John, Eucha, OK, 47; 16694, Susan, W, 50; George S, 15
- **7890** SAPSUCKER, Levi, Kansas, OK, 53; 7892, Aggie, W, 42; Arlie, S, 14; Jinnie, D, 12
- **172** SAPSUCKER, Luke, Zena, OK, 59; Lena, D, 12; Sissie, D, 10; Enda, D, 5
- **43253** SAPSUCKER, Price, Eucha, OK, 24
- **16417** SAR-WE-GU-YAH, Bullett, Campbell, OK, 17

[SATTERWHITE, Elizabeth. See #25291]
                         (Note: entry separate from other family groups)

[SAUNDERS, Mary M, See #1344]   *(Note: entry separate from other family groups)*

- **6238** SAWNEY [Tickaneeski], Stilwell, OK, 80; Mike, S, 11

CHEROKEE DESCENDANTS RESIDING WEST OF MISSISSIPPI RIVER.
VOLUME III (N – Z)

Key: Guion Miller Application Number; Name; Address, Relation (to Head); Age in 1906

5894 SAWNEY, Alex, Stilwell, OK, 35; 15634, Lizzie, W, 22; Lula, D, 5; Annie, D, 2; Noney, D, 1/6

[SAWNEY, Anna. See #16353]   *(Note: entries separate*
[SAWNEY, Colnay. See #16353]   *from other family groups)*

6235 SAWNEY, Celia, Evansville, AR, 55; Anna, D, 18; Lizay, D, 16; Nancy, D, 10
1914 SAWNEY, Jack, Stilwell, OK, 45; 22655, Susie, W, 40; John, S, 20; Lydia, D, 13; Joe, S, 9; Annie, D, 5; Tom, S, 2
6592 SAWNEY, Jennie, Evansville, AR, 39; John, S, 17; Peter, S, 14; Laura, D, 12; Susie, D, 8; Sawney, Stand, Evansville, AR, S, 2
9399 SAWNEY, Lucy, Stilwell, OK, 47; Annie, D, 15; Lizzie, D, 10

[SAWNEY, Robert. See #30827]   *(Note: entries separate*
[SAWNEY, Roy. See #30827]   *from other family groups)*

29193 SAWYER, Allen, Eucha, OK, 29
11883 SCACEWATER, James, Stilwell, OK, 29; 11913, Murtie M, W, 27; Lucien B, S, 6; Clara E, D, 4; Jack, S, 1
17103 SCARCEWATER, Ross, Vian, OK, 18; Jimmie, Bro, 16; By Wm. E. McConnell, Gdn.
983 SCALES, Amanda P, Webbers Falls, OK, 69
34490 SCALES, Ethel, Flint, OK, 20

[SCALES, Joseph A, Jr, See #10302]   *(Note: entries separate*
[SCALES, Frank V. See #10302]   *from other family groups)*

34463 SCALES, Mattie, Flint, OK, 38; Grover, S, 17; Joseph, S, 15; Lillie, D, 12; Louisa, D, 10; George, S, 7; Ann L, D, 3; Mary E, D, 5/12
14132 SCAR-GEE-NEE, Loonie, Locust Grove, OK, 31;   By David Fixing, Gdn.
2740 SCHAFFER, Annie, Moodys, OK, 53
25735 SCHAMBLIN, Julia C, Warner, OK, 31; John R, S, 3
23493 SCHARBLE, Joseph O, Tahlequah, OK,   28
1871 SCHELL, Tennessee, Nowata, OK, 20; Irwin Earl, S, 4; Margaret Viola, D, 3
24820 SCHLIECKER, Lucy C, Vinita, OK, 25; August F, S, 4; Herman A, S, 2
23442 SCHOONOVER, Frank, Keefeton, OK, 27; Vesta V, D, 5; Annie R, D, 2; Frank M, S, 1/6
23445 SCHOONOVER, Tom, Keefeton, OK,   20
26160 SCHRADER, Susan A, Southwest City,   MO, 25; Josephine E, D, 4; Frederick W, S, 3; Charles F, S, 1
14767 SCHRIMISHER, Elizabeth B, Claremore, OK, 33
5963 SCHRIMSHER[sic], Newton Jasper, Wagoner, OK, 57; Josephine, D, 11; Marie, D, 10; Nellie P, D, 5
31458 SCHRIMSHER, Susan P, Claremore, OK, 28; Loletia, D, 2; Maxine, D, 2; John G, S, 1

CHEROKEE DESCENDANTS RESIDING WEST OF MISSISSIPPI RIVER.
VOLUME III   (N – Z)

Key: Guion Miller Application Number; Name; Address, Relation (to Head); Age in 1906

- **791** SCHRIMPSHER, Juliette M, Webbers Falls, OK, 65
- **9420** SCHUTH, Eva S, Blue Jacket, OK, 23; Walter G, S, 3
- **4335** SCHUTH, Vinnie M, Chetopa, KS, 32; Elizabeth Irene, D, 8; Ruby Evaline, D, 5; Gladys Ermina, D, 1
- **24621** SCOGGINS, Effie, Pryor Creek, OK, 22; Louis, S, ½
- **8143** SCOGGINS, Georgia A, Bartlesville, OK, 20; Florence P, D, 4; Clarence E, S, 2; Veva B, S, 2/3
- **9957** SCOGGINS, Lucy J, Pryor Creek, OK, 43; Lola D, D, 14; Jesse E, W, 12; Una, D, 10; Willie, S, 8; Marion, S, 2
- **7673** SCONTI, Cornelius, Sallisaw, OK, 32; 7672, Emma, W, 34; 8111, Lassley, Sarah, D of W, 16; 7673, Sconti, Lydia, D, 5; Thomas, S, 3
- **28589** SCOTT, Alfred A, McLain, OK, 29
- **2157** SCOTT, Amanda C, Vinita, OK, 56; James W, S, 20; Charles D, S, 14
- **16677** SCOTT, Ananias, Warner, OK, 3;   By William W. Scott, Gdn.
- **23690** SCOTT, Anna, Rose, OK, 33; Cornelius, S, 12; Gertie, D, 11; William, S, 9; Myrtle, D, 8; Nannie, D, 5; Riley, S, 4; Lou C, D, 2
- **9159** SCOTT, Belle H, Ft. Gibson, OK, 51; Allen H, S, 14
- **33776** SCOTT, Calvin C, Muskogee, OK, 31
- **9709** SCOTT, Charlie Bunch, OK, 46; 15630, Nancy, W, 54; 9709, Dora, D, 20; Ned, S, 17; Charley, S, 15; Maud, D, 12
- **270** SCOTT, Charlotte, Nowata, OK, 25
- **26958** SCOTT, Cherokee, Nowata, OK, 31; Jesse, S, 14; William, S, 11; David, S, 8; Looney, S, 5; Cora, D, 3
- **31721** SCOTT, Chester A, Muskogee, OK, 25; Laura V, D, 2
- **20246** SCOTT, Daniel, Stilwell, OK, 29; 5341, Annie, W, 23; 20237, Lincoln, S, 8; 20246, He-ke [Hickey], S, 1
- **24612** SCOTT, Dennis, Chance, OK, 23
- **7458** SCOTT, Eli, Stilwell, OK, 59
- **7896** SCOTT, Elizabeth O, Ft. Gibson, OK, 80
- **23242** SCOTT, Ella N, Tahlequah, OK, 30; Anna M, D, 5; Milo B, S, 2
- **709** SCOTT, Elmira, Coffeyville, KS, 26; Orville E, S, 7; Clarence R, S, 5; Ruth A, D, 2

[SCOTT, Emma. See #26356]
[SCOTT, Mary. See #26356]
[SCOTT, John. See #26356]
[SCOTT, Bulah. See #26356]

(Note: entries separate from other family groups)

- **12913** SCOTT, Eura, St. Louis, MO, 909 Chestnut St, 26
- **7478** SCOTT, George, Stilwell, OK, 68; 7454, Lucinda, W, 74
- **9644** SCOTT, George, Bunch, OK, 50
- **16544** SCOTT, George, Ross, OK, 18
- **24049** SCOTT, Gibson R, Vian, OK, 29; 24050, Minnie, W, 26; 24049, Gladys H, D, 4; Gibson R, Jr, S, 2
- **26071** SCOTT, Henry, Talala, OK, 26; John W, S, 4

CHEROKEE DESCENDANTS RESIDING WEST OF MISSISSIPPI RIVER.
VOLUME III (N – Z)

Key: Guion Miller Application Number; Name; Address, Relation (to Head); Age in 1906

4792 SCOTT, Ida L, Muskogee, OK, 41; Patterson M, S, 14; Lucy A, D, 12; Helen May, D, 10; Naomi, D, 8; Geo W, Jr, S, 5; Fite B, S, 3; Ida Nola, D, 1
22900 SCOTT, Jack S, Ft. Gibson, OK, 22
1594 SCOTT, Jennie, Chance, OK, 52; 23159, Susie, D, 18; 1594, Tom, S, 15; Rufus, S, 12; Margaret, D, 9; Fannie B, D, 6
6734 SCOTT, John, Stilwell, OK, 37; 6732, Emeline, W, 38
9637 SCOTT, John, Bunch, OK, 59; 13193, Laura, W, 59
24152 SCOTT, John B, Vinita, OK, 35; Charles F, S, 4; Bertha E, D, 2
6232 SCOTT, Kate, Bunch, OK, 50; 14271, Murphy, Watt, S, 17; Emma [or Amy], D, 15
31723 SCOTT, Lee Rex, Muskogee, OK, 28
11632 SCOTT, Linnie, Chance, OK, 21
13467 SCOTT, Lula, Wimer, OK, 31; Ethel N, D, 13; George E, S, 12; James A, S, 10; Myrtle E, D, 6; Marion T, S, 5; Millard E, S, 3; Iva L, D, 1
36313 SCOTT, Martin B, Webbers Falls, OK, 27; Bonnie C, D, 5; Reginald, S, 3; Gus C, S, 1
11226 SCOTT, Mary E, Tahlequah, OK, 54; Grover Harris, S, 14
28753 SCOTT, Moses J, McLain, OK, 31; Lena, D, 3

[SCOTT, Nancy. See #12589]
[SCOTT, Jennie. See #12588]
(Note: entries separate from other family groups)

4857 SCOTT, Peter, Locust Grove, OK, 40; 5287, Betsy, W, 30; 4857, Gaw-ye-na-ey, D, 5; Nancy, D, 2
8979 SCOTT, Polly, Stilwell, OK, 80 [Died 12-1-1908]
16563 SCOTT, Polly Ann, Rose, OK, 50; 31889, Armindas, D, 19; 16563, George, S, 15
13751 SCOTT. Riley, Cookson, OK, 14;   By Chas. Bendabout, Gdn.
22803 SCOTT, Robert, Stilwell, OK, 24
10924 SCOTT, Roxie, Rose, OK, 25; Buster, S, 7; Edna, D, 6; Eva, D, 4; Ida, D, 2; Rena, D, 1
412 SCOTT, Sabrina, Maysville, AR, 47; Mattie E, D, 14
9386 SCOTT, Son-e-qu-yah, Lometa, OK, 59
39775 SCOTT, Sue, Sallisaw, OK, 29; Willie, S, 12; Belle, D, 10; Claude, S, 8; Ernest, S, 6; Jessie, D, 4; David E, S, 2
29301 SCOTT, Susie V, Maysville, AR, 24
11483 SCOTT, Susan F, Sallisaw, OK, 35; Carry E, D, 10; Sue J, D, 7; Arthur L, S, 3; George S, S, 1
27124 SCOTT, Thomas A, Braggs, OK, 29; Beatrice H. Y, D, 3; Robert Mayes, S, ¾
13395 SCOTT, Wah-la-ne-tah, Braggs, OK, 19;   By Nellie Josiah Ned, Gdn.
4059 SCOTT, Walter, Ft. Gibson, OK, 34
22826 SCOTT, William, Uniontown, AR, 20
28341 SCOTT, William A, McLain, OK, 32; Francis M, S, 10; James S, S, 9; Hazel I, D, 4; Theodore M, S, 2
29300 SCOTT, William T, Maysville, AR, 26
9729 SCRAPER, Betsy, Proctor, OK, 38; 9728, Oliver, S, 16; John, S, 15

CHEROKEE DESCENDANTS RESIDING WEST OF MISSISSIPPI RIVER.
VOLUME III (N – Z)

Key: Guion Miller Application Number; Name; Address, Relation (to Head); Age in 1906

  9230 SCRAPER, Charley, Tahlequah, OK, 72
13292 SCRAPER, Dick, Bunch, OK, 27; Ellen, D, 4; Bob, S, 2
25908 SCRAPER, Elijah, Southwest City, MO, 22
  6269 SCRAPER, Fields, Bunch, OK, 49; 13124, Lucy, W, 34; 42188, Jennie, D, 16; 6269, Jesse, S, 13; John, S, 11; Annie [Anewake], D, 8; Nannie, D, 5; Ice, S, 2
  433 SCRAPER, Henry, Southwest City, MO, 52; 573, Lydia, W, 51; 25909, Fannie, D, 17; 433, Ernest, S, 13
  3244 SCRAPER, Nancy, Bunch, OK, 25
  3245 SCRAPER, Ned, Bunch, OK, 27; 5690, Susie, W, ?; Te-hee, Charlie, S of W, 14; Miller or Mills, Lizzie, D of W, 12; Scraper, Nellie, D 9; Ben, S, 7; Narcy, D, 3
13103 SCRAPER, Paulina, Southwest City, MO, 26

[SCRAPER, Polly. See #604]   *(Note: entry separate from other family groups)*

  431 SCRAPER, Tom, Southwest City, MO, 30 [Died 12-20-'06]; 13182, Nancy, D, 20; 13098, Lewis, S, 14
16652 SCRAPER, William, Baron, OK, 26; 10762, Sallie E, W, 22; Lula, D, 4; Alice, D, 3
  1782 SCRAPPER, Jim, Baron Fork, OK, 21
27186 SCREWES, Lavada, Sallisaw, OK, 19; Linnie Vola, D, 2; Joseph Henry, S, ¼

[SCRUGGIN, Grape. See #526]   *(Note: entry separate from other family groups)*

13310 SCRUGGS, Charley, Blackgum, OK, 12;   By Sarah M. Smith, Gdn.
31550 SCRUGGS, Red Cloud, Edna, KS, 32; 34489, Cora, W, 22; David, S, 5; Jack, S, 3; Revord, S, 1
34486 SCRUGGS, Sarah F, Adair, OK, 25; Julia M, D, 1
  8989 SCUDDER, Alfred B, Texanna, OK, 22
25458 SCUDDER, Annie C, Chelsea, OK, 19
  8988 SCUDDER, Cherokee G, Texanna, OK, 26
29351 SCUDDER, Gordon H, Dewey, OK, 29
  8990 SCUDDER, Jacob M, Texanna, OK, 35;   Hermon G, S, 5; Clifford H, S, 2
  8991 SCUDDER, Maggie B, Texanna, OK, 16
25461 SCUDDER, Nellie V, Chelsea, OK, 20
22522 SCUDDER, Newton G, Chelsea, OK, 25
  888 SCUDDER, Wm. H. H, Chelsea, OK, 65; Wm. H. H. Jr, S, 16; Julia R, D, 14; Louis B, S, 10; Farrar, Oliver M, GS, 11; Gaskey, John R, GS, 7

[SCULLAWL. See SKUL-LOR-LE.]

11279 SCULLAWL, James, Hulbert, OK, 75 [Deceased] (By) Joe M. Tahay, Admr, Claremore, OK
  6781 SCULLAWL, William, Catoosa, OK, 66; 6770, Caroline, W, 37; Tucker, Mary, D of W, 16; Hawkins, John, S of W, 12; 9649, McKinsey, Annie, D of W, 10; 6781, Scullawl, Dare, D, 1

CHEROKEE DESCENDANTS RESIDING WEST OF MISSISSIPPI RIVER.
VOLUME III   (N – Z)

Key: Guion Miller Application Number; Name; Address, Relation (to Head); Age in 1906

28194 SEABOLT, Albert, Long, OK, 22; Ida M. A, D, 4; Bellzora, D, 1/12
598 SEABOLT, Alfred P, Muldrow, OK, 36; Alfred L, S, 14; Ottaway, S, 12; Martin L, S, 10; Robert W E, S, 5; Vera M, D, 2; Ura E, D, 1
9973 SEABOLT, Anderson B, Long, OK, 35; Susanna, D, 12; Sarah L, D, 10
601 SEABOLT, Bean, Long, OK, 46; Ora, D, 7
16615 SEABOLT, Benj, Stilwell, OK, 27; Nancy, D, 1
2122 SEABOLT, Christopher C, Hanson, OK, 53; Dovey, D, 7; Minnie, D, 1; Tommy L, S, 12
9890 SEABOLT, Claremore, Long, OK, 61
33217 SEABOLT, Dewey D, Long, OK, 3;   By Robert Smith, Gdn.
15632 SEABOLT, Eliza, Stilwell, OK, 18
12497 SEABOLT, Elvira, Hanson, OK, 31; Quinton, Myrtle C, N, 5
600 SEABOLT, James, Maple, OK, 48
9968 SEABOLT, James M, Long, OK, 49; 16777, Ollie, W, 48; Lucy L, D, 17; Bertha A, D, 14; Levi D, S, 11; Mary E, D, 9; Clayton M, S, 5
9395 SEABOLT, Joe, Stilwell, OK, 20
9885 SEABOLT, John, Long, OK, 33
12496 SEABOLT, John E, Hanson, OK, 35
6919 SEABOLT, John M, Stilwell, OK, 30; Loy H, S, 5; Carrie M, D, 1
9974 SEABOLT, Josiah, Long, OK, 52; Minnie M, D, 16; Charles E, S, 14; Nancy A, D, 12; Trilby L, D, 10; Joseph M, S, 7; Daniel H, S, 3
9889 SEABOLT, Lucy, Long, OK, 16;   By Claremore, Seabolt, Gdn.
599 SEABOLT, Luny, Maple, OK, 33; Sam H, S, 6
28599 SEABOLT, Mary, Evansville, AR, 17
6587 SEABOLT, Minnie B, Stilwell, OK, 23
1893 SEABOLT, Nancy, Long, OK, 80
4066 SEABOLT, Polly, Stilwell, OK, 49; 43787, Chuckalate Hyatt or Hyde, S, 3; Chuckalate, Ose or Oscar, S, 2   [Died 2-1907]
10953 SEABOLT, Scott, Muldrow, OK, 31; Levi Wofford, S, 11; Lizzie, D, 8; Charlie, S, 7; Ella May, D, 4; Linnie Emma, D, 2
9888 SEABOLT, Stephen, Long, OK, 29; 9972, Joanna, W, 22; Lassley, Cecil M, S, 4; Seabolt, Raymond G, S, 2; Willie L, S, 1
9175 SEABOLT, Thomas, Hanson, OK, 22
28196 SEABOLT, Timothy E, Long, OK, 47
8260 SEABOLT, William R, Stilwell, OK, 53
6579 SEABOLT, Willie E, Stilwell, OK, 17
25390 SEABOURN, Sadie L, Southwest City, MO, 35; Joy C, D, 11; Joseph D, S, 10
31315 SEARS, David, Pryor Creek, OK, 21
[SEARS, Peggie. See #8732]   *(Note: entry separate from other family groups)*

32285 SEARS, Sam, Pryor Creek, OK, 21
31314 SEARS, Stephen, Webb City, MO, 25; 28839, Ada, W, 29

CHEROKEE DESCENDANTS RESIDING WEST OF MISSISSIPPI RIVER.
VOLUME III (N – Z)

Key: Guion Miller Application Number; Name; Address, Relation (to Head); Age in 1906

[SECONDI, Cornelius. See #7673]
[SCONDI[sic], Emma. See #7672]
[SECONDI, Lydia. See #7673]
[SECONDI, Thomas. See #7673]   *(Note: entries separate from other family groups)*

17498 SECREST, John O, Ozona, TX, 33

[SEEING, Ben. See #7023]   *(Note: entry separate from other family groups)*

[SEEING, Ollie. See #7024]
[SEEING, Mary. See #7024]   *(Note: entries separate from other family groups)*

[SEEING, Charlotte. See #7024]
[SEEING, Willie. See #7024]
[SEEING, Peggie. See #7024]   *(Note: entries separate from other family groups)*

[SEEING, Starr. See #15973]   *(Note: entry separate from other family groups)*

16900 SEEKINGS, Dannie, Muskogee, OK, 26; William T, S, 6; Nancy Jane, D, 2; Robert, S, 1
3711 SEILER[sic], Mary A, Blue Jacket, OK, 26; Kathleen Ione, D, 1
4737 SELLERS, Chichalulu, Evansville, AR, 52; 1697, Peggy, W, 40; Richard, S, 14; Maud, D, 9
28153 SELLERS, Laura J, Sageeyah, OK, 26; Ruth, D, 2
9398 SELLERS, Patsy, Evansville, AR, 23; John, S, 2

[SELLOUT, Polly. See #2298]   *(Note: entry separate from other family groups)*

5487 SELVIDGE, John B, Cherokee City, AR, 34; Goldie S, D, 13; Percy L, S, 11; Katey A, D, 7; Dolpha E, S, 5
28345 SENDLIN, Lydia, Gans, OK, 26; Miller, Pearl L, D, 3
16185 SE-QUAH-YAH, Doosda, Campbell, OK, 23
14800 SE-QUAH-YAH, Eja-ger, Campbell, OK, 19; Buster, George, S, 2
14807 SE-QUAH-YAH, Scarlupka, Campbell, OK, 21
14808 SE-QUAH-YAH, Tom, Campbell, OK, 25
4688 SEQUICHIE, Arch, Chelsea, OK, 32; Arch, Jr, S, 9; Nina K, D, 7; Alma, D, 4; Nellie L, D, 2

[SEQUICHE, Emma. S#3550]   *(Note: entry separate from other family groups)*

4687 SEQUICHIE, Joseph R, Chelsea, OK, 35; 31782, Annie L, W, 28; 31782, Marion L, S, 7; J. Oris, S, 4

[SEQUICHIE, Squirrel. See #12405]   *(Note: entry separate from other family groups)*

CHEROKEE DESCENDANTS RESIDING WEST OF MISSISSIPPI RIVER.
VOLUME III (N – Z)

Key: Guion Miller Application Number; Name; Address, Relation (to Head); Age in 1906

4294 SEQUOYAH, Daniel, Hadley, OK, 26
9271 SEQUOYAH, Dick, Lometa, OK, 46; 9270, Lucy, W, 46; Betsy, D, 10
9410 SEQUOYAH, Stute, Lometa, OK, 34; 1268, Sarah, W, 54; Adams, Richard, S of W, 16
9409 SEQUOYAH, Thos, Lometa, OK, 62; 9413, Alley [Ella], D, 17
22448 SETSER, Francis M, Pryor Creek, OK, 45; Walter M, S, 20; Martha J, D, 16; Willie F, S, 14; Waneta M, D, 11; Albert A, S, 8; Lillie Ann, D, 5
4019 SETSER, Martha A, Tahlequah, OK, 71
26909 SETSER, Maud L, Tahlequah, OK, 15; Ella M, S (Sis), 12; David F, B (Bro), 10; Lily E, S (Sis), 7;   By Sarah A. Frederick, Mother
11792 SEVEN, Rufus, Grove, OK, 29
14041 SEVENS, Joseph S, Grove, OK, 36; Georgia N, D, 2; Deward L, S, 1/6
6050 SEVENSTAR, Ella, Melvin, OK, 18
10334 SEVENSTAR, Larken, Ochelata, OK, 26
17177 SEVENSTAR, Sam, Long, OK, 26
24282 SEVERS, Bessie M, Muskogee, OK, 24
29368 SEVERS, Charles J, Jefferson Barracks,   MO, 21
15722 SEVERS, Samuel B, Little Rock, AR, 52
15722 SEVERS, Samuel B, Jr, Muskogee, OK, 19 [Died 6-14-1906]; Emma M, S (Sis), 17; Bartow F, B, (Bro), 12;   By W. B. Butz, Gdn.
25675 SEVIER, Anna E, Webbers Falls, OK, 25
25677 SEVIER, Callie O, Webbers Falls, OK, 26
5855 SEVIER, Daniel, Copan, OK, 36
25674 SEVIER, Jerry A, Webbers Falls, OK, 22
33103 SEVIER, Jesse, Tahlequah, OK, 18;   By Harry L. Sanders, Gdn.
25673 SEVIER, Jos. C, Webbers Falls, OK, 22
11225 SEVIER, Jos. J, Webbers Falls, OK, 48; 25676, Alice B, D, 19; 11225, Charles Fowler, S, 18; Leo Earnest, S, 14; Nelson A. M. S, 8
17005 SEVIER, William P, Hulbert, OK, 34; 36483, Ida E, W, 31; Alma E, D, 3; Thompson C, S, 1
29107 SEXTON, Mary M, Mount Judea, AR, ?; Isaac A, S, 12; Joseph M, S, 8; David R, S, 6; Maudie M, D, 3
27639 SHACKLEFORD, Jessie B, Paw Paw, OK, 19
12817 SHACKLEFORD, Martha F, Cherokee City, AR, 38; Effie E, D, 18; Charley L, S, 13
27640 SHACKLEFORD, Maude E, Paw Paw,   OK, 21
14666 SHACKLEFORD, Peachie R, Joplin, MO, 23; Robert E, S, 1/3
6074 SHADE, Adam, Melvin, OK, 56; 9428, Arlie [Ollie], W, 28; Josie, D, 7; Betsy, D, 5; Stricker, S, 3; Aggie, D, 1/6
29789 SHADE, Henry, Tulsa, OK, 31; 7007, Maggie, W, 25
7659 SHADE, Isaac, Tahlequah, OK 61; Coony, S, 16 [Died 4-1908]; Isaac, S, 14
32857 SHADE, John, Tulsa, OK, 25
1291 SHADE, Joseph, Peggs, OK, 64; 1942, Peggy, W, 50
22020 SHADE, Thomas, Jr, Tahlequah, OK, 37; 8314, Betsy, W, 32; Lilie, D, 14; Joseph, Jr, S, 8

CHEROKEE DESCENDANTS RESIDING WEST OF MISSISSIPPI RIVER.
VOLUME III   (N – Z)

Key: Guion Miller Application Number; Name; Address, Relation (to Head); Age in 1906

- **1891** SHAKINGBUSH, Geo, Uniontown, AR, 39; 8261, Susie, W, 34; Aggie, D, 13; Lela, D, 9; Levi, S, 5; William, S, 2
- **12657** SHAMBLIN, Geo. W, Coffeyville, KS, 41; Plese F, D, 14; Stephen D, S, 11; Bert A, S, 7; Annie E, D, 4; Geo. Clark, S, 2; Arnold P, S, 1/12
- **23865** SHAMBLIN, Lou E, Remy, OK, 16; Dock H, S, ½
- **23866** SHAMBLIN, Ollie May, Remy, OK, 14
- **25595** SHAMBLIN, Rebecca E, Long, OK, 18; Emma May, D, 2
- **8008** SHANAHAN, Jennie, Vinita, OK, 39; 30371, Margaret, D, 18; 8008, Jennie, D, 10; Timothy, S, 4
- **10661** SHANKS, Nannie E, Vian, OK, 16; 10663, Jessie J, S, 17; 10664, John Ed, Bro, 12; 10662, Narcissa, S, 14;   By John C. Cotner, Gdn.
- **23225** SHANNON, Ophelia B, Evansville, AR, 25; Jesse W, S, 3; Mary O, D, 1/12
- **17105** SHARP, Clifford, Vian, OK, 10;   By George Kiddy, Gdn.
- **26154** SHARP, Edward L, Bluejacket, OK, 29; Rebecca L, D, 1; Cora N, D, 1
- **8968** SHARP, Fannie, Vian, OK, 30; Mike, S, 7; Dan, S, 6; Alma Thay, D, 2
- **8630** SHARP, Jim, Stilwell, OK, 18
- **9009** SHARP, John, Locust Grove, OK, 47
- **11194** SHARP, John W, Tahlequah, OK, 53; Albert, S, 17; Caroline, D, 15; Grover, S, 13; George W, S, 4; 44338, John, S, 20
- **27723** SHARP, Margaret E, Chance, OK, 24; Franklin B, S, 2; George T, S, 1
- **14173** SHARP, Peggy, Mark, OK, 72
- **7562** SHARP, Ratler, Southwest City, MO, 34; Mary, D, 12; Huckleberry, S, 1
- **33414** SHARP, Richard H, Tahlequah, OK, 28
- **9903** SHARP, Too-late, Spavinaw, OK, 53; 9905, Ella [Aily], D, 18; 9903, Davis, S, 15; Buck, S, 13; Nelson, S, 8
- **17091** SHARP, Worcester, Ketchem, OK, 24
- **805** SHARYER, Mary M, Ballard, OK, 25; Stella, D, 1
- **13223** SHAVER, Betsy, Bunch, OK, 91

[SHAW, Bertha M. See #7445]   *(Note: entries separate*
[SHAW, Bessie B. See #7445]   *from other family groups)*

- **24984** SHAW, Bettie, Pryor Creek, OK, 22
- **24995** SHAW, Lena Ann, Bokchito, OK, 16; Wm Ernest, Bro, 11; By Sarah E. Shaw, Mother.
- **22200** SHAW, Mary P, Chelsea, OK, 34
- **906** SHAY, Minnie, Henryetta, OK, 37; Jessie L, D, 4; Minnie T, D, 2
- **4440** SHEARER Ella, Moody, OK, 26; Laura S, D, 5; John M, S, 3; Joseph T, S, 1
- **10758** SHEARHART, Nannie, Texanna, OK, 23; Cale M, S, 2
- **27705** SHELDON, Wm. T, Grove, OK, 31; Walter M, S, 12; Willie M, D, 9

[SHELL, Ada. See #28289]   *(Note: entries separate*
[SHELL, Florence May. See #28289]   *from other family groups)*

CHEROKEE DESCENDANTS RESIDING WEST OF MISSISSIPPI RIVER.
VOLUME III   (N – Z)

Key: Guion Miller Application Number; Name; Address, Relation (to Head); Age in 1906

9285 SHELL, Charley, Stilwell, OK, 41; 9284, Rebecca, W, 37; 42190, Lula, D, 16; 9285, Susie, D, 11; Nannie, D, 9; Charlotte, D, 6; Lucinda, D, 4; Charley, S, 1; Lucinda, D, 4; Charley, S, 1
4919 SHELL, James, Westville, OK, 45; Susie E, D, 8; Ennice V, D, 6; Earnest, S, 3; Pearlie E, D, 1/3
1615 SHELL, Jennie, Stilwell, OK, 55
17280 SHELL, Richard, Stilwell, OK, 26; 15662, Wuttie D, W, 19; James, S, 6; Thompson, S, 3; Emma, D, 1
11919 SHELL, Sallie, Stilwell, OK, 46; Arch, S, 18
1617 SHELL, Samuel, Stilwell, OK, 30; 2872, Lucy, W, 28; Huckleberry, S, 11; Jack, S, 10; Luke, S, 8; Charley, S, 6; Stand, S, 3; Howell L, S, 1
3722 SHELL, Tash, Baron, OK, 60; 24508, Jennie, W, 54; 24507, Johanna, D, 18; 3722, Jessie, S, 11; 27435, Adair, Floyd, GS, 8
24509 SHELL, William, Baron, OK, 34; 1830, Nancy J, W, 34; David, S, 11; John, S, 7; Elmer C, S, 4; Callie M, S, 4
2422 SHELTON, Andromache, B, Vinita, OK, 75 [Died 11-28-1906]
13699 SHELTON, Claude S, Centralia, OK, 46; 13698, Mary Z, W, 35; Johnnie B, S, 15
13700 SHELTON, Harvey W. C, Centralia, OK, 43; Harvey, Jr, S, 9
29693 SHELTON, James A, Nowata, OK, 30 [Deceased] By Bradie Shelton, Wife; Raymon S, S, 7; Mary Jane, D, 5; Sadie M, D, 3
13543 SHELTON, Norman B, Big Cabin, OK, 48; Mayme Lorine, D, 4
42817 SHELTON, Robert L, Nowata, OK, 24
325 SHELTON, Spencer, Nowata, OK, 58
4021 SHELTON, Susie A, Tahlequah, OK, 26
30380 SHEPPARD, Mollie, Ft. Gibson, OK, 40; Elizabeth, D, 15
14000 SHEPPARD, Rich B, Warner, OK, 32
13551 SHERLEY, John L, Welling, OK, 50; 13561, Annie, D, 20; 13551, Viola, D, 2

[SHERLEY, Mattie. See #3151]   *(Note: entry separate from other family groups)*

23216 SHERLEY, Nancy M, Stilwell, OK, 27
18144 SHERLEY, Willie, Proctor, OK, 16
6589 SHERMAN, Mary J, Vinita, OK, 39
1057 SHERILL, William, Wolf Point, MT, 27
28922 SHETLEY, Eliza, Warner, OK, 34; Nancy, D, 11;   Sarah, D, 2
24384 SHIMP, Louisa J, Talala, OK, 31; Bernice R, D, 12; George B, S, 10; Louisa P, D, 6; Mary A, D, 4; Lydia E, D, 1
14771 SHINN, Alexander, Warner, OK, 19
13707 SHINN, Columbus M, Warner, OK, 37; 29877, Mary J, W, 22; Jessie J, D, 10; Frank J, S, 6; Emma, D, 3; Arthur, S, 1
13709 SHINN, John J, Warner, OK, 30; Gladis Lee, D, ½ [Deceased 4-14-'07]
11873 SHINN, Marion R, Webbers Falls, OK, 18;   By W. H. Shinn, Gdn.
26655 SHIRLEY, Maggie, Evansville, AR, 22; Flosey May, D, 3; James E, S, 1
2871 SHOAP, Mary J, Welch, OK, 40

CHEROKEE DESCENDANTS RESIDING WEST OF MISSISSIPPI RIVER.
VOLUME III (N – Z)

Key: Guion Miller Application Number; Name; Address, Relation (to Head); Age in 1906

9718   SHOEMAKER, John W, Southwest City, MO, 12; Franklin, Bro, 10; David W, Bro, 9; By Wm J. Shoemaker, Gdn.
6941   SHOEMAKER, Mary, Collinsville, OK, 19; Herbert N, S, ½
9679   SHOOTER, Lucy, Stilwell, OK, 64
26736 SHORT, Guess, Vian, OK, 25

[SHORT, Joe. See #8996]   *(Note: entries separate*
[SHORT, Hugh [Housten]. See #8996]   *from other family groups)*

42978 SHOTPOUCH, Beky, Zena, OK, 30; Hildebrand, Karlardee, D, 7; Guess, Victoria [Clud], D, 3
16453 SHOTPOUCH, Bird, Zena, OK, 13;   By Boney Raven, Gdn.
17630 SHOWERS, Mary J, Pensacola, OK, 46; William P, S, 5
12847 SHUGART, Sophronia, Claremore, OK, 16
4000   SHUTT, Clementine W, Pryor Creek, OK, 58
23177 SHUTT, John W, Pryor Creek, OK, 36; Georgia, D, 11; Virginia, D, 6

[SILCOX, Eliza. See #2825]   *(Note: entry separate from other family groups)*

28754 SILCOX, James, Row, OK, 25; Dolly, D, 2
1454   SILK, Aggie, Akins, OK, 80
16764 SILK, Betsy, Long, OK, 19

[SILK, Charles. See #13369]   *(Note: entries separate*
[SILK, Susan. See #13369]   *from other family groups)*
[SILK, Jennie. See #13369]

10954 SILK, George, Muldrow, OK, 45
1214   SILK, George W, Akins, OK, 35; Susan N, D, 8; Rosa L, D, 6; Sam, S, 4; Geo W. J, S, 2; Ted, S, 1/6
2378   SILK, John, Maple, OK, 39; Lueana, D, 6
13371 SILK, Johnson, Cookson, OK, 21; 8795, SILK, Levi, Claremore, OK, 62; 8794, Melvina, W, 63

[SILK, Lizzie. See #14263]   *(Note: entry separate from other family groups)*

14751 SILK, Nancy, Claremore, OK, 28

[SILK, Sarah. See #4404]   *(Note: entry separate from other family groups)*

22480 SILK, William, Claremore, OK, 27; Edna, D, 3
16344 SILVERSMITH, Adolphus, Needmore,   OK, 30

[SILVERSMITH, Bettie. See #1971]

(Note: entry separate from other family groups)

CHEROKEE DESCENDANTS RESIDING WEST OF MISSISSIPPI RIVER.
VOLUME III (N – Z)

Key: Guion Miller Application Number; Name; Address, Relation (to Head); Age in 1906

1970 SILVERSMITH, John, Southwest City, MO, 55; 1735, Katie, W, 42; Bettie May, D, 17; Amanda L, D, 16; Mary A, D, 13; Steve, S, 11; Earnest, S, 9; 1735, Silversmith, Sarah Susan, D, 6; Lizzie E. B, D, 3; Pearl, D, 1

[SIMERSON, John. See #12539]   *(Note: entry separate from other family groups)*

24073 SIMINGTON, Patsy, Locust Grove, OK, 24; Thompson, Lorina, D, 6; Rattlingourd, Judy, D, 2

[SIMMONS, Geo. See #17237]   *(Note: entry separate from other family groups)*

5656 SIMLIN, Rachel, Maysville, AR, 55
11551 SIMMON, Ada, Marble City, OK, 22

[SIMMONS, Columbus. See #10462]   *(Note: entry separate from other family groups)*

8368 SIMMONS, Johnson, Stilwell, OK, 63; 5337, Nancy, W, 53

[SIMMONS, Maggie. See #10462]   *(Note: entry separate from other family groups)*

11644 SIMMONS, Millie M, Westville, OK, 25; Mamie, D, 1/6
5337 SIMMONS, Nancy, Stilwell, OK, 53
26436 SIMMONS, Thomas B, McLain, OK, 21
471 SIMON, David, Eucha, OK, 27; 23843, Caroline [or Kline], W, 20; Anna, D, 3; Post, S, 1
16183 SIMON, Ka-he-dah, Campbell, OK, 11;   By Nellie Buster, Gdn.
470 SIMON, May, Spavinaw, OK, 24; George, S, 5
16184 SIMON, Susie, Campbell, OK, 13;   By Nellie Buster, Gdn.
28612 SIMPSON, Cora L, Kansas, OK, 18
26341 SIMPSON, James A, Chelsea, OK, 20
26339 SIMPSON, Kate, Chelsea, OK, 40; Hugh, S, 16; Grover, S, 14; Minnie, D, 12; John, S, 10; George, S, 6; Thomas A, S, 4; Jos. R, S, 2
26340 SIMPSON, Mary F, Chelsea, OK, 20

[SIMPSON, Oma. See #22635]   *(Note: entry separate from other family groups)*

4645 SIMPSON, Polly, Ft. Smith, AR, 45
23189 SIMPSON, Undena, Warner, OK, 27; Fannie, D, 10; Lee, Julius P, S, 4; Simpson, George, S, 1/12; Fredie, S, 1/12
9372 SIMS, Eliza Jane, Ft. Gibson, OK, 47
17880 SIMS, Lowell, Rose, OK, 20
9488 SINNIG, Mary, Braggs, OK, 53; Clay, Henry, S, 18
33801 SIPES, Orah J, Ft. Gibson, OK, 26
6605 SI-QUA-LI-SI, Lesie, Oaks, OK, 60

CHEROKEE DESCENDANTS RESIDING WEST OF MISSISSIPPI RIVER.
VOLUME III (N – Z)

Key: Guion Miller Application Number; Name; Address, Relation (to Head); Age in 1906

29183 SISCO, Darcus Riller J, Vivian, LA, 27, R.F.D. #1; Green, Arthur, S, 8; Marcus Benj, S, 6; Sisco, Jennie Lee, D, 1

2415 SISSON, Harry, Rex, OK, 47; Chas. H, S, 11; Jesse May, D, 9; Sue, D, 7; 2415, May, D, 5; Pauline, D, 3

28611 SISSON, Lady, Kansas, OK, 23; Hattie N, D, 5; Tom W, S, 3; David, S, 1

25567 SITSLER, George W, Tip, OK, 13; James L, Bro, 7;   By Henry Sitsler, Gdn.

11911 SITTEN, Naomi A, Maple, OK, 24; Theo L, S, 5; Jeanie I, D, 1

10323 SITTINGDOWN, Stephen, Sallisaw, OK, 33; James, S, 13; Thadius, S, 11; Minnie, D, 10; Agnes, D, 8; Edgar, S, 5; Emma, D, 3

16613 SITTINGDOWN, Wm, Evansville, AR, 20

224 SIX, Enoch, Southwest City, MO, 40; 1869, Ida, W, 38

12700 SIX, John, Afton, OK, 11;   By Thomas M, McGlue, Gdn.

5319 SIXKILLER, Abraham, Ballard, OK, 63; 5316, Margaret, W, 49; Dennis, S, 20; Sarah, D, 17; Kate, D, 15; Lincoln, S, 14; Retta, D, 7

24713 SIXKILLER, Arch, Stilwell, OK, 30; 24710, Charlotte, W, 32; Goodrich, Jack, S of W, 13; Sixkiller, George, S, 6; Lulu M, D, 2

5723 SIXKILLER, Blueford, Kansas, OK, 51; 5727, Annie, W, 59

43245 SIXKILLER, Charles, Muskogee, OK,   24

5975 SIXKILLER, Charley, Maysville, AR, 34; 1710, Eliza, W, 31; Rufus, S, 8; Sampson, S, 5; Houston, S, 3; Lilia, D, 1/12

23397 SIXKILLER, Emma, Stilwell, OK, 20

2236 SIXKILLER, Ethel, Tahlequah, OK, 16;   By Sarah Sixkiller, Gdn.

[SIXKILLER, Gafford. See #785]   *(Note: entry separate from other family groups)*

[SIXKILLER, Pearl. See #16594]   *(Note: entries separate*
[SIXKILLER, Nellie. See #16594]   *from other family groups)*

[SIXKILLER, Laura. See #16594]   *(Note: entries separate*
[SIXKILLER, Harvey. See #16594]   *from other family groups)*

24715 SIXKILLER, Geo, Stilwell, OK, 25; 8977, Annie, W, 25; Sadie, D, 2

44034 SIXKILLER, Glover, Echo, OK, 14; Samuel, Charles F, ½ B, 1; By Carrie Samuel, Gdn

6694 SIXKILLER, Henry, Ballard, OK, 34; 11926, Linnie M, W, 34; 6694, Wm F, S, 7; Artemecie, D, 5; Ruth, D, 2

8632 SIXKILLER, James, Collinsville, OK, 45; 8633, Nancy, W, 32; Carrie, D, 11; Pearly, D, 6; Joseph, S, 1

3806 SIXKILLER, Jesse, Tahlequah, OK, 34;   2227, Sarah, W, 52

1539 SIXKILLER, John, Stilwell, OK, 60; 177, Winnie, W, 66

39163 SIXKILLER, John B, Bunch, OK, 29; 14255, Peggie, W, 26; Cicero, S, 6; Dora, D, 6; Mary, D, 2; Ganer, S, 1

6484 SIXKILLER, Johnson, Westville, OK, 44

684 SIXKILLER, Joseph, Locust Grove, OK, 39; 10631, Jennie, W, 29; Lucy, D, 7; Gracie, D, 5; Cherokee, D, 3

CHEROKEE DESCENDANTS RESIDING WEST OF MISSISSIPPI RIVER.
VOLUME III (N – Z)

Key: Guion Miller Application Number; Name; Address, Relation (to Head); Age in 1906

226 SIXKILLER, Joshua, Brushy, OK, 51; 30177, Sallie, W, 36; 226, Johnnie, S of H, 15; 30177, Sanders, Jennie, D of W, 10; Sixkiller, William, S, 2; Annie, D, 1/12

[SIXKILLER, Josie. See #2940] *(Note: entry separate from other family groups)*

[SIXKILLER, Kathleen. See #2233] *(Note: entry separate from other family groups)*

21044 SIXKILLER, Lola, Choteau, OK, 20 [Died 2-28-1908]; By Belle Sixkiller, Mother
4550 SIXKILLER, Luke, Afton, OK, 56; 1664, Emma, W, 51
23516 SIXKILLER, Lynch, Stilwell, OK, 27; 2873, Maggie, W, 27; Felix, S, 3
5590 SIXKILLER, Mable, Choteau, OK, 15; Henry, B, 9; Mary A, S, 7; By Belle Sixkiller, Gdn
23927 SIXKILLER, Martha, Stilwell, OK, 21
27967 SIXKILLER, Mattie B, Afton, OK, 32
16583 SIXKILLER, Nancy, Baptist, OK, 89
761 SIXKILLER, Samuel, Stilwell, OK, 47; 786, Nancy, W, 58; 761, Ned, S, 17; Delia, D, 13
16721 SIXKILLER, Samuel, Baptist, OK, 13; Henry, B, 10; By Johnson Sixkiller, Gdn.
16328 SIXKILLER, Samuel R, Muskogee, OK, 29
770 SIXKILLER, Walter, Stilwell, OK, 51; Henry, S, 19; Frank, S, 13; Ella M, D, 10; Walter R, S, 8; 23928, Narcissa, D, 17
7462 SKAGGS, Myrtle A, Ramona, OK, 21; Roy, S, 8
6476 SKINNER, Betsey A, Adair, OK, 18

[SKAH-GIN-NE, Lacy. See #1700] *(Note: entry separate from other family groups)*

[SKAH-GIN-NE, Lizzie. See #631] *(Note: entry separate from other family groups)*

23839 SKAHGINNE, Mollie, Chloeta, OK, 18
23838 SKAHGINNE, Samuel, Chloeta, OK, 23; 1823, Celie, W, 17
23841 SKAHGINNE, Scott, Spavinaw, OK, 28
23840 SKAHGINNE, Walker, Chloeta, OK, 20
8276 SKIDMAN, Sarah E, Big Cabin, OK, 43; Bessie D, D, 17; John O, S, 6
7669 SKINNER, John K, Lenapah, OK, 24
3483 SKINNER, Mary A, Adair, OK, 12; By James W. Skinner, Gdn.
26553 SKINNER, Mattie R, Vinita, OK, 26; Mary Pauline, ?, 1
4994 SKINNER, Morgan D, Adair, OK, 22
377 SKINNER, Roy M, Talala, OK, 22
8217 SKINNER, Thomas F, Pueblo, CO, 617 West St, 24
22928 SKIRVIN, Jennie Cowart, Muskogee, OK, 20
29219 SKIRVIN, Rhoda L, LaBelle, MO, 18
9682 SKITT, Ella, Stilwell, OK, 35; 16354, Maggie, D, 16; Alice, D, 14; Mattie, D, 12; Calvin, S, 6; Vena, D, 1

CHEROKEE DESCENDANTS RESIDING WEST OF MISSISSIPPI RIVER.
VOLUME III (N – Z)

Key: Guion Miller Application Number; Name; Address, Relation (to Head); Age in 1906

4900 SKITT, Martha, Bunch, OK, 56; 42174, Nancy, D, 18; Lucy, D, 12
42175 SKITT, Sam, Bunch, OK, 24; 32745, Sallie, W, 26; Thomas, S, 1; Hewing, Ruth, D of W, 6; Starr, Rena, D of W, 2
1700 SKUCKINNE, Lacy, Eucha, OK, 49; 631, Lizzie, W, 48; Wiley, S, 16; Charity, D, 7
13054 SKUL-LOR-LEE, Bear, Bartlesville, OK, 38
765 SKUL-LOR-LE[sic], John, Ochelata, OK, 39; 2299, Jennie, W, 54; Willie, S, 16; Richard, S, 14
23734 SLAPE, Laura, Gideon, OK, 17; Evert E, S, 1
29266 SLAUGHTER, Bird, Collinsville, OK, 25; Oscar, S, 3
13599 SLAUGHTER, Josie, Webbers Falls, OK, 26; Tommy, S, 3; Sidney E, S, 1
6983 SLEEPER, Minnie, Wagoner, OK, 34; Julia, D, 11; Gideon D, Jr, S, 9; Walter J, S, 7; Martha E, S, 5
12583 SLEEPER, Nannie, Ft. Gibson, OK, 23; Nannie, D, 5; Margaret, D, 3; Louis, S, 2
3717 SLOAN, Edward Estel, Big Cabin, OK, 56; Samuel, S, 17; Eva L, D, 15; James E, S, 12; Nina P, D, 10; Florence Cherokee, D, 7
387 SLOAN, Mary E, Baptist, OK, 67
30004 SLOAN, Minnie E, Big Cabin, OK, 22
33210 SLOAN, William A, Adair, OK, 28; Naomia[sic] C, D, 2; James E, S, 1
4623 SLOCUM, Mary Pearl, Grove, OK, 20
30678 SMALLEY, Susan, Nowata, OK, 47; Manahan, Emma, D, 16; Mary E, D, 15; Frank, S, 14; Viola, D, 12; Charles, S, 11; Wm. McK, S, 9
6487 SMALLWOOD, Catherine, Westville, OK, 66; Horn, Florence, GD, 8
3580 SMALLWOOD, David E, Rose, OK, 38; 22479, Louisa, W, 32; Samuel M, S, 11; Patsy E, D, 9
1668 SMALLWOOD, Samuel, Porum, OK, 31; 1667, Lena, W, 22; Annie, D, 4; Richard, S, 2
1669 SMALLWOOD, William, Porum, OK, 31; Mary L, D, 6
8670 SMART, Henry, Muskogee, OK, 35; Nelson, S, 9; William A, S, 7; James F, S, 5; Hattie E, D, 4; Cora B, D, 1
7030 SMITH, Adeline, Stilwell, OK, 23
2172 SMITH, Alice, Grove, OK, 37
29206 SMITH, Allie V, Chetopa, KS, 23; Wayne M, S, 1
2061 SMITH, Benjamin, Eucha, OK, 24; 1186, Olkin, W, 16
26368 SMITH, Bunch [or Mose], Campbell, OK, 19; Smith, Spears, S, 2
26229 SMITH, Callie, Nowata, OK, 29; 8678, Callie M, D, 6
29625 SMITH, Carrie E, Caney, KS, 22; Mable, D, 1/6
1841 SMITH, Charley, Stilwell, OK, 58; 1839, Eliza, W, 57; Kate, D, 18; Henry, S, 16

[SMITH, Charley. See #2230]
[SMITH, Annie. See #2230] *(Note: entries separate from other family groups)*

25480 SMITH, Charley, Peggs, OK, 30
42954 SMITH, Charley C, Campbell, OK, 24

CHEROKEE DESCENDANTS RESIDING WEST OF MISSISSIPPI RIVER.
VOLUME III (N – Z)

`Key: Guion Miller Application Number; Name; Address, Relation (to Head); Age in 1906

4499 SMITH, Charlie, Locust Grove, OK, 36; 2140, Susie, W, 36; James, S, 11; Jesse, S, 2
5971 SMITH, Charlie, Spavinaw, OK, 24
23837 SMITH, Clearcy, Okoee, OK, 35; 23836, Cora P, D, 18; Ruth L, D, 20; Bertha B, D, 17; James L, S, 7
5062 SMITH, Daniel, Stilwell, OK, 32; 12654, Lizzie, W, 23; 5062, Lucy, D, 6; Jennie, D, 4; Fannie, D, 2
31575 SMITH, Datus, Okoee, OK, 21
6662 SMITH, Dennis, Coffeyville, KS, 26; 25276, Bessie B, W, 16
10651 SMITH, Dick, Locust Grove, OK, 51; 16918, Lizzie, W, 55 [Died 3-25-1907]
6921 SMITH, Eli, Stilwell, OK, 26
9402 SMITH, Eliza, Webbers Falls, OK, 25
16908 SMITH, Eliza, Locust Grove, OK, 4; By Dick Pheasant, Gdn.
23487 SMITH, Eliza, Wann, OK, 40; Westover, Warren F, S, 14; Smith, Louis C, S, 7; Smith, James R, Wann, OK, S, 5; Anton N, S, 2
6498 SMITH, Elizabeth J, Coffeyville, KS, 31; Susie, D, 11; Mamie E, D, 8; John R, S, 6; George C, S, 4
1738 SMITH, Emma, Grove, OK, 45; Oscar C, S, 16
23378 SMITH, Emma, Stilwell, OK, 26; Jesse J, S, 5; George W, S, 4; Ada, D, 1/6
7877 SMITH, Emma S, Coffeyville, KS, 22

[SMITH, Emmett. See #9971] *(Note: entry separate from other family groups)*

27900 SMITH, Emmett B, Southwest City, MO; 31
6667 SMITH, Esther S, Sallisaw, OK, 58
28385 SMITH, Etta, Sallisaw, OK, 25
10265 SMITH, Famous, Webbers Falls, OK, 53
17149 SMITH, Famous, Warner, OK, 16; Juney, Sis, 11; By Kiahua Smith, Gdn.
3159 SMITH, Florence C, Southwest City, MO, 58
15922 SMITH, Florence F, Webbers Falls, OK, 23
10264 SMITH, Frank, Webbers Falls, OK, 20; Dave, B, 17; Cherokee, S, 15; By Famous Smith, Gdn.
7491 SMITH, Frederick B, Big Cabin, OK: 40
1224 SMITH, George, Tahlequah, OK, 48; 1223, Betsy, W, 47; Daniel, S, 20; Levi, S, 13
26335 SMITH, George, Blackgum, OK, 21; 13544, Sarah, W, 17
28388 SMITH, George, Sallisaw, OK, 32; By Tilman Smith, Gdn.
641 SMITH, George W, Rose, OK, 40; 1274, Nannie B, W, 40; Walter, S, 17; James, S, 14; Rose Etta, D, 12; Narcissa, S, 9; Scott, S, 6; Flossie, D, 3
5611 SMITH, Geo. W, Stilwell, OK, 30; 27641, Jennie M, W, 21; 5611, Grover P, S, 1
27251 SMITH, Geo. W, Wann, OK, 29
27802 SMITH, Grover C, Oaks, OK, 21
28829 SMITH, Henry B, McAlester, OK, 35; Lelia, D, 11; Mary A. B, D, 6; Francis B, S, 5; James L, S, 3

CHEROKEE DESCENDANTS RESIDING WEST OF MISSISSIPPI RIVER.
VOLUME III   (N – Z)

Key: Guion Miller Application Number; Name; Address, Relation (to Head); Age in 1906

24955 SMITH, Henry J, Grove, OK, 51; Willie May, D, 16; Robert L, S, 15; Percy W, S, 12; Margaret R, Grove, OK, D, 10; Alice D, D, 8; Jesse H, S, 6; Franklin S, S, 4
24277 SMITH, Homer L, Owasso, OK, 27; Bonnie Kathleen, D, 3; Thelma Florence, D, ½
23252 SMITH, Ivy N, Grove, OK, 21
 851 SMITH, James, Peggs, OK, 69; 850, Nellie, W, 59; Lizzie [Non comp.], D, 30
 886 SMITH, James, Bushyhead, OK, 35
1864 SMITH, James, Moody, OK, 55; 1875, Mary, W, 39; Thomas, S, 18; Louie, S, 15
24750 SMITH, James, Braggs, OK, 21
 473 SMITH, James O, Coffeyville, KS, 37; Ola J, D, 10; Shelly K, D, 10; Betty, D, 4; Evelyn, D, 1
16385 SMITH, James R, Hoffman, OK, 39
22988 SMITH, James W, Grove, OK, 26; Homes, S, 6; Hazel M, D, 3
 6661 SMITH, Jasper M, Coffeyville, KS, 14;   By Dennis Smith
 4935 SMITH, Jessie, Chloeta, OK, 19; George J, S, 5/12
24516 SMITH, Jessie, Ketchum, OK, 20

[SMITH, Jim. See #10258]   *(Note: entry separate from other family groups)*

[SMITH, Jim. See #16164]   *(Note: entry separate from other family groups)*

 4209 SMITH, John, Vian, OK, 44; 15998, Maggie, W, 38; 4209, Wilson, S, 18; Miller, William, S of W, 16; Martha, D of W, 10; Lizzie, D of W, 8; Andrew, S of W, 7; Smith, Susie, D, 5; Ellis, S, 3; Mesis, D, 1/12
 4621 SMITH, John, Nowata, OK, 16;   By Oscar H. Mayfield, Gdn.
 7979 SMITH, John, Cherokee City, AR, 52; Sam, S, 11; Dave, S, 4

[SMITH, John. See #11188]   *(Note: entry separate from other family groups)*

14101 SMITH, John, Welling, OK, 50; 9188, Too-ka, W, 30; 14102, Jossie, D, 11; Ellen, D, 5; Alex, S, 1
28375 SMITH, John, Sallisaw, OK, 23
 7493 SMITH, John B, Moodys, OK, 37; 27389, Ada G, W, 27; Maggie, D, 11; Anna B, D, 9; James, S, 8; Eaton, John E, S of W, 6
33557 SMITH, John Q, Broken Arrow, OK, 27
25526 SMITH, John R, Campbell, OK, 32; 6231, Lizzie, W, 21
10588 SMITH, Joseph, Webbers Falls, OK, 31
 613 SMITH, Joseph E, Claremore, OK, 29
23818 SMITH, Josephine, Pryor Creek, OK, 24; James W, S, 4
25645 SMITH, Kate, Webbers Falls, OK, 21; Richard, S, 1
17150 SMITH, Kiahue, Warner, OK, 25
25555 SMITH, Lamech, Oaks, OK, 32; 9664, Nellie, W, 28; Lee, S, 8; Byron, S, 6; Daniel, S, 1
 7876 SMITH, Laura L, Coffeyville, KS, 19
11862 SMITH, Lee, Braggs, OK, 17; Arch, B, 14; Mattie, S, 11;   By Sarah Smith, Gdn.

CHEROKEE DESCENDANTS RESIDING WEST OF MISSISSIPPI RIVER.
VOLUME III   (N – Z)
Key: Guion Miller Application Number; Name; Address, Relation (to Head); Age in 1906

1190 SMITH, Lila, Oaks, OK, 36; Foreman, Reuben, S, 19; 1426, Smith, Bessie, D, 10

[SMITH, Lila. See #26137]   *(Note: entry separate from other family groups)*

23052 SMITH, Lillie T, Ramona, OK, 22; Julius P, S, 6; Floyd, S, 4
656 SMITH, Liza, Rose, OK, 71
17908 SMITH, Lizzie, Cookson, OK, 16
27727 SMITH, Lizzie, Tahlequah, OK, 31; Hendricks, Louisa, D, 12; Katherine, D, 7; Smith, John, S, 5; Jennie Evaline, D, 3
29650 SMITH, Lizzie, Big Cabin, OK, 34; Fred E, S, 12; Richard L, S, 7; Julian, S, 3
26089 SMITH, Louisa, Vinita, OK, 27; Mary J, D, 3
15923 SMITH, Louise, Muskogee, OK, 27

[SMITH, Love G. See #1866]
[SMITH, Wm A. See #1866]   *(Note: entries separate*
[SMITH, Pearl E. See #1866]   *from other family groups)*

10599 SMITH, Lucinda, Stilwell, OK, 38
8791 SMITH, Lucy, Claremore, OK, 29; Walter A, S, 4
12835 SMITH, Lucy, Blackgum, OK, 53; Kiah, S, 17; Stoke, S, 15
3956 SMITH, Lutitia, Keefeton, OK, 34; William, S, 16
9297 SMITH, Lydia, Cherokee City, AR, 40
710 SMITH, Mahala, Wann, OK, 58
1357 SMITH, Margaret, Maysville, AR, 70
28349 SMITH, Martha, Campbell, OK, 49; Minnie, D, 17; Rufus, S, 14; John, S, 12
4796 SMITH, Mary C, Lincoln, NE, 1236 T. St, 78
9152 SMITH, Mary E, Campbell, OK, 41
26793 SMITH, Mary J, Oologah, OK, 33; John A, S, 15; Elizabeth R, D, 14; Ada M, D, 12; Elmer T, S, 9; Clarence B, S, 6; Richard E, S, 2
17189 SMITH, Maud, Tahlequah, OK, 30
26843 SMITH, Minnie J, Cleora, OK, 44; Hugh E, S, 19; William E, S, 14; Eliza V, D, 10; Sydney L, S, 8; Earl F, S, 3
26741 SMITH, Minta, Oseuma, OK, 38
8915 SMITH, Nancy, Moody, OK, 50; Tom, S, 20; Lewis, S, 14
139 SMITH, Nancy J, Claremore, OK, 64
9403 SMITH, Nannie, Webbers Falls, OK, 22
11863 SMITH, Nannie, Braggs, OK, 22
4461 SMITH, Nannie V, Adair, OK, 35; Cochran, Sallie P, D, 13; Henry C, S, 5
27312 SMITH, Nathaniel D, Owasso, OK, 29; Nathaniel D, Jr, S, 2
5063 SMITH, Nellie, Stilwell, OK, 22
26690 SMITH, Otha, Stilwell, OK, 19; Ruthie, D, 1
27901 SMITH, Othie A, Vinita, OK, 38; Lee B, S, 12; Lelia L, D, 10; Ruby E, D, 8; Owen, S, ¼
10269 SMITH, Peter, Rose, OK, 48; 5771, Betsey, W, 59
860 SMITH, Polly, Peggs, OK, 66

CHEROKEE DESCENDANTS RESIDING WEST OF MISSISSIPPI RIVER.
VOLUME III (N – Z)
Key: Guion Miller Application Number; Name; Address, Relation (to Head); Age in 1906

- **5667** SMITH, Richard, Ft. Gibson, OK, 26; 27401, Carrie, W, 19
- **25528** SMITH, Richard, Campbell, OK, 26
- **5306** SMITH, Rosa, Evansville, AR, 48
- **13236** SMITH, Sallie, Oaks, OK, 21; Jennie, D, 2
- **25392** SMITH, Sallie, Tahlequah, OK, 23; Hick, Walter, S, 3; Sanders, Jesse, S, 1/12 [Born 3-2-'06 Died 10-2-'06]
- **28248** SMITH, Saloe, Ft. Gibson, OK, 24; Saloe, Jr, S, 6
- **5747** SMITH, Sam, Hulbert, OK, 30; Lizzie, D, 7

[SMITH, Samuel. See #2107]   *(Note: entries separate from other family groups)*
[SMITH, Joseph. See #2107]

- **25527** SMITH, Samuel, Blackgum, OK, 31; 13311, Sarah M, W, 27
- **5896** SMITH, Samuel L, Ft. Gibson, OK, 33; 30423, Elmira, W, 28; Sirrissia E, D, 6; Texanna, D, 3
- **2044** SMITH, Sarah, Kansas, OK, 50
- **4641** SMITH, Sarah, Oaks, OK, 51; Lucy, D, 18; Floy, D, 15; Rebecca, D, 13
- **11865** SMITH, Sarah, Braggs, OK, 40; Lee, S, 16; Archie, S, 13; Mattie, D, 10
- **7873** SMITH, Sarah E, Afton, OK, 43; Smith, Maud, D, 12; Eliza, D, 9
- **4413** SMITH, Sarah J, Foyil, OK, 29; Laura K, D, 8
- **1341** SMITH, Sarah P, Maysville, AR, 64; Walter F, S, 36[Insane]; Wm. L, GS, 20; Pearl H, GD, 19
- **3838** SMITH, Susan C, Chelsea, OK, 66
- **22764** SMITH, Theodore, Wann, OK, 31
- **864** SMITH, Thomas, Peggs, OK, 62
- **16393** SMITH, Thomas F, Keefeton, OK, 22
- **28386** SMITH, Tildon, Sallisaw, OK, 28
- **28882** SMITH, Tom, Blackgum, OK, 23; 8343, Sallie, W, 20; Redflag, S, 2
- **2907** SMITH, Walter, Fairland, OK, 51; Amanda, D, 17; Rachel, D, 15; Calicayah, S, 12; Isaac, Fairland, OK, S, 10; Maggie, D, 5; Walter, Jr, S, 2
- **43257** SMITH, Walter D, Oaks, OK, 28
- **27903** SMITH, Walter E, Collinsville, OK, 33; Mildred B, D, 6; Paul A, S, 4
- **5697** SMITH, Walter F, Ft. Gibson, OK, 29; Jesse E, S, 6; Willie N, S, 5; Gladys, D, 3
- **5061** SMITH, William, Stilwell, OK, 27; 8646, Annie, W, 34; Lizzie, D, 10; Betsey, D, 7
- **10271** SMITH, William, Oaks, OK, 55; 13237, Stan, S, 17; 13233, Dave, S, 15; 13234, Eli, S, 20
- **25568** SMITH, William, Moody, OK, 23; Emma, D, 2; Ray, S, 1
- **29862** SMITH, William, Braggs, OK, 23
- **1600** SMITH, William A, Cleora, OK, 47; Della, D, 14; Lewyn, S, 7; William A, S, 4
- **27313** SMITH, William L, Owasso, OK, 41; Sophrona P, D, 11; Omie L, D, 9; John W B, S, 7
- **14184** SMITH, Wm S, Angels Camp, CA, 32; Rolston F, S, 5; Geneva C, D, 3
- **5666** SMITH, Willie, Ft. Gibson, OK, 18; Lizzie, S, 17;   By Frank Smith, Gdn.

CHEROKEE DESCENDANTS RESIDING WEST OF MISSISSIPPI RIVER.
VOLUME III   (N – Z)

Key: Guion Miller Application Number; Name; Address, Relation (to Head); Age in 1906

[SMITH, (Wilson). See #6709]   *(Note: entry separate from other family groups)*

31988 SMITH, Wilson, Tahlequah, OK, 25
 4856 SMOKE, Grant, Locust Grove, OK, 30

[SMOKE, Eve. See #8299]   *(Note: entry separate from other family groups)*

11408 SMOKE, Lewis, Spavinaw, OK, 29; 10428, Polly [Wah-le], W, 30; Chah-wah-you-gah [or Mary], D, 11; Oo-you-tih, S, 6; William, S, 2
16788 SMOKE, Lewis, Leach, OK, 35; 16782, Mary, W, 35; Lizzard, S, 1/3
 9883 SMOKER, Nancy, Long, OK, 40; Guineyhead, Emma, D, 14
  481 SNAIL, Sarah, Southwest City, MO, 19

[SNAKE, Tom. See #16498]   *(Note: entry separate from other family groups)*

[SNAKE, Annie. See #10964]   *(Note: entry separate from other family groups)*

[SNAKE, Richard [or Ezekiel]. See #17669]
   (Note: entry separate from other family groups)

  834 SNEED, James P, Moody, OK, 45; Leora, D, 12; Myrtle, D, 7
 4924 SNELL, Annie, Southwest City, MO, 68
27799 SNELL, Bertha, Oaks, OK, 19
 5029 SNELL, Charlie, Southwest City, MO, 26
 5729 SNELL, Charley, Kansas, OK, 27; 7868½, Ina, W, 23
 1503 SNELL, Coming, Oaks, OK, 48; 1187, Snell, Anna, W, 43
 5030 SNELL, Coon, Southwest City, MO, 29; 11970, Susie, W, 24; Nora, D, 6; Bud, S, 3
 1196 SNELL, Eli, Kansas, OK, 39; 5658, Dann, Oaks, OK, S, 10
 1867 SNELL, Eli, Southwest City, MO, 51; 1569, Katie, W, 51; Alice, D, 19
 5028 SNELL, Ellick, Southwest City, MO, 24; 29194, Rachel, W, 22
 1925 SNELL, George, Kansas, OK, 24; 17062, Ella Leach, W, 35; Rooster, Maggie, D of W, 18; Dirt Dobber, N of W, 10
 1409 SNELL, Gilbert, Kansas, OK, 31; 4902,   Susan, W, 26; Swimmer, S, 7; Jennie, D, 3; Bertha, D, 1
 9618 SNELL, Joe, Kansas, OK, 35; Emma, D, 5; Ida, D, 1
 5715 SNELL, John, Kansas, OK, 50
  168 SNELL, Katie, Southwest City, MO, 62
17975 SNELL, Looney, Kansas, OK, 13;   By Nellie Y. Snell, Gdn.
27798 SNELL, Lydia, Oaks, OK, 22
 2419 SNELL, Nancy, Southwest City, MO, 20
 5728 SNELL, Nellie Y, Kansas, OK, 58; 16927, Snell, Nancy, D, 16; 17976, Walker, GS, 8
16503 SNELL, Sam, Kansas, OK, 25; [For Wife, See Eliza Youngwolf. See #5718]
 1502 SNELL, Sarah, Oaks, OK, 54

CHEROKEE DESCENDANTS RESIDING WEST OF MISSISSIPPI RIVER.
VOLUME III (N – Z)

Key: Guion Miller Application Number; Name; Address, Relation (to Head); Age in 1906

16928 SNELL, Sarah, Kansas, OK, 24

[SNELL, Youngbird. See #16987½] *(Note: entry separate from other family groups)*

9971 SNELLING, Lonia, Akins, OK, 23; Smith, Emmett, S, 5; [By former husband.]
1637 SNIDER, Annie B, Chelsea, OK, 45; Thomas B, S, 15; Perry E, S, 13; Jerry R, S, 11; Walton L, Chelsea, OK, S, 7
14239 SNIP, Charley, Westville, OK, 22
5097 SNIP, Nancy, Westville, OK, 19
1973 SNIP, Nick, Westville, OK, 56; 5133, Susie, W, 32; Josie, D, 11; Rufus, S, 8; Bessie, D, 6; Kinnie[sic], S, 1
26701 SNITZLER, Edna M, Canehill, AR, 20; Hutchings, Agnes P, D, 3; Carthul O, S, 1
11721 SNODGRASS, Matilda A, Denver, CO, 2310 Welton St, 49

[SNOW, Flora C. See #13366] *(Note: entry separate from other family groups)*

3246 SNOW, Mary Ann, Dutch Mills, AR, 63
13623 SNYDER, Jacob E, Vinita, OK, S, 19; Jas. Floyd, S, 16; Roy Clinton, S, 14; Freeman, Cecil, S, 8;   By Andrew J. Snyder, Gdn.
7650 SOAP, Betsy, Stilwell, OK, 54; Moses, S, 11; Katy, D, 15
14316 SOAP, George, Stilwell, OK, 35; 9638, Polly, W, 35
35588 SOAP, Mary, Stilwell, OK, 24; Samney [Sah-ne], S, 4
1463 SOAP, Nick, Stilwell, OK, 51; 1428, Nellie, W, 66; Charley, S, 20
1784 SOAP, Rachel, Baron, OK, 71
6730 SOAP, Rachel, Stilwell, OK, 83
17176 SOAP, Tom, Long, OK, 36
30198 SOAP, Willie, Stilwell, OK, 23
1824 SOLDIER, Peter, Eucha, OK, 33; 365, Susan, W, 31; Whitaker, S, 11; Julia, D, 7
5554 SOLDIER, Rachel, Southwest City, MO, 72
4408 SOLDIER, Taylor, Locust Grove, OK, 32; 4501, Nancy, W, 48; Annie, D, 10; Martha, D, 7

[SOPHER, Pliney. See #24700] *(Note: entry separate from other family groups)*

32392 SORTORE, Jennie, Claremore, OK, 19; Mabel C, D, 2
9771 SOSBEE, Lugie P, Campbell, OK, 21; Juanita, D, 1
11198 SOURJOHN, Albert, Braggs, OK, 33; 17044, Oo-lu-ja, W, 30; Levi, S, 11; Anderson, S, 10; Silk, S, 5; Charlie, S, 2
7865 SOURJOHN, Annie, Oaks, OK, 25
3662 SOURJOHN, Isaac, Locust Grove, OK, 26; 14299, Maggie, W, 23
7868 SOURJOHN, Lewis, Oak, OK, 17; By Nancy Goingsleep, Gdn.
7864 SOURJOHN, Levi, Oaks, OK, 9; By Nancy Goingsleep, Gdn.
7866 SOURJOHN, Lizzie, Oaks, OK, 15; By Nancy Goingsleep, Gdn.
9251 SOURJOHN, Sarah, Tahlequah, OK, 57

CHEROKEE DESCENDANTS RESIDING WEST OF MISSISSIPPI RIVER.
VOLUME III (N – Z)

Key: Guion Miller Application Number; Name; Address, Relation (to Head); Age in 1906

16089 SOURJOHN, Susan, Tahlequah, OK, 17; William, B 11; Eli, B, 7; By Mary Smith, Gdn
 3736 SOUTH, Susie, Chelsea, OK, 27; Edwin Clifford, S, 1
 1811 SOUTHERLAND, Arabella, Vinita, OK, 49
 2267 SPADE, Annie, Christie, OK, 50; 20321, Hitcher, Wilson, Baron, OK, S, 12
44464 SPADE, Cau-tes-kee [or Ned], Proctor, OK, 2;   By John Spade, Gdn.
33147 SPADE, Ella, Baron, OK, 19

[SPADE, Emma. See #30362]   *(Note: entry separate from other family groups)*

16603 SPADE, Frank, Kansas, OK, 28; 16693, Lucy, W, 31; 16603, Nannie, D, 6; Redbird, S, 2
 6433 SPADE, James, Proctor, OK, 43; 6495, Jennie, W, 35; Robert, S, 11; Charley, S, 9; Ruskey, S, 6; Lacy, S, 4; Susie, D, 1
26164 SPACE, John, Welling, OK, 35; 2735, Josie, W, 26; Sam, S, 14; Nannie, D, 10; Jennie, D, 8; Watt, S, 6; Rosie, D, 4
  135 SPADE, Johnson, Proctor, OK, 72; 1609, Rachel, W, 46
 1470 SPADE, Leonard, Moodys, OK, 40; 40694, Alice P, W, 27; 1470, White, S, 17; Oo-na-soo-kah, S, 12; Lula, D, 9
16597 SPADE, Nannie, Kansas, OK, 52; 16600, Sarah [or Saggie], D, 18; 16691, Jennie, D, 17; 16601, Naggie [Takie], D, 15; 16630, Maria, D, 13; 16632, Sallie, D, 12

[SPADE, Rachel. See #16990]
[SPADE, Nellie. See #16990]   *(Note: entries separate from other family groups)*

[SPADE, Robert. See #9444]   *(Note: entry separate from other family groups)*

  134 SPADE, Watson, Proctor, OK, 37; Johnson, S, 4; Jack, S, 1/6
25975 SPANIARD, Eliza, Campbell, OK, 38

[SPANIARD, Lizzie. See #4932]   *(Note: entries separate*
[SPANIARD, Lydia. See #4932]   *from other family groups)*

16697 SPANIARD, Richard, Vian, OK, 28; Hazel, D, 4; Buck Richard, S, 2
13108 SPANIARD, Zeke, Stilwell, OK, 37; 13276, Sarah, W, 28; Mose, S, 4; Lila, D, 2; Young, Lydia, D of W
 7661 SPANIARD, Teacher, Vian, OK, 21
26069 SPARKS, Johnsie A, Brushy, OK, 25; William W, S, 6; John R, S, 4; Lettie H, D, 2; James P, S, 7/12
13228 SPARROWHAWK, Nannie, Tahlequah, OK, 26
 5507 SPEAKER, Jennie, Welling, OK, 46; Sunday, S, 16; Suske, D, 12; Lydia, D, 9
16766 SPEAKER, Arch, Stilwell, OK, 33

CHEROKEE DESCENDANTS RESIDING WEST OF MISSISSIPPI RIVER.
VOLUME III   (N – Z)

Key: Guion Miller Application Number; Name; Address, Relation (to Head); Age in 1906

[SPEAKER, Samuel. See #1124]
[SPEAKER, Dick. See #1124] *(Note: entries separate from other family groups)*
[SPEAKER, Joe. See #1124]

[SPEAKER, Willie. See #6456] *(Note: entries separate from other family groups)*
[SPEAKER, Sam. See #6456]

16812 SPEARS, Amos, Vera, OK, 28; Edward J. T, S, 1
33415 SPEARS, Arch, Tahlequah, OK, 39
 5529 SPEARS, Charlotte E, Melvin, OK, 20
13028 SPEARS, Dennis S, Hominy, OK, 27; Floyd, S, 2
11292 SPEARS, Eli Day, Melvin, OK, 24; John Albion, S, 2; Daniel Eli, S, 1/3
13026 SPEARS, James, Hominy, OK, 20;   By Mary J. Spears, Gdn.
13029 SPEARS, John, Hominy, OK, 25
10170 SPEARS, Robert, Melvin, OK, 33; 5206, Lizzie, W, 35; Arthur, D, 13; Minnie, D, 11; Dora, D, 9; Charlie, S, 7; Croosly, S, 5; Mary, D, 2
17065 SPEARS, Walter, Tahlequah, OK, 27
24068 SPEIGHTS, Viola, Wilburton, OK, 27; Thompson, Henry C, S, 5

[SPENCER, Allen. See #1205]   *(Note: entry separate from other family groups)*

11229 SPENCER, Emma, Kansas, OK, 24
32028 SPENCER, Nancy J, Maysville, AR, 22; Gonia, D, 5
 1552 SPLITNOSE, Thomas, Porum, OK, 38; 1553, Susan, W, 27; Henry, S, 9; Jennie, D, 6; Martha, D, 1
26914 SPRADLIN, Ada, Moodys, OK, 15
 9765 SPRIGGS, Alexander A, Wagoner, OK, 47; Mamie P, D, 16; Henry A, S, 13; Judge Leo, S, 10; Seaburn P, S, 8; Lucy L, D, 5
28796 SPRIGGS, John B, Wagoner, OK, 21
 7810 SPRINGER, Nina W, Grand Saline, TX, 28; Gertrude, D, 10; Owen, S, 3
  447 SPRINGSTON, John L, Vian, OK, 63; William P. B, S, 19

[SPRINGWATER, Lucy. See #29487]   *(Note: entry separate from other family groups)*

23329 SPRINGWATER, Columbus, Vian, OK, 30; 6513, Katie, W, 27
11487 SPRINGWATER, Ida, Long, OK, 25; Augerhole, Eli, S, 7
10908 SPRINGWATER, Jennie, Stilwell, OK, 23; Lizzie, D, 5; Eliza, D, 4; Richard, S, 1/12
13505 SPRINGWATER, Johnson, Vian, OK, 52; Wah-li-ne, D, 8
42194 SPRINGWATER, Levi, Bunch, OK, 27; 9660, Lula, W, 25; John, S, 6; Arthur, S, 2
 1866 SPRINGWATER, Minnie A, Gans, OK, 34; Smith, Love G, D, 16; William A, S, 14; Pearl E, D, 12; Bethel, Clarence W, S, 8; Springwater, Troy H, S, 4; William R, S, 1
 8969 SPRINGWATER, Susan, Vian, OK, 50

CHEROKEE DESCENDANTS RESIDING WEST OF MISSISSIPPI RIVER.
VOLUME III (N – Z)
Key: Guion Miller Application Number; Name; Address, Relation (to Head); Age in 1906

[SPURLOCK, Louis. See #3162] } *(Note: entries separate*
[SPURLOCK, Harden. See #3162] } *from other family groups)*

8745 SQUIRREL, Daniel, Locust Grove, OK, 52; 8744, Gur-u-jay, W, 50
16963 SQUIRREL, George, Locust Grove, OK, 21
1097 SQUIRREL, Jack, Afton, OK, 44; Willie, S, 8; Peter A, S, 6; Nancy, D, 1; Joe, S, 4
11600 SQUIRREL, Jack F, Cookson, OK, 34; 11665, Jennie, W, 36
5035 SQUIRREL, James, Locust Grove, OK, 28
34959 SQUIRREL, Jennie, Eucha, OK, 24; Lylia[sic], D, 4
16983 SQUIRREL, Lina, Oaks, OK, 26
26529 SQUIRREL, Malinda, Dragger, OK, 20; Walter, S, 1
3585 SQUIRREL, Martin, Locust Grove, OK, 39
174 SQUIRREL, Mary, Locust Grove, OK, 21
3584 SQUIRREL, Mitchel, Locust Grove, OK, 55; 5587, Roselia, W, 53; 5558, Downing, Joe, S of W, 18; Lafayette, S of W, 16
17048 SQUIRREL, Nancy, Oaks, OK, 4; 17049, Lillie, Sis, 5; Susie, Sis, 3; By Polly O'Field, Gdn.
6606 SQUIRREL, Peter, Oaks, OK, 47; 6603, Betsy, W, 41
639 SQUIRREL, Sam, Spavinaw, OK, 53
10258 SQUIRREL, Sequiche, Cookson, OK, 66
12405 SQUIRREL, Sequiche, Cookson, OK, 33; 3550, Emma, W, 29; Bettie, D, 6; Jackson, S, 4; Jennie, D, 2; Eliza, D, 5/12
409 SQUIRREL, Walter, Locust Grove, OK, 67
16588 STADEHOME, Alie, Stilwell OK, 59
26237 STALLCUP, Sarah K, Salina, OK, 31; Florence, D, 13; Mary A, D, 11; Dicey D, D, 10; Cullice, S, 7; Sealie, D, 5; Ida, D, 3
27803 STALLER, Carrie, Whitmire, OK, 24
17203 STALLER, James, Pryor Creek, OK, 46; 17202, Martha, W, 19; Windy, S, 20; Jesse, S, 14; Samuel, S, 10; 17203, Looney, S, 7; 17202, Polan, Ochelata, S, 2; Steller[sic], Lizzie, D, 1/3
218 STALLSWORTH, Lena, Talala, OK, 49; Mamie C, D, 14
23898 STAND, Robin B, Stilwell, OK, 44; 23915, Lucy, W, 34; Peggie, D, 18; Sallie, D, 15; Richard C, S, 12; Taylor B, S, 7; Katie, D, 4; John Henry, S, 1/6
13019 STANDINGDEER, Dagadose, Wauhillau, OK, 15
17027 STANDINGDEER, Davis, Wauhillau, OK, 22
6660 STANDINGDEER, Jackson, Wauhillau, OK, 35

[STANDINGDEER, Nannie. See #8136]
(Note: entry separate from other family groups)

15087 STANDINGDOOR, Ailsey, Moodys, OK, 69
7867 STANDING DOOR, Goose, Locust Grove, OK, 56
6977 STANDINGWATER, Charlotte, Locust Grove, OK, 62
14290½ STANDINGWATER, Dave, Locust Grove, OK, 20

CHEROKEE DESCENDANTS RESIDING WEST OF MISSISSIPPI RIVER.
VOLUME III (N – Z)

Key: Guion Miller Application Number; Name; Address, Relation (to Head); Age in 1906

23046 STANDLEY, Minnie, Centralia, OK, 19
11534 STANLEY, Annie, Flint, OK, 33; Bessie Ann, D, 13; Jefferson H, S, 10; Mabel, D, 7; Barney, S, 3; Alva, S, 1
 3982 STANLEY, Nannie, Vian, OK, 24
  199 STANSILL, Hill, Baron, OK, 27; 26110, Jennie, W, 21; Archilla, S, 7; Bertha, D, 5; Minnie J, D, 1
 7727 STANSILL, John, Baron, OK, 30; 7728, William K, S, 18; Joel B, S, 15
25172 STAPLER, Anna B, Tahlequah, OK, 20
  65 STAPLER, John B, Tahlequah, OK, 46; 5869, Ellen Z, W, 46; Nellie M, D, 12; John B, S, 8
  47 STAPLER, James S, Tahlequah, OK, 50; Otway H, S, 16; John W, S, 9
25173 STAPLER, Lorena O, Tahlequah, OK, 21
40297 STARK, Annie V, Dawson, OK, 21

[STARK, Mattie S, See #404]   (Note: entry separate from other family groups)

[STARKEY, Willie. See #31049] ⎫   (Note: entries separate
[STARKEY, Henry. See #31049] ⎭   from other family groups)

23299 STARKS, Edna L, Hillside, OK, 22; Cynthia A, D, 3; Alfred G, S, 1
13415 STARNES, Jessie E, Pryor Creek, OK, 21
11869 STARNES, John, Ft. Gibson, OK, 47; 24718, Bessie, D, 47; Thomas, S, 19; Mary E, D, 13; Emma, D, 11; Lelia, D, 7; Margie, D, 1
 5979 STARR, Albert, Southwest City, MO, 23; 26065, Nannie E, W, 27
16564 STARR, Alice, Westville, OK, 12;   By Frank Howard, Gdn.
17252 STARR, Alice, Briertown, OK, 48
29698 STARR, Archibald N, Claremore, OK, 29; Andy T, S, 8; Tony B, S, 6; Edwin B, S, 3
29315 STARR, Bettie Stilwell, OK, 23

[STARR, Caleb. See #1283]   (Note: entry separate from other family groups)

10962 STARR, Caleb E, Stilwell, OK, 52; 9133, Louvenia, D, 18; 9473, Nannie L, D, 13; Hooley [Lucian], S, 15
10943 STARR, Charles, Braggs, OK, 29; 29864, Georgie A, W, 26; Pocahontas, S, 8; R. Juanita, D, 6; Jack R, S, 1
11667 STARR, Charles L, Stilwell, OK, 28; 27911, Amy, W, 24; Cherry, D, 4; Ezekiel, S, 3; Lula, D, 1
10691 STARR, Charlie, Catoosa, OK, 21
15048 STARR, Clem R, McKey, OK, 10;   By Lugie Starr, Gdn.
 8948 STARR, De'ilah[sic], Baron, OK, 18
10770 STARR, Eldee, Tahlequah, OK, 34

[STARR, Ellen C. See #12850]   (Note: entry separate from other family groups)

CHEROKEE DESCENDANTS RESIDING WEST OF MISSISSIPPI RIVER.
VOLUME III (N – Z)
Key: Guion Miller Application Number; Name; Address, Relation (to Head); Age in 1906

2926 STARR, Ellis, Sallisaw, OK, 48; 2925, Martha, W, 52; 2926, Charles C, S, 16; Hulda, D, 10
12931 STARR, Ellis, Porum, OK, 31
5582 STARR, Emma J, Vinita, OK, 64
32254 STARR, Etta, Porum, OK, 8;   By Ellis Starr, Gdn.
17063 STARR, Ezekiel, Blackgum, OK, 27
40500 STARR, Ezekiel, Vinita, OK, 25
2270 STARR, Fannie, Stilwell, OK, 50; Callie, D, 17
10352 STARR, Fannie G, Porum, OK, 51; 16769, Margaret, D, 11; Cherokee, D, 12

[STARR, Florence. See #9586] (Died, 1908)
(Note: entry separate from other family groups)

32911 STARR, George E, Stilwell, OK, 22
9969 STARR, George W, Uniontown, AR, 34; 8165, Rachel, W, 27
10192 STARR, George W, Sallisaw, OK, 45; 29952, Florence E, W, 39; David R, S, 9; Washington H, S, 7
9137 STARR, Georgia A, Stilwell, OK, 22
10300 STARR, Henry D, Braggs, OK, 26
12362 STARR, Henry G, Muskogee, OK, 33; 9376, Olive, W, 24; Roosevelt I, S, 2
14737 STARR, Isabelle, Porum, OK, 40; Richard, S, 16; Polly, D, 19
28734 STARR, Jack, Stilwell, OK, 26; 2864, Lizzie [Lucinda], W, 24; Rufus, S, 5; Jossie, D, 1/12
14784 STARR, Jacqueline, Braggs, OK, 13;   By Elizabeth Sanders, Gdn.
2265 STARR, James, Evansville, AR, 53; Lilly, D, 16; Charley, S, 14; Neuty, S, 14; Akey, D, 11; Callie, D, 9; Rosa, D, 6
653 STARR, Jesse, Eucha, OK, 47; 419, Jennie, W, 47
34499 STARR, Joe, Rose, OK, 25; 23691, Margueritte[sic], W, 21; Lillie, D, 3; Felix, S, 1
10772 STARR, Joel Mays, Tahlequah, OK, 19; Callie L, Sis, 17; J. Ruth, Sis, 14; Ezekiel E, Bro, 10;   By Maggie E. Starr, Gdn.
430 STARR, John, Grove, OK, 34; Nellie, D, 2; Elizabeth, D, 1 [Died 6-15-1906]
39164 STARR, John C, Vinita, OK, 36; Jesse B, S, 11; James C, S, 6; Martha E, D, 1/12; Charles J, S, 1/12
13697 STARR, Katie, Sallisaw, OK, 62
16723 STARR, Katie, Porum, OK, 22
4410 STARR, Lucy, Locust Grove, OK, 22; Lizzie, D, 2/3
25752 STARR, Lucy, Sallisaw, OK, 23
15046 SARR[sic], Lugie W, McKey, OK, 41
10771 STARR, Maggie E, Tahlequah, OK, 49
32912 STARR, Martin C, Evansville, AR, 21
10769 STARR, May Belle, Tahlequah, OK, 21
4794½, STARR, Nancy J, Claremore, OK, 11; Caleb L, Bro, 10;   By Emmett Starr, Gdn.
9126 STARR, Nathaniel, Stilwell, OK, 26; 28979, Sarah E, W, 23; Eugene F, S, 2; Mary B, D, 1/3

CHEROKEE DESCENDANTS RESIDING WEST OF MISSISSIPPI RIVER.
VOLUME III   (N – Z)

Key: Guion Miller Application Number; Name; Address, Relation (to Head); Age in 1906

11444 STARR, Rachel, Cove, OK, 14;   By Na-ke Hilderbrand, Gdn.

[STARR, Rena. See #32745]   *(Note: entry separate from other family groups)*

 9136 STARR, Samuel J, Stilwell, OK, 26
10589 STARR, Samuel J, Evansville, AR, 39; Joseph, S, 10
12849 STARR, Samuel S, Porum, OK, 29; 12850, Carrie E, W, 27
16770 STARR, Spy [Thomas B.], Porum, OK, 21; 32428, Willie H, W, 19
16598 STARR, Tarnah, Westville, OK, 74

[STARR, Thomas. See #3880]   *(Note: entry separate from other family groups)*

32044 STARR, Tobe, Stilwell, OK, 23; 8975, Katie, W, 20
10693 STARR, William, Catoosa, OK, 23; Carl M, S, 4; Ernest W, S, 2
42186 STARR, William, Rose, OK, 28; Jim, S, 4
  327 STARR, William, Grove, OK, 50 [Dead];   By Sarah Starr, Wife
 3135 STATHAM, Nancy M, Bartlesville, OK, 36; Dona[sic] E, D, 17; Leonidas A, S, 15; Edmond R, S, 10; Cleo B, S, 6
16357 STAY-AT-HOME, Joe, Stilwell, OK, 17
13666 STAY-AT-HOME, John, Stilwell, OK, 38; 14273, Eliza [Warlice], W, 23
13245 STAY-AT-HOME, Sarah, Stilwell, OK, 28; Nancy, D, 14; Ned, S, 9; Lewis, S, 1
16356 STAY-AT-HOME, William, Stilwell, OK, 21
 3468 STEALER, Annie, Tahlequah, OK, 22
11163 STEALER, Ben, Ochelata, OK, 11;   By Dave Hendricks, Gdn.
11995 STEALER, George, Marble City, OK, 28; 11881, Kate, W, 28; William Angel, S, 4

[STEALER, Lewis. See #3877]   *(Note: entries separate*
[STEALER, Niecer. See #3877]   *from other family groups)*

 3087 STEALER, Louis, Locust Grove, OK, 27; 3173, Charlotte, W, 21; Mollie, D, 1
14296 STEALER, Ned, Locust Grove, OK, 29

[STEALER, Sallie. See #2936]
[STEALER, Jimmie. See #2936]   *(Note: entries separate*
[STEALER, Lizzie. See #2936]   *from other family groups)*
[STEALER, Sara. See #2936]

 1421 STEELE, Robert V, Tahlequah, OK, 61
14791 STEERE, Annie, Coffeyville, KS, 14;   By William Steere, Gdn.
14793 STEERE, Minnie, Coffeyville, KS, 12;   By William Steere, Gdn.
14790 STEERE, Sarah, Coffeyville, KS, 15;   By William Steere, Gdn.
 9235 STEETHEE, Doodaner, Melvin, OK, 59
31403 STEGER, Maudie M, Hillside, OK, 17

CHEROKEE DESCENDANTS RESIDING WEST OF MISSISSIPPI RIVER.
VOLUME III (N – Z)

Key: Guion Miller Application Number; Name; Address, Relation (to Head); Age in 1906

27101 STEPHENS, Alice, Briertown, OK, 19; Bertha, D, 4 [Died 10-4-1906]; Clyde, S, 3

15034 STEPHENS, Betsy, Chelsea, OK, 31; Cynthia B, D, 9; George H, S, 6; Lee M, S, 4; Eugene L, S, 2; Homer, S, 1

1485 STEPHENS, Elmira, Park Hill, OK, 49

32866 STEPHENS, Ernest L, Lometa, OK, 34; Spencer H, S, 8; Ernest L, S, 6; Sarah R, D, 3

4033 STEPHENS, James, Tahlequah, OK, 18; Albert, Bro, 13; By Jesse Sanders, Gdn.

4111 STEPHENS, Levi, Tahlequah, OK, 29; William L, S, 4

12564 STEPHENS, Mary H, Murphys, CA, 43; James Raymond, S, 20; Earl Benjamin, S, 17; Della Ann, D, 12

614 STEPHENS, Nancy M, Oolagah, OK, 27; Allie M, D, 10; Willie D, D, 7; Thelma G, D, 6; Ruth, D, 4; Lewis G, S, 2

25758 STEPHENS, Nellie M, Grove, OK, 36

2376 STEPHENS, Spencer, Lometa, OK, 69; 1953, Sarah, W, 76

23250 STEPHENS, Spencer A, Claremore, OK, 38; Foreman Spencer, S, 10; Ola E, D, 8; Inez [Leona], D, 6; Sarah M, D, 3; Cherokee, D, 1

29188 STEPHENS, Steven, Park Hill, OK, 23; Claud W, S, 1

24518 STEPHENSON, Rosa L, Ketchum, OK, 24; Mary A, D, 5; Roxie M, D, 3

15623 STEPP, Charley, Evansville, AR, 51; 2827, Polly, W, 44; George, S, 18; Jeaney, D, 16; Ellis, S, 13

24065 STEPP, Laura A, Claremore, OK, 32; George C, S, 13; Ernest L, S, 10; Leonard, S, 7; Charles B, S, 5

4388 STERLING, Ella Welch, OK, 30; Lilly E, D, 13; Nettie, D, 11; Ethel M, D, 4; Adah B, D, 1

17135 STEVENS, Carrie Lee, Vinita, OK, 17

1090 STEVENS, Flora, Fairland, OK, 29; Barnes, Maud L, D, 12; Stevens, William E, S, 8; Rubbie M, D, 6

23486 STEVENS, Josephine, Wann, OK, 16

4719 STEVENS, Lucy, Cookson, OK, 29 [Dead]; Cochran, George, S, 12; Parnell, Jesse, S, 6; Floyd, S, 4

17133 STEVENS, Marshall C, Vinita, OK, 27

17134 STEVENS, Mary E, Vinita, OK, 17

9611 STEVENS, Mary Jane, Salina, OK, 25; Joe Mac, S, 7; David Leslie, S, 3; Jessie Jewel, D, 2

[STEVENS, Stephens[sic]. See #29188]

10699 STEVENSON, Mary Elizabeth [Lizzie], Tahlequah, OK, 44; John A, S, 16; Clyde [William C], S, 12

8322 STEVENSON, William F, Southwest City, MO, 29

8300 STEWART, Catherine, Akins, OK, 55; John T, S, 19; David C, S, 14

31995 STEWART, Celina K, Grove, OK, 60

CHEROKEE DESCENDANTS RESIDING WEST OF MISSISSIPPI RIVER.
VOLUME III (N – Z)

Key: Guion Miller Application Number; Name; Address, Relation (to Head); Age in 1906

35941 STEWART, Ella Locust Grove, OK, 22; Newton, S, 6; Lettie L, D, 4; Mrytie[sic] M, D, 2
31998 STEWART, George W, Bluejacket, OK, 24
31996 STEWART, John H, Bluejacket, OK, 34; Max, S, 6
31346 STEWART, Nancy R, Sallisaw, OK, 25; Teautla, S, 1
33761 STEWART, Sallie, Sallisaw, OK, 16; Eva L, Sis, 15; By Winfield Stewart, Gdn.
10461 STEWART, William H, Warner, OK, 50; 5082, Annie, W, 57
31997 STEWART, William W, Grove, OK, 31; 27659, Sallie K, W, 26; Eugene R, S, 3
35532 STICK, Eli, Cove, OK, 22; 13180, Annie, W, 22; Lacy, Starr, S[sic] of W, 3
10160 STICKES, Emily, Zena, OK, 88
6989 STICKS, Joe, Southwest City, MO, 46; 7020, Nancy, W, 45; Spade, S, 12; Sallie, D, 9; Tom, S, 6
5201 STILES, Charlotte E, Pryor Creek, OK, 38; Emma J, D, 10; Clarinda E, D, 8; Elsie J, D, 3
24358 STILL, Asia, Cherokee City, AR, 29; Chester, S, 12; Cornelius, S, 4
4635 STILL, Clarence, Vinita, OK, 19; Beulah, Sis, 18; William, Bro, 16; By Ida Cobb, Gdn.
1374 STILL, Cook, Peggs, OK, 24; 23449, Bertha, W, 26; 1374, Ella, D, 10; Curtis, S, 8; Chester, S, 6; Laura, D, 1
6692 STILL, Cook, Tahlequah, OK, 30
25521 STILL, David, Vian, OK, 28
3941 STILL, Dick, Stilwell, OK, 35; 13139, Eliza, W, 32; 3941, Tobe, S, 2

[STILL, Enos. See #3607]   *(Note: entry separate from other family groups)*

2060 STILL, Ezekiel, Hadley, OK, 50; 11440, Mollie E, W, 43; May E, D, 19; Clem L, S, 15; Flora G, D, 14; Pocahontas, D, 11
30051 STILL, Frank J, Hadley, OK, 22; 26170, Amanda L, W, 23

[STILL, General. See #499]   *(Note: entry separate from other family groups)*

1929 STILL, George, Leach, OK, 62
24359 STILL, Green, Cherokee City, AR, 42; May, D, 12; Geneva, D, 9; Clyde, S, 5
4290 STILL, James, Hadley, OK, 26
25604 STILL, James L, Rose, OK, 32; 25603, Emma A, W, 26; Joe Ivey, S, 3; Mack Edna, S, 2
3678 STILL, Jack [Ose], Sallisaw, OK, 24; 13792, Jennie, W, 20; Mary, D, 1
2792 STILL, Jim, Flint, OK, 44
13704 STILL, John, Wagoner, OK, 28; Emmet, S, 6; James, S, 4; Leveta, D, 1
17112 STILL, John, Sallisaw, OK, 32
25523 STILL, John, Campbell, OK, 19
33437 STILL, John N, Leach, OK, 34; James, S, 15; Mary E, D 12
9253 STILL, Jonas, Gideon, OK, 45; Emma, D, 16; Ollie, D, 13; Thomas J, S, 10
16686 STILL, Luella, Tahlequah, OK, 12; By Lucy Henson, Gdn.

CHEROKEE DESCENDANTS RESIDING WEST OF MISSISSIPPI RIVER.
VOLUME III (N – Z)

Key: Guion Miller Application Number; Name; Address, Relation (to Head); Age in 1906

[STILL, Margaret. See #5279]   *(Note: entry separate from other family groups)*

13091 STILL, Mary, Sallisaw, OK, 27; Nellie, D, 4; Polly, D, 2
5326 STILL, Marv E, Leach, OK, 62
3036 STILL, Sallie, Tahlequah, OK, 15;   By Edward Still, Gdn.
25199 STILL, Sam, Oologah, OK, 26; 6668, Louisa M, W, 24; John Thomas, S, 3
22766 STILL, Sampson, Campbell, OK, 32; Lelah May, D, 2
5343 STILL, Thomas, Westville, OK, 58; 5342, Lucy, W, 57
23672 STILL, Thomas, Jr, Westville, OK, 24; Noble, S, 1
25522 STILL, William, Campbell, OK, 25; Pearl, D, 3
2807 STILL, William, Flint, OK, 54
24000 STILL, William Jackson, Peggs, OK, 21
23733 STILL, Willie, Westville, OK, 22
3522 STINE, May, Oologah, OK, 31; John V, S, 13; Edie J, S, 5; Mattie Lane, D, 3
29073 STINGER, Albert, Edna, KS, 24
11435 STINGER, Louisa, Edna, KS, 63
23593 STINSON, Lena M, Adair, OK, 33; Willie May, D, 10; Violet V, D, 6
3011 STOCKTON, Clara, Copan, OK, 32; Bernice, D, 2
3011 STOCKTON, Sarah, Pryor Creek, OK, 26; Ada, D, 7; Roy, S, 3
23334 STOGSDILL, Augusta, Grove, OK, 21; Bertha M, D, 1/6
27356 STOGSDILL, Bettie, Grove, OK, 24; Ernest, S, 1
22802 STOKES, Alice, Muskogee, OK, 29; Nannie Ruth, D, 1
44422 STOKES, Ewing M, Bushyhead, OK, 26
28918 STOKES, Herschel, Bushyhead, OK, 24
5046 STOKES, Mary M, Chelsea, OK, 45; Robert Y, S, 17; Jennie E, D, 12; Carl N, S, 5

[STOKES, Mattie B. See #27967]   *(Note: entry separate from other family groups)*

23130 STOKES, Mattie L, Afton, OK, 24
25778 STOKES, Maude M, Claremore, OK, 20
28919 STOKES, William T, Bushyhead, OK, 22
51 STONE, Elizabeth Emily, Southwest City, MO, 56
3141 STONE, Mary E, Ochelata, OK, 26; Rena, D, 1/6
27706 STONE, Mary E, Southwest City, MO, 29; Opal M, D, 9; Pearl, D, 7; William F, S, 5; Fay, D, 3; Lucile[sic], D, 2
8782½, STONEBARGER, Rose M, Braggs, OK, 15;   By J. H. Stonebarger, Gdn.
15957 STOO-GI, Peggy, Wauhillau, OK, 56
5694 STOOL, Sam, McKey, OK, 34
19079 STOP, Adam, Tahlequah, OK, 27
21029 STOP, Annie, Tahlequah, OK, 29
6481 STOP, Blue, Proctor, OK, 53
6483 Mary [Che-cor-na-lah], W, 28; 6481, Ida, D, 11; Lee, S, 8; Bird, S, 4; William, S, 1
13205 STOP, Gah-ne-you-eh, Stilwell, OK, 23

CHEROKEE DESCENDANTS RESIDING WEST OF MISSISSIPPI RIVER.
VOLUME III (N – Z)

Key: Guion Miller Application Number; Name; Address, Relation (to Head); Age in 1906

1003 STOP, Gilbert, Choteau, OK, 36; 1283, Mary, W, 30; Star, Caleb, S of W, 14; 1003, Stop, Flora, D, 8
4600 STOP, Johnson, Tahlequah, OK, 19
4498 STOP, Lucy, Choteau, OK, 42; Potts, Samuel, S, 18; Potts, John, S, 16; Potts, Sallie, D, 5; Potts, Mary, D, 2
2753 STOP, Sallie, Peggs, OK, 60
5972 STOP, Sallie, Maysville, AR, 65
1002 STOP, Sam, Choteau, OK, 46; 980, Sallie, W, 52
2823 STORTS, Margaret, Siloam Springs, AR, 30; Beulah, D, 8; Clara M, D, 6; Lyda V, D, 5; Ada V, D, 3; George F, S, 1
42100 STORY, Minerva, Afton, OK, 19
2042 STOVER, Lewis, Oaks, OK, 25
7553 STOVER, Lizzie, Tahlequah, OK, 30; DeGrott, Carrie H, D, 4 [Dead]
23421 STOUT, Louisa J, Wagoner, OK, 24
4784 STOUT, Martha, Collinsville, OK, 36; Russell S, S, 8
9255 STOUT, Mary Ann, Wagoner, OK, 54; 23422, Susan M, D, 18; Samuel J, S, 16; James William, S, 13; John Henry, S, 9
26207 STOUT, Minnie, Texanna, OK, 17
9600 STOYALL, Susan C, Choteau, OK, 33; Keekee T, S, 11; Lubirdie, D, 5
10681 STOVER, Madison, Oaks, OK, 21
24521 STOVER, Rose Ella, Chelsea, OK, 25; Samuel Louis, S, 3; Mattie Elizabeth, D, 1
2116 STOVER, William R, Needmore, OK, 33; 29782, Edith L, D, 19; 2116, Roger I, S, 16; William A, S, 13; Ralph B, S, 10; Ola, D, 5
11232 STRAINER, Aggie, Oaks, OK, 64
1062 STRAND, Nora M, Welch, OK, 25; Joseph R, S, 4; Earl D, S, 3; John R, S, 1/3
7497 STRANGE, Mary R, Chelsea, OK, 37
22752 STRANKS, Jane, Muskogee, OK, 43
8154 STRATTON, Ada, Tahlequah, OK, 38; Myrtle M, D, 16; Samuel T, S, 13; John M, Jr, S, 10; Jesse H, S, 8; William W, S, 5; Thomas D, S, 2
1377 STRECKLER, Maggie, Hadley, OK, 7; Fred, S, 12; Aley, D, 10; Frank, S, 6; Lee, S, 4
22602 STRICKLAND, Elizabeth L, Coffeyville, KS, 24
22604 STRICKLAND, Kate C, Coffeyville, KS, 27
3154 STRICKLAND, Sarah, Coffeyville, KS, 52; Rogers, S, 14

[STRINGER, Louisa. See #11435] *(Note: entry separate from other family groups)*

31457 STRONG, Augusta C, Nowata, OK, 35; Phillips, S, 14; Susan Virginia, D, 12; Ross, S, 10; Dewey, S, 8; Koto A, S, 6; Willie V, S, 4; Ahniwake, D, 1
10931 STROUP, Clara B, Inola, OK, 36; Earl, S, 17; Theo. Pearl, D, 15; Jesse, S, 12; Ruby, D, 9; Willie, S, 6; Johnnie, S, 4; Fredie, S, 1
813 STRONT, Eliza A, Vinita, OK, 51
830 STUBBS, John S, Muskogee, OK, 27

CHEROKEE DESCENDANTS RESIDING WEST OF MISSISSIPPI RIVER.
VOLUME III (N – Z)

Key: Guion Miller Application Number; Name; Address, Relation (to Head); Age in 1906

13090 STUDY, Bill [William], Southwest City, MO, 54; 11972, Lid-di [Lydia], W, 44; Benjamin, S, 19; Andy, S, 16 ; Robert, S, 12; Katie, D, 8; Ka-ya-ji [Guyuche], D, 6

[STUDY, John. See #4873]   *(Note: entry separate from other family groups)*

31364 STUDY, John, Southwest City, MO, 24; 13106, Mary, W, 21; Smokes, S, 7; John D, S; 2
29469 STURDIVANT, Aaron, Albia, OK, 33; Preston M, S, 9; Alvia C, D, 6; Eva E, D, 4; Carl T, S, 3
249 STURDIVANT, John, Cherokee City, AR, 67; 250, Elizabeth S, W, 65
29468 STURDIVANT, John, Albia, OK, 31
23494 STURDIVANT, Joseph F, Cowskin, MO, 28; 22821, Zilphia E, W, 23
4690 STURDIVANT, Martin B, Grove, OK, 62
27708 STURDIVANT, Nancy, Grove, OK, 29; Mollie L, D, 13
27707 STURDIVANT, Richard, Grove, OK, 25
9465 SUAGE, Stan, Spavinaw, OK, 34; 9608, Yok-sa [York-sie], W, 34; Jennie, D, 8; Nannie, D, 1
35814 SUAGEE, Dennis B, Wann, OK, 22; 32207, Maud A, W, 22; Stella M, D, 1
13626 SUAGEE, Joel, Bartlesville, OK, 35; Evaline, D, 12; Floyd, S, 10; David, S, 7; Madeline M, D, 1
4414 SUAGEE, Laura I, Foyil, OK, 32
856 SUAGEE, Peter C, Lenapah, OK, 34; Clella I, D, 2; Gladys W, D, 1
21609 SUAGEE, Robert, Keifer, OK, 27
6502 SUAGEE, Sam, Southwest City, MO, 36; 432, Nellie, W, 47; Henry, S, 9
714 SUAGEE, Stand, Coffeyville, KS, 59; Stand [Watie], S, 19; Bessey May, D, 16; Ray Lee, S, 13
38567 SUAGEE, Thomas, Coffeyville, KS, 21
10898 SUAGEE, Thomas Wilson, Foyil, OK, 19; Louisa Amanda, Sis, 16;   By Louisa Suagee, Gdn
5716 SUAGGY, Swimmer, Oaks, OK, 51

[SUAKE, Katie. See #8736]   *(Note: entry separate from other family groups)*

[SUAKE, Jennie (Jane). See #17086]
[SUAKE, James. See #17086]
[SUAKE, Ah-no-hee. See #17086]   *(Note: entries separate*
[SUAKE, Lillie. See #17086]   *from other family groups)*
[SUAKE, Mary. See #17086] (Died 4-1908)
[SUAKE, Swimmer. See #17086]

16599 SUAKE, Jim, Chance, OK, 26
12614 SUAKE, Lawyer, Ballard, OK, 14;   By Betsy Suake, Mother
11925 SUAKE, May, Chance, OK, 17;   By Betsy Suake, Mother

CHEROKEE DESCENDANTS RESIDING WEST OF MISSISSIPPI RIVER.
VOLUME III (N – Z)

Key: Guion Miller Application Number; Name; Address, Relation (to Head); Age in 1906

16498 SUAKE, Tom, Whitmire, OK, 27; 10964, Annie Bearpaw, W, 35; 17669, Richard [Ezekiel], S, 11; 17671, Chewie, Lucy, D of W, 8

9275 SUAKEE, Dave, Tahlequah, OK, 41

13405 SUAWATT, William, Grove, OK, 32

28373 SUDDERTH, Louisa, Nowata, OK, 34; Hallie B, D, 14; Delia F, D, 12; Theodore B, S, 10; Edgar S, S, 8; Lloyd W, S, 5; Evelyn, D, 3

451 SUGAR, Sallie, Spavinaw, OK, 59

11785 SUGGS, Dolly J, Pryor Creek, OK, 32; William A, S, 12; Zelma G, D, 10; F. M, S, 7; Elliott, S, 1

23819 SUITER Martha, Pryor Creek, OK, 21

[SULLATESKEE, Annie. See #6068]   *(Note: entry separate from other family groups)*

[SULLATESKEE, Emily [Chewaney] See #13174]
(Note: entry separate from other family groups)

[SULLATESKEE, Charlotte. See #13175]
(Note: entry separate from other family groups)

4849 SULLATESKEE, Watt, Locust Grove, OK, 35; Nancy, D, 11; Sullateskee [Oo-stay-lah], S, 8; George, S, 4; Betsie, D, 2; Dowie, S, 1

2295 SULLIVAN, Frank, Claremore, OK, 28; 2294, Peggie, W, 31; 2295, James B, S, 10

931 SULLIVAN, Sarah, Proctor, OK, 53; Ellis, S, 19

1570 SULSAH, Sparrow, Southwest City, MO, 54; 380, Lucinda, W, 53; Wilburn, S, 16

9335 SULTEESKEE, George, Melvin, OK, 31

6068 SULTEESKEY, Annie, Melvin, OK, 64; 13174, Emily [Chewaney], D, 17

13175 SULTEESKEY, Charlotte, Melvin, OK, 21; Milo, Lizzie, D, 1

1000 SULTUSKY, John, Choteau, OK, 49

[SULTZER, Sparrow. See #1570]   *(Note: entry separate from other family groups)*

[SULTZER, Lucinda. See #380] } *(Note: entries separate from other family groups)*
[SULTZER, Wilburn. See #380]

10164 SUMMERFIELD, Ah-see-ni, Southwest City, MO, 15; By Sam Summerfield, Brother

11456 SUMMERFIELD, A-wi, Southwest City, MO, 54; Daisy [Cowati], D, 17; Aggie, D, 16

10165 SUMMERFIELD, Celia, Southwest City, MO, 24

7558 SUMMERFIELD, Charley, Southwest City, MO, 30

630 SUMMERFIELD, Isaac, Spavinaw, OK, 56; 629, Ta-ky, W, 55

4854 SUMMERFIELD, Jack, Fairland, OK, 31; 1645, Samantha, W, 30; 4854, Joe, S, 12; Clem, D, 9; Malinda, D, 7; Nancy, D, 3

CHEROKEE DESCENDANTS RESIDING WEST OF MISSISSIPPI RIVER.
VOLUME III (N – Z)

Key: Guion Miller Application Number; Name; Address, Relation (to Head); Age in 1906

28227 SUMMERFIELD, Jesse, Zena, OK, 25; 5984, Lucy, W, 21; Arlie [Olie], D, 3; Ed, S, 2

10163 SUMMERFIELD, Leach, Southwest City, MO, 22

10166 SUMMERFIELD, Sam, Zena, OK, 32; 10161, Betsy, W, 43; 10166, Scott, S, 8

28237 SUMMERFIELD, Swimmer, Zena, OK, 22; 27472, Mollie, W, 16

4399 SUMMERLIN, Armine, Braggs, OK, 27; Noah C, S, 3; Virgil D, D, 2; Pearly M, D, 1/6

994 SUMMERLIN, Bessie F, Muskogee, 812 S. Cherokee St, OK, 20; Edna Mae, D, 1

217 SUMMERS, Amanda C, Talala, OK, 61

28004 SUMMERS, Calvin, Vinita, OK, R.F.D. #1, 23; 21815, Maggie L, W, 23; Wynama L, D, 2; Williams, William P, S of W, 8

[SUMMERS, Frederick. See #2977]   *(Note: entry separate from other family groups)*

5289 SUMMERSET, Locust Grove, OK, 60; 5288, Ah-li-sah, W 57

43418 SUMMERSETTE, Lena, Rose, OK, 23

43417 SUMMERSETTE, William, Rose, OK, 21

27834 SUMPTER, Altie M, Sallisaw, OK, 9; Raymond L, Bro, 7; By John E. Sumpter, Gdn.

28601 SUMPTER, Georgia A, Braggs, OK, 45; William R, S, 18; Alice Bell, D, 16; Labany Lee, D, 14; Mattie V, D, 12; Susie E, D, 9; Amanda C, D, 7; George M, S, 5

12636 SUNDAY, Andy, Peggs, OK, 30; Mary, D, 8; Elva, D, 6; Lois, D, 3; Laura, D, 1 [Died 10-19-1906]; 17129, Betsy, Sis, 14

6529 SUNDAY, David, Chapel, OK, 21

[SUNDAY, Dick. See #2953]   *(Note: entry separate from other family groups)*

11930 SUNDAY, Edward, Jr, Oologah, OK, 21
11929 SUNDAY, Edward, Sr, Oologah, OK, 52
10086 SUNDAY, Eliza, Pryor Creek, OK, 57
9651 SUNDAY, Elizabeth, Oaks, OK, 55; 2212, Laura, D, 19
2207 SUNDAY, Jane, Oaks, OK, 32; Dina, D, 6
10610 SUNDAY, Jane, Tulsa, OK, 30
13802 SUNDAY, John, Lowrey, OK, 18; Annie, Sis, 12;   By William B. Foreman, Gdn.
4552 SUNDAY, Josie, Cleora, OK, 41
22839 SUNDAY, Lewis, Cleora, OK, 22; Sunday, Opal T, D, 1/12
16930 SUNDAY, Louella, Oaks, OK, 28
1670 SUNDAY, Mary, Porum, OK, 30; Bunch, Eli, S, 12

[SUNDAY, Nancy. See #1825]   *(Note: entries separate*
[SUNDAY, Levi. See #1825]   *from other family groups)*

CHEROKEE DESCENDANTS RESIDING WEST OF MISSISSIPPI RIVER.
VOLUME III (N – Z)

Key: Guion Miller Application Number; Name; Address, Relation (to Head); Age in 1906

10791 SUNDAY, Nick, Locust Grove, OK, 21
1938 SUNDAY, Peggie, Locust Grove, OK, 67
11778 SUNDAY, Silas, Cookson, OK, 19;   By R. C. Fuller, Gdn.
16104 SUNDAY, Speaker, Proctor, OK, 53; 16074, Betsy, W, 60

[SUNDAY, Susie. See #17470]   *(Note: entry separate from other family groups)*

1555 SUNDAY, Thomas, Porum, OK, 49; 1556, Malinda, W, 49; Eva, D, 16; Kelley, S, 14; Katie, D, 11
2209 SUNDAY, William, Oaks, OK, 28; 5264, Betsy, W, 33; Galcatcher, Wesley, S of W, 16; Maud, D of W, 13; Ruth, D of W, 10; Bluebird, Elias, S of W, 7; Galcatcher, Lilly, D of W, 4; Mollie, D of W, 2
11932 SUNDAY, William, Oologah, OK, 28
33141 SUNDAY, William, Tulsa, OK, 50; 33142, Neppie, W, 26; Jake, S, 9; Ellis, S, 8; Leroy, S, 6; Jessie, D, 4; William, S, 7/12
13162 SUNSHINE, Lucy, Tahlequah, OK, 50
1690 SUNSHINE, Ollie, Evansville, AR, 51; 6281, Mary, D, 14
11446 SURRELL, Mattie B, Atoka, OK, 22; Mildred D, D, 4; John R, S, 2
10757 SUTAWAKEE, Charlie, Campbell, OK, 22; 17170, Gahoge, D, 4; 7169, A-to-la-ha, S, 1
13493 SUTAWAKEE, John, Campbell, OK, 24
18328 SUTHERLAND, Abby M, Pryor Creek, OK, 26
6746 SUTHERLIN, Pollie, Chelsea, OK, 38; Sammie A, S, 18; Lee Roy, S, 16; Hurbert F, S, 13; Jesse E, S, 10; William O, S, 8; Alice L. D, D, 4; James M, S, 2
1284 SUTTEER, George, Marble City, OK, 45; Maud, D, 12
2888 SUTTON, Alexander, Grove, OK, 43
13773 SUTTON, Bettie, Hanson, OK, 44; 12441, Pearlie, D, 19; 12440, Joel E, S, 17; 12443, Esther F, D, 15; 12442, Anna L, D, 11
22845 SUTTON, David H, Grove, OK, 22
4807 SUTTON, John S, Miami, OK, 40; George F, S, 9; John R, S, 6
13661 SUTTON, Sallie, Hanson, OK, 21
4920 SUTTON, William H, Grove, OK, 51; Edward A, S, 20; John A, S, 18; Hattie M, D, 12; Claud, S, 9; Otis W, GS, 7; Bertha, D, 6
13498 SUTTON, Willis J, Hanson, OK, 24
15958 SU-WA-LA, Quaitsy, Wauhillau, OK, 40

[SUWATT. See SWATT.]

[SUWATT, Wm. See #13405]   *(Note: entry separate from other family groups)*

9221 SWAGERTY, Lucy, Hudson, OK, 34; Kelley, Claude, S, 14
8005 SWAIN, Rebecca McN, Vinita, OK, 42
4926 SWALLOW, Sarah, Grove, OK, 29; William J, S, 7; Elizabeth, D, 4
2263 SWAN, Boudinot, Bushyhead, OK, 41; 814, Alley, W, 33; John, S, 8
22606 SWAN, Neal, Foyil, OK, 37

CHEROKEE DESCENDANTS RESIDING WEST OF MISSISSIPPI RIVER.
VOLUME III (N – Z)

Key: Guion Miller Application Number; Name; Address, Relation (to Head); Age in 1906

- **22637** SWAN, Paul, Bushyhead, OK, 24
- **815** SWAN, Susan, Foyil, OK, 65
- **5084** SWARTS, Nannie, Warner, OK, 20
- **4950** SWATT, Easter, Grove, OK, 58
- **5913** SWATT, Oliver, Grove, OK, 23; 37700, Elmira, W, 18; Ruth, D, ¼
- **8274** SWATT, Thomas, Honey Creek, OK, 26; Beulah, D, 4; Zada, D, ½
- **5914** SWATT, Wesley A, Grove, OK, 21
- **823** SWEANEY, John T, Eugene, MO, 32
- **942** SWEETWATER, William, Zena, OK, 65; John, S, 12; Goldie, D, 9; Viola, D, 6
- **31057** SWIFT, Frank T, Muskogee, OK, 39; Crystie, S[sic],15; Frank B, S, 12; Mabel, D, 10
- **35338** SWIFT, James T, Muskogee, OK, 36
- **5540** SWIFT, Mattie, Girard, KS, 60
- **5806** SWIMMER, Adam, Tahlequah, OK, 34; 5746, Ellen, W, 34; 5806, Nelly, D, 13; Arch, S, 11; Lizzie, D, 9; Bettie, D, 8; Jim, S, 5; Sunday, S, 2
- **9290** SWIMMER, Charles A, Pitts, OK, 25

[SWIMMER, Cul. See #658]   *(Note: entry separate from other family groups)*

- **4198** SWIMMER, George, Cookson, OK, 36; 13126, Akey, W, 37; Eliza, D, 15; Tom, S, 8; Lucy, D, 1
- **13246** SWIMMER, Henry, Bunch, OK, 20
- **7667** SWIMMER, James S, Blackgum, OK, 18
- **7665** SWIMMER, Joe, Blackgum, OK, 21
- **2943** SWIMMER, John, Locust Grove, OK, 34; 8971, Elsie, W, 31; Ella, D, 10; Crutchfield, Nannie, D of W, 11; Canoe, Martin, S of W, 7; Nancy, D of W, 3
- **8736** SWIMMER, Katie, Locust Grove, OK, 46; 17086, Jennie [Jane], D, 14; James, S, 16; Ah-no-hee, D, 8; Lillie, D, 4; Mary, D, 4 [Died 4-1908]; Swimmer, S, 2
- **1344** SWIMMER, Lizzie, Stilwell, OK, 45; Saunders, Mary M, D, 13

[SWIMMER, Lizzie. See #6233]   *(Note: entry separate from other family groups)*

[SWIMMER, Lizzie. See #11197]
[SWIMMER, Ned. See #11197]   *(Note: entries separate from other family groups)*

- **26810** SWIMMER, Lydia, Cookson, OK, 23
- **16079** SWIMMER, Martha, Braggs, OK, 18
- **6471** SWIMMER, Mary J, Muldrow, OK, 53
- **2272** SWIMMER, Nancy, Stilwell, OK, 55
- **5809** SWIMMER, Nellie, Oaks, OK, 65
- **853** SWIMMER, Steeler, Tahlequah, OK, 55; 852, Sarah, W, 50 [Died 8-1908]; French, [Frank], S, 15; Jesse Lee, S, 8
- **28061** SWIMMER, Thomas, Kansas, OK, 28; 43401, Charlotte, W, 25; Grace, D, 3; Lincoln, S, 1

CHEROKEE DESCENDANTS RESIDING WEST OF MISSISSIPPI RIVER.
VOLUME III (N – Z)

Key: Guion Miller Application Number; Name; Address, Relation (to Head); Age in 1906

 7410 SWIMMER, Tom, Stilwell, OK, 50; 15661, Jennie, W, 50; 7411, Eva, D, 14; 7409, Nancie, D, 12
 682 SWIMMER, Wash, Rose, OK, 59; 175, Betsy, W, 56; Cull, S, 20; Louisa, D, 17; Jennie, D, 15; Peak, Connell, GS, 9
 7563 SWIMMER, William, Blackgum, OK, 24
26701 SWITZLER, Edna M, Canehill, AR, 20; Hutchins, Agnes, D, 3; Carther, S, 1

[SWIMS, Hannah. See #16642]   *(Note: entry separate from other family groups)*

 9019 SYKES, Alexander, Muskogee, OK, 36; Bertie Anderson, D, 9; Leander, S, 7; Delilah, D, 3

[SYKES, Bertha O. See #2848]   *(Note: entry separate from other family groups)*

 8897 SYKES, Frederick, Muskogee, OK, 30
28311 SYKES, Nora, Porum, OK, 18

35331 TABER, Margaret Okla, Little Rock, AR, 19
43890 TACKETT, Bert A Owasso, OK, 17; Maud P, Sis, 14; Walter E, Bro, 11; By L. H. Tackett, Gdn.
 1414 TADPOLE, Eli, Wellston, OK, 41; 8133, Dorcas Foreman, W, 36; Lelia, D, 16; Emma, D, 14; Wm H, S, 9; Annie, D, 6
 8972 TADPOLE, Polly, Choteau, OK, 73
 4460 TADPOLE, Rufus, Hulbert, OK, 45; Grover, S, 13; Elmer, S, 12
10959 TADPOLE, Thos. J, Tahlequah, OK, 34; Commodore P, S, 11
 8271 TADPOLE, Tiger, Choteau, OK, 40; Lydia, D, 8; Curtarney, D, 6; Betsy, D, 3; Lizzie, D, 1
14143 TAG, John, Spavinaw, OK, 47; 19646, Esther, W, 36; 14143, Maud, D, 10; Ollie, D, 8; Dutch, S, 14; Arch, S, 5; Henry, S, 3

[TAGG, Soggee. See #2968]   } *(Note: entries separate*
[TAGG, Ida. See #2968]   *from other family groups)*

[TAH-LA-LA, Chee-goo-wa. See #9010]
    (Note: entry separate from other family groups)

  785 TAH-NOO-WEE, Gafford, Marble City, OK, 33; 16594, Susie, W, 29; Pearl, D, 11; Nellie, D, 9; Laura, D, 7; Harvey, S, 3
 2842 TAHQUETT, John, Hulbert, OK, 53; 1203, Annie, W, 39
13203 TAIL, Amos, Bunch, OK, 21; 39160, Rosie, W, 23
11909 TAIL, French, Leach, OK, 38; 26515, Lucy, W, 36; Jim or Ezekiel, S, 6; Lewis, S, 2; Eli or Cusarnee, S, 1; Manus, Maggie, D of W, 14
13766 TAIL, George, Bunch, OK, 23

CHEROKEE DESCENDANTS RESIDING WEST OF MISSISSIPPI RIVER.
VOLUME III (N – Z)
Key: Guion Miller Application Number; Name; Address, Relation (to Head); Age in 1906

[TAIL, Henry. See #43362] *(Note: entries separate*
[TAIL, Sallie. See #43362] *from other family groups)*

[TAIL, Nancy. See #13236] *(Note: entry separate from other family groups)*

11288 TALBERT, Abbie E, Claremore, OK, 57
 9432 TALBERT. Mary, Claremore, OK, 19; Ellen, Sis, 18; Carrie, Sis, 16; George, Bro, 15; Grover, Bro, 13; By Geo. W. Talbert, Gdn.
 5883 TALBOT, Jesseca Bird R, Santa Cruz, 81 Branciford Ave, CA, 42; 31841, Nivens, Helen Elizabeth, D, 18; Archibald R, S, 15
 4789 TALBOT, John W, Row, OK, 29
 4786 TALBOT, Thornton S, Row, OK, 27
28377 TALBOTT, James Albert, Flint, OK, 13; By Geo. W. Talbott, Gdn.
30377 TALLY, Andrew, Ft. Gibson, OK, 37; Maggie, D, 5; Rosseta, D, 2; 22087, James W, Nep, 6
 6793 TALLY, Betty, Ft. Gibson, OK, 66
 4368 TALLY, Cynthia, Tahlequah OK, 53; Dewitt C, S, 19
41526 TALLY, James W, Ft. Gibson, OK, 6; By Andrew Tally, Gdn.
23625 TALLY, Rachel, Tahlequah, OK, 21
23499 TALLY, Walter E, Tahlequah, OK, 27; 7554, Ellie, W, 22; Ethel M, D, 4
   19 TANKERSLEY, August H, Pryor Creek, OK, 54; Henry A, S, 11; Alexander, S, 8; Jane L, D, 4; Lee Austin, S, 2
23075 TANKERSLEY, Egbert, Pryor Creek, OK, 29
31962 TANKERSLEY, Ella, McAlester, OK, 29
23739 TANKERSLEY, John A, Kansas City, 718 Wabash Ave. MO, 34
28331 TANNER, Allen, Eucha, OK, 7; Stacey, Sis, 6; By Moses D, Field, Gdn.
 1563 TANNER, Charley, Grove, OK, 33; 1558,Betsey, W, 38; Sarah, D, 12; Lena, D, 8; Clark, S, 2
  420 TANNER, James, Eucha, OK, 38; 651, Annie, W, 31; Mary, D, 14; Jas, Jr, S, 8; Ollie, D, 6; Aaron or Allen, S, 4; John, S, 2
 6726 TANNER, Jennie, Inola, OK, 25; Vera C, D, 7; Olan R, S, 5; Jessey Harold, S, 2
 2479 TANNER, Margaret A, Albuquerque, NM, 36; Green, Ernestine L, D, 15; Ethel R, D, 13; Herbert L, S, 12; Tanner, Sabra L, D, 8; Willie W, S, 4
25166 TANNER, Mary E, Claremore, OK, 27
  339 TANNER, Phesant, Maysville, AR, 59; 5992, Martha, W, 50; Minnie, D, 13; Scott, S, 10; White, Alice, D of W, 16; Okalr[sic], D of W, 8

[TANNER, Sequoyah. See #9007] *(Note: entry separate from other family groups)*

36508 TANNER, Taylor, Maysville, AR, 25; 23352, Mary A, W, 21; Eucha, S, 1
 1714 TANNER, Thos. Eucha, OK, 38; 1711, Nancy, W, 25; Jennie, D, 3; Lucy, D, 1; Ridge, Nellie, D of W, 6
10936 TAPP, Elnora, Ft. Gibson, OK, 60
 3978 TAPP, James, Ft. Gibson, OK, 30

CHEROKEE DESCENDANTS RESIDING WEST OF MISSISSIPPI RIVER.
VOLUME III (N – Z)

Key: Guion Miller Application Number; Name; Address, Relation (to Head); Age in 1906

[TAREPIN. See TERRAPIN.]

13714 TAREPIN, Charlie, Wauhillau, OK, 30; 12634, Callie, W, 30; 13714, Henry W, S, 1/6
2609 TAREPIN, Gabriel, Stilwell, OK, 23
3681 TAREPIN, James, Bartlesville, OK, 47; 3495, Betsey, W, 35; Mollie, D, 13 [Died 8-26-'06]; Lydia, D, 11; Sallie, D, 9
26392 TAREPIN, Jesse, Tahlequah, OK, 25; Ollie, D, 2; Dollie, D, 2
7009 TAREPIN, Joe, Tahlequah, OK, 49; 6512,Wilda, W, 50; Ellen, D, 14
2754 TAREPIN, Ollie, Peggs, OK, 54
2701 TARRAPIN, Lizzie, Stilwell, OK, 48; Jennie, D, 15 [Dead, 9-1907]; Wilson, GS, 3
9324 TARRAPIN, Lydia, Melvin, OK, 60
7695 TARRAPIN, Polly, Tahlequah, OK, 76
9476 TERRAPINHEAD, Kate, Vian, OK, 52; 9381, John, S, 18; 9477, Nancy, D, 20
27709 TATE, Josephine D, Muskogee, OK, 21
4193 TATUM, Lula, Vian, OK, 19

[TATUM, Sitting Bull. See #3934]
[TATUM, Thomas. See #3934]
[TATUM, Jay. See #3934]   *(Note: entries separate from other family groups)*
[TATUM, Dock. See #3934]
[TATUM, Earl. See #3934]

4952 TAU-U-NEA-CIE, Daniel, Grove, OK, 34; Jeffie, D, 9; Berchie, D, 6; Lewis, S, 4; Lexie, D, 4
4918 TAU-U-NEA-CIE, Jane, Grove, OK, 59
13207 TAYLOR, Albert A, Tahlequah, OK, 36; Allie B, D, 12; Susie P, D, 10; Albert A, Jr, S, 8; Shelly K, S, 3; Gilbert T, S, ½
23920 TAYLOR, Alfred, Pryor Creek, OK, 36; Gertie, D, 13; Pearl, D, 11; Sallie, D, 9; David, S, 7; Carl, S, 5; Stacy Ann, D, 3; Mitchell T, S, 1
31556 TAYLOR, Alma R, Choteau, OK, 22
22925 TAYLOR, Annie E, Stilwell, OK, 24
34834 TAYLOR, Annie L, Bluejacket, OK, 21; Elwyn F, S, 3; Laura A, D, 1
13975 TAYLOR, Campbell H, Muskogee, OK, 24
14990 TAYLOR, Campbell H, Coffeyville, KS, 68; Stacy Belle, D, 14; Campbell H, Jr, S, 13; George A.M, S, 11; Grayson F, S, 7; Regina N, D, 4; Millard B, S, 1; Mildred B, D, 1
5670 TAYLOR, Chas. F, Rex, OK, 24
838 TAYLOR, Charlotte T, Muskogee, OK, 39
1382 TAYLOR, David, Dawson, OK, 33
13547 TAYLOR, David, Sr, Chelsea, OK, 80
33811 TAYLOR, Edward, Chelsea, OK, 46; Roy, S, 17; Mabel, D, 15; Edward C, S, 13; Fletcher, S, 12; Mary E, D, 11; Sarah, D, 9; Flora C, D, 5
4831 TAYLOR, Ellen, Lynch, OK, 48; Benge, John D, S, 12

CHEROKEE DESCENDANTS RESIDING WEST OF MISSISSIPPI RIVER.
VOLUME III (N – Z)

Key: Guion Miller Application Number; Name; Address, Relation (to Head); Age in 1906

25345 TAYLOR, Emma Lane, Chelsea, OK, 20; Robt. D, S, 2
11216 TAYLOR, Eva, Christie, OK, 36; Rider, S, 19; Shadock, S, 12; Betsy, D, 6; John, S, 1
30166 TAYLOR, George, Vinita, OK, 26; 23269, Nannie, W, 24
22211 TAYLOR, Isom, Pryor Creek, OK, 34 [Died, 1908]
116 TAYLOR, James, Pryor Creek, OK, 85 [Died 1-14-1907]
2489 TAYLOR, James, Evansville, AR, 29; 2507, Annie, W, 31; 2489, Columbus, S, 7; Mary, D, 5
18866 TAYLOR, James E, Oologah, OK, 51; Samuel C, S, 20; Bennie E, S, 16; Bertha B, D, 15; Emma I, D, 13; Walter A, S, 8; Mary I, D, 5; Bernard, S, 1; 25044, Clyde E, S, 18
17493 TAYLOR, Jas. L, Pryor Creek, OK, 45; Nellie B, D, 9; Alice M, D, 7; Margarette, D, 4; Wm J, S, 1
33634 TAYLOR, Jessie, Tulsa, OK, 19
6716 TAYLOR, John, McKey, OK, 54; John Cornelius, S, 19; Myrtle G, D, 14; James F, S, 13; Juanita, D, 11; Mark Hanna, S, 9; Soper B, S, 6; Clifford B, S, 5
23862 TAYLOR, John, Vian, OK, 35; 10900, Maria, W, 37; Downing, Jesse, S of W, 16
32744 TAYLOR, John Booth, McKey, OK, 27; Neta, D, 2
28822 TAYLOR, John D, Gideon, OK, 52; Wyly, S, 14; Andrew C, S, 12
23506 TAYLOR, Jno F, Chelsea, OK, 45; Mack, S, 13; Albert, S, 11; Richard, S, 9; Fred, S, 8; Annie, D, 6; Amanda, D, 4; Malinda, D, 2
26 TAYLOR, John M, Jr, Claremore, OK, 46; Blaine S, S, 12; Murell, D, 11; Robert C, S, 9; Florence T, D, 4; McCutchen, S, 2
32847 TAYLOR, John M, Jr, Lowell, AR, 34
3038 TAYLOR, John W, Ft. Smith, AR, R.F.D. #3 Box 178, 70
31580 TAYLOR, Jno. O, Bartlesville, OK, 31
6998 TAYLOR, Laura E, Ochelata, OK, 67
5581 TAYLOR, Lewis, Baron, OK, 47
8116 TAYLOR, Lydie, Vian, OK, 56
23769 TAYLOR, Lydia K, Vinita, OK, R.F.D. #1 Pheasant Hill, 48; Alma Lane, D, 6
22677 TAYLOR, Margaret E, Vinita, OK, 19
2343 TAYLOR, Martha, Afton, OK, 52; Frank R, S, 17; William H, S, 14; 23936, Georgia M, D, 18
22924 TAYLOR, Mary A, Stilwell, OK, 23
40462 TAYLOR, Mary Elizabeth, Claremore, OK, 18; James G, Bro, 12; Joseph Wesley, Bro, 9; By J. Ryan, Gdn.
8657 TAYLOR, Mina, Melvin, OK, 14; Bessie, Sis, 12; Zachey, Bro, 8; By Jennie Lindsey, Gdn.
13632 TAYLOR, Nancy, Vinita, OK, 43; Effie, D, 20; Henry, S, 18; Delora, D, 16; Betty, D, 13; John, S, 12; Joseph, S, 9; Fred, S, 8; Walter, S, 4; Ufa, D, 3
13642 TAYLOR, Nancy, Braggs, OK, 34; Levi, Adam, S, 12
8752 TAYLOR, Nancy L, Akin, OK, 15; Mary A, Sis, 13;   By Jas C. Taylor, Gdn.
29318 TAYLOR, Narcissa, Stilwell, OK, 27
4286 TAYLOR, Peggy, Stilwell, OK, 81

CHEROKEE DESCENDANTS RESIDING WEST OF MISSISSIPPI RIVER.
VOLUME III   (N – Z)

Key: Guion Miller Application Number; Name; Address, Relation (to Head); Age in 1906

2493 TAYLOR, Richard L, Stilwell, OK, 51; 3291, Margaret E, W, 50; Susie B, D, 17; Richard L, Jr, S, 15; Martha C, D, 12; Wm B, S, 14
23051 TAYLOR, Robt, Ochelata, OK, 28; Laura E, D, 5; Wm E, S, 3
44358 TAYLOR, Robert O, Afton, OK, 22
30253 TAYLOR, Robert R, Tahlequah, OK, 2
29280 TAYLOR, Sallie, Chelsea, OK, 15; Herbert, Bro, 14; Mattie, Sis, 12; Wm J. B, Bro, 10; Gracie, Sis, 8; Mandie, Sis, 5;   By Laura Taylor, Gdn.
31416 TAYLOR, Theodore, McKey, OK, 22
29269 TAYLOR, Thos D, Collinsville, OK, 33; Daniel O, S, 11; Thomas V, S, 3
10890 TAYLOR, Thos. F, Tahlequah, OK, 28
1207 TAYLOR, Thomas J, Tahlequah, OK, 88;   By Rebecca A. Johnson, Gdn.
6968 TAYLOR, Timothy, Coffeyville, KS, 29; Flocy Gladys, D, 5; Roy, S, 3; Hazel May, D, 1/12
6 TAYLOR, Wiley, Pryor Creek, OK, 79
5753 TAYLOR, William, Stilwell, OK, 45; 1618, Sarah, W, 33; 5753, William, Jr, S, 20; Jackson, S, 15; Jennie, D, 12; John, S, 10; Eliza, D, 8; George, S, 2; Rachel, D, 1/12
31628 TAYLOR, Wm F, Leach, OK, 45; Herman J, S, 18; Julia M, D, 17; Zacharia, S, 14; Columbus, S, 12; Frank J, S, 10; Rachel G, D, 4
13711 TAYLOR, Wm H, Tahlequah, OK, 38
25600 TAYLOR, Wm M, Dewey, OK, 26; Laura B, D, 2
30 TAYLOR, Wm T, Claremore, OK, 40; Beulah M, D, 10; Lelah M, D, 9; Ruth M, D, 4; Rachel M, D, 2

[TEAGUE, Myrtle. See #17684]   *(Note: entry separate from other family groups)*

3812 TECAHNEYESKE, Richard, Whitmire, OK, 64
17412 TECUMSEH, George, Braggs, OK 22
30736 TECUMSEH, Jackson, Braggs, OK, 24
26525 TEEL, Mary R, Warner, OK, 19; Plenny, D, 2
15664 TEE-NOO-WEE-, Nancy, Stilwell, OK, 55
35012 TEHEE, Bird, Cherokee City, AR, 21
14699 TEHEE, Charles, Jr, Tahlequah, OK, 48; 26912, Lizzie, W, 28; 14700, Florence, D, 17; 14701, Ada, D, 14; 14702, Hoke, S, 13; 14699, Maggie, D, 7; Mary, D, 3
9295 TEHEE, Charles, Sr, Cherokee City, AR, 81 [Died 2-1909]; 26261, Annie, W, 20
6474 TEHEE, Charley, Locust Grove, OK, 29; 8916, Ellen, W, 20; Eva, D, 5

[TEE-HEE, Charlie. See #2505]   *(Note: entry separate from other family groups)*

8295 TEEHEE, Charley, Cherokee City, AR, 40; 9298, Lese, W, 48; Mary, D, 19; George, S, 15; Eliza, GD, 5/6

[TE-HEE, Charlie. See #5690]   *(Note: entry separate from other family groups)*

10376 TEHEE, Christian, Rose, OK, 11;   By Lizzie Tehee, Gdn.

CHEROKEE DESCENDANTS RESIDING WEST OF MISSISSIPPI RIVER.
VOLUME III (N – Z)

Key: Guion Miller Application Number; Name; Address, Relation (to Head); Age in 1906

13635 TEHEE, Ellen, Braggs, OK, 30; Whitewater, Geo, S, 10; Tehee, Jim, S, 4; Jack, S, 1
35011 TEHEE, Ellick, Cherokee City, AR, 25

[TEHEE, Elmira. See #16859] ⎱ *(Note: entries separate*
[TEHEE, Dora. See #16859] ⎰ *from other family groups)*

8294 TEHEE, Ely, Cherokee City, AR, 33; 8296, Sallie, W, 56; Nellie, D, 16; George, S, 14; Grant, S, 12; Elsie, D, 9
16606 TEHEE, Felix M, Rose, OK, 21
13079 TEEHEE, Houston B, Tahlequah, OK, 32
9732 TEHEE, John, Tahlequah, OK, 66

[TEEHEE, Katie. See #1129]   *(Note: entry separate from other family groups)*

7442 TEHEE, Lee, Wynoma, OK, 42; Henry, S, 18; Moses, S, 14; Charlie, S, 11; Colbert, S, 9
9130 TEHEE, Lizzie, Rose, OK, 57
16083 TEHEE, Martin, Tahlequah, OK, 24
40377 TEHEE, Moody M, Rose, OK, 15;   By Lizzie Tehee, Gdn.

[TEHEE, Peggy. See #10320] ⎱ *(Note: entries separate*
[TEHEE, Jess. See #10370] ⎰ *from other family groups)*

[TEHEE, Charley. See #10371]   *(Note: entry separate from other family groups)*

[TEHEE, Rosie. See #38484]   *(Note: entry separate from other family groups)*

13383 TEHEE, Stephen, Tahlequah, OK, 68; Schofield, S, 15; Lizzie, D, 13; Monroe, S, 11; Levi, S, 9; Sequoyah, S, 6; Davis, S, 3
16162 TEHEE, Stephen B, Jr, Tahlequah, OK, 27

[TEEHEE, Susie. See #5916]   *(Note: entry separate from other family groups)*

[TEHEE, Treaskie. See #4730]   *(Note: entry separate from other family groups)*

17181 TEHEE, War-lar-you-gar, Campbell, OK, 24; Annie, D, 4; Charlie, S, 3
16863 TELL, Sarah E, Choteau, OK, 32; Adair, Frankie M, S, 12; Tell, Alice C, D, 6; Benj. G, S, 3
2486 TELLER, Ceily, Stilwell, OK, 57
2866 TELLER, Eve, Bunch, OK, 49
26842 TENBROOK, Mattie J, Fairland, OK, 46; Earling, S, 19; Ida Juanita, D, 14
14810 TENKILLER, Della, Campbell, OK, 26
14811 TENKILLER, Lee, Campbell, OK, 24
14809 TENKILLER, Nancy, Campbell, OK, 56; Layee, D, 15

CHEROKEE DESCENDANTS RESIDING WEST OF MISSISSIPPI RIVER.
VOLUME III (N – Z)

Key: Guion Miller Application Number; Name; Address, Relation (to Head); Age in 1906

34923 TENNISON, Elizabeth, Gravette, AR, 23; Jessy V, D, 6; George W, S, 4; Sallie A, D, 3

[TERRAPIN. See TAREPIN.]

10713 TERRAPIN, Catherine, Baron, OK, 66
5334   TERRAPIN, Jennie, Westville, OK, 47; 16350, Lydia, D, 16; Charlie, S, 10

[TERRELL, Charles. See #9186]
[TERRELL, Wm. See #9186]   *(Note: entries separate*
[TERRELL, Dennis. See #9186]   *from other family groups)*
[TERRELL, Lucinda. See #9186]

23590 TERRELL, John, Vinita, OK, 22
28219 TERRELL, John, Eureka, OK, 52; 1979, Samantha, W, 50; Jackson, S, 16; 28219, Ellis, S, 20
29043 TERRELL, John Albert, Tahlequah, OK, 26
28220 TERRELL, Mary E, Eureka, OK, 22
3635   TERRELL, Polly, Tahlequah, OK, 91
8336   TERRELL, Robt. M, Vian, OK, 34; Emma, D, 4
28221 TERRELL, Samuel, Eureka, OK, 28
17041 TERRELL, Sarah E, Baron, OK, 22
25008 TERRELL, Wm, Cookson, OK, 52; 25847, Elizabeth, W, 34; Katie, D, 12; Joseph, S, 10; Ella, D, 9; Susan, D, 6; Viola, D, 5; Chas. L, S, 1; Etta, D, 1

[TESQUANTEE. See DE-S-QUA-NI.]

3667   TETER, Alice, Pryor Creek, OK, 37; Clara, D, 15; Myrtle, D, 12; Walter, S, 10; Edna, D, 8; Goldie Ethel, D, 4; Leon, S, 1/12
10335 THARP, Maud E, Ramona, OK, 34; Bussey, Emma B, D, 12; Brown, Jesse B, S, 9
6934   THEURER, Alta V, Ft. Smith, AR, 47; Lena, D, 18; Alta V, D, 7
8031   THOMAS, Annie, Vinita, OK, 52; Terrell, Joseph, S, 20; Richard, S, 17; Samuel, S, 14; Cintha, D, 12
23592 THOMAS, Annie, Vinita, OK, 6;   By P. C. Thomas, Gdn.
25486 THOMAS, Bessie, Pryor Creek, OK, 16; Clarence, S, 1
3060   THOMAS, Eliza G, Evansville, AR, 10; George F, Bro, 7; Jimmie T, Bro, 4; By Alice C. Fenburg, Gdn.
10666 THOMAS, Eugenia, Tulsa, OK, 32; Viola B, D, 13; George H, S, 9; Arvol V, S, 7; Theron T, S, 5; Gladys M, D, 1
3042   THOMAS, George E, Stilwell, OK, 30; Lettie L, D, 8; Mary M, D, 5; Annie M, D, 3; Callie D, D, 1/6
8703   THOMAS, Henry R, Vinita, OK, 25; Louise, D, 7/12
3859   THOMAS, Jennie, Bartlesville, OK, 21

CHEROKEE DESCENDANTS RESIDING WEST OF MISSISSIPPI RIVER.
VOLUME III   (N – Z)

Key: Guion Miller Application Number; Name; Address, Relation (to Head); Age in 1906

- **877** THOMAS, John L, Vinita, OK, 18; Thura, Sis, 17; Ellis P, Bro, 14; Elizabeth T, Sis, 8; By Jesse A. Thomas, Gdn.
- **30662** THOMAS, Johanna, Vinita, OK, 52 [Died 7-27-1906];   By Jesse Thomas, Adm.
- **5928** THOMAS, Lizzie, Muldrow, OK, 58
- **3771** THOMAS, Lucius F, Stilwell, OK, 28; John B, S, 5; Geo. Lee, S, 2; Lucius S, S, 3
- **23634** THOMAS, Lucy, Oaks, OK, 18
- **4704** THOMAS, Lydia, Talala, OK, 16;   By A. J. Rider, Gdn.
- **33641** THOMAS, Martha J, Siloam Springs, AR, 48; Burk, William R, S, 20; John S, S, 17; Walter R, S, 14
- **12702** THOMAS, Mary L, Afton, OK, 25; Sopha E, D, 10; Wm B, S, 9; Mable, D, 6
- **29667** THOMAS, May L, White Oak, OK, 18; Roswell E, S, 1
- **24747** THOMAS, Melvina S, Spavinaw, OK, 21
- **25678** THOMAS, Mollie, Chetopa, KS, 24; Nellie, D, 1
- **5191** THOMAS, Napoleon F, Vinita, OK, 23
- **696** THOMAS, Nicholas, Vinita, OK, 73
- **9736** THOMAS, Samuel, Maple, OK, 15;   By Wm N. Miller, Gdn.
- **6987** THOMAS, Thomas C, Vinita, OK, 27; Vera L, D, 4
- **13286** THOMASON, Daniel W, Westville, OK, 15; Freddie D, Bro, 11;   By Wm H. Thomason, Gdn.
- **24856** THOMASON, Elsey A, Siloam Springs, AR, 19
- **12703** THOMASON, Rachel, Vinita, OK, 37; George L, S, 16; 26844, Bertha, D, 18
- **26784** THOMPSON, Ada, Vinita, OK, 24
- **37206** THOMPSON, Alexander, Dousette, TX, 24; Moselle, D, 1
- **5493** THOMPSON, Alfred B, Trinity, TX, 46; 25107, Celia L, D, 20; Archie W, S, 14; Virgil E, S, 3
- **31392** THOMPSON, Alice, Pensacola, OK, 25
- **27935** THOMPSON, Alice M, Hanson, OK, 20; Marvin J, S, 2; William, S, 1/6
- **34691** THOMPSON, Allison, Cleburne, TX, 40; Ernest W, S, 15; Mamie, D, 13; Allison A, S, 4; Maurice C, S, 2
- **23901** THOMPSON, Caleb A, Gideon, OK, 44; Florence L, D, 17; Gertrude M, D, 12; Jesse C, S, 8; Gracey L, D, 6; James A, S, 4
- **1122** THOMPSON, Caleb S, Ahniwake, OK, 77
- **4013** THOMPSON, Catharine, Ft. Gibson, OK, 32; McEnery, Fred B, S, 13; Hazel, D, 11
- **32244** THOMPSON, Charley, Choteau OK, 21
- **7508** THOMPSON, Claude A, Muskogee, OK, 27; Frances Pauline, D, ½
- **27886** THOMPSON, Clem, Row, OK, 25; Lucy M, D, 6; Jesse, S, 5
- **27437** THOMPSON, David L, Valeda, OK, 28; George W, S, 5; John H, S, 4; Norma V, D, 1
- **26343** THOMPSON, Ethel A, Chelsea, OK, 16
- **39567** THOMPSON, Felix, Siloam Springs, AR, 28; Helen, D, 8
- **12852** THOMPSON, Florence E, Warner, OK, 15; Nora B, D, 14; Nellie F, D, 12; Ira L, S, 10; Ella M, D, 5; Mary M, D, 3;   By John W. Thompson, Father

CHEROKEE DESCENDANTS RESIDING WEST OF MISSISSIPPI RIVER.
VOLUME III (N – Z)

Key: Guion Miller Application Number; Name; Address, Relation (to Head); Age in 1906

11640 THOMPSON, Francis B, Niagara, KS, 19; Richard L, Bro, 17; Alfred D, Bro, 11; By Lydia S. Thompson, Gdn.
6439 THOMPSON, George, Muldrow, OK, 2; By Arch Thompson, Gdn.
7509 THOMPSON, Gilbert T, Tahlequah, OK, 59
25272 THOMPSON, Gilbert T, Jr, Muskogee, OK, 28
3881 THOMPSON, Henry, Eucha, OK, 43; 914, Sarah, W, 34; Judge, S, 16; Ellen, D, 8; Lacey, S, 6; Thomas, S, 4

[THOMPSON, Henry. See #24068] *(Note: entry separate from other family groups)*

37205 THOMPSON, Harry H, Houston, TX, 27
29148 THOMPSON, Hicks E, Kilgore, TX, 21
11639 THOMPSON, Hiram A, Niagara, KS, 29; By Jno M, Thompson, Gdn.
37197 THOMPSON, Hooley D, Edna, KS, 38
1073 THOMPSON, James Allen, Vinita, OK, 58; 8785, Sarah, W, 37
32308 THOMPSON, Jas. A, Taylor, TX, 52; Alex M, S, 20; Lucile, D, 17; John A, S, 11
32735 THOMPSON, Jas C, Row, OK, 28; Elbert, S, 2
25011 THOMPSON, Jas. Kidd, Muskogee, OK, 32; Joseph Gilbert, S, 5
27497 THOMPSON, Jas. M, Nowata, OK, 24
7472 THOMPSON, Jas. P, Tahlequah, OK, 29; 25925, Maggie M, W, 27; James M, S, 5; Claude E, S, 2
27441 THOMPSON, James W, Valeda. OK, 54; David C, S, 17; Della L, D, 14; Bertha L, D, 11
1230 THOMPSON, Jesse D, Stilwell, OK, 37; Robert H, S, 16; William T, S, 14; Louis A, S, 12; John, S, 10; Mary, D, 8; Jesse C, S, 6; Alma, D, 4; Ola, D, 4; James, S, 2
23902 THOMPSON, John D, Gideon, OK, 20; Mary E, D, 1
35969 THOMPSON, Jno. J, Corley, AR, 28; Mattie H, D, 5; John H, S, 3; Lois M D, 1
37203 THOMPSON, John L, Waco, TX, 32; John L, S, 5; Ben, S, 4
6532 THOMPSON, John M, Pryor Creek, OK, ?; Buna Vista, D, 4; Bonnie Lee, S(?), 2
26342 THOMPSON, John M, Chelsea, OK, 18; By Mary J. Thompson, Gdn.
1598 THOMPSON, John M, Sherman, TX, 76 [Died, 5-1907]; 37207, Anna M, D, 20
26577 THOMPSON, John N, Tahlequah, OK, 23; 8132, Sallie E, W, 24; Ruby M, D, 3
26574 THOMPSON, John T, Tahlequah, OK, 53; Margaret L, D, 17; Jesse C, S, 11
30255 THOMPSON, Joseph C, Row, OK, 22
5022 THOMPSON, Joseph F, Tahlequah, OK, 65
13628 THOMPSON, Joseph L, Pensacola, OK, 69; Ollie B, D, 10; Anna K, D, 6
7435 Thompson, Joseph M, Tahlequah, OK, 46; Anna C, D, 17; Eddie H, S, 15; Mamie L, D, 11
37204 THOMPSON, Liggett N, Houston, TX, 29
15985 THOMPSON, Lettie, Pryor Creek, OK, 35; Collier, Charlotte, D, 12; Edgar, S, 8; Thompson, Letha, D, 2; Leala, D, 1
23926 THOMPSON, Lihu F, Ahniwake, OK, 39; Georgia A, D, 16; Katy M, D, 8; William C, S, 4; Bud E, S, 2

CHEROKEE DESCENDANTS RESIDING WEST OF MISSISSIPPI RIVER.
VOLUME III (N – Z)

Key: Guion Miller Application Number; Name; Address, Relation (to Head); Age in 1906

13627 THOMPSON, Louis Kell, Pensacola, OK, 32; Jas. Robert, S, 5; Louis LeRoy, S, 2
 2476 THOMPSON, Maggie L, Centralia, OK, 26; Albert L, S, 6; Harley C, S, 2
 3731 THOMPSON, Mary E, Fowler, CO, 34; Letitia V, D, 15; Mary Ann, D, 14; Francis L, S, 10; Joseph H, S, 8
12969 THOMPSON, Margy M, Muldrow, OK, 4; By Arch Thompson, Gdn.
23880 THOMPSON, Matthew A, Muskogee, OK, 23
26254 THOMPSON, Milton K, Muskogee, OK, 35; 7467, Louise, W, 31; Katharine, D, 6; Louise E, D, 3
23048 THOMPSON, Myrtle, Centralia, OK, 22; Sanders, Lena, D, 4; Thompson, John, S, 2
  975 THOMPSON, Narcissa, Row, OK, 59; Ethel, D, 17
26576 THOMPSON, Nellie, Tahlequah, OK, 20

[THOMPSON, Newton. See #822]   *(Note: entry separate from other family groups)*

 1507 THOMPSON, Ollie, Oaks, OK, 85
 1693 THOMPSON, Peggy, Siloam Springs, AR, 50; Joel B. M, S, 19; Lena, D, 14
 6966 THOMPSON, Polly, Stilwell, OK, 19
  418 THOMPSON, Rachel, Eucha, OK, 65
 5224 THOMPSON, Rachel M, Row, OK, 47; Wm C, S, 19; Susie, D, 16; Calvin H, S, 15; Andrew J, S, 11
 8770 THOMPSON, Reuben C, Kansas City, 1100 N 10th St, KS, 36; Ollie R, F, 25; George A, S, 12; Floyd O, S, 11; Lottie M, D, 8; Clarence E, S, 4; Opal F, D, 2
28713 THOMPSON, Robert F, Valeda, KS, 35; James W, S, 9; Lark A, S, 7; John L, S, 5; Harvey F, S, 2; Shelly L, S, 1/6
27885 THOMPSON, Robert H, Row, OK, 32; Ethel T, D, 11; Robert L, S, 9; Ettie M, D, 8; Mary Ester, D, 4
 6800 THOMPSON, Robert J, Tahlequah, OK, 46; 4588, Rosa, W, 44; Eloise, D, 10; Ida Frances, D, 8; Susie, D, 4; Thomas F, S, 2
30909 THOMPSON, Robt. W, Corley, AR, 28
30679 THOMPSON, Ruthie V, Moody, OK, 26; Ivey A, D, 2
 1088 THOMPSON, Thomas F, Vinita, OK, 60; 1087, Susan C, W, 61
 4580 THOMPSON, Thos. F, Vinita, OK, 35; Maurine, D, 5; Maurice, S, 2
 3211 THOMPSON, Walter A, Tahlequah, OK, 41; 23350, Emily J, W, 28
21121 THOMPSON, Weakie, Vian, OK, 16; By Annie Byers, Gdn.
43517 THOMPSON, Will, Siloam Springs, AR, 26
 8105 THOMPSON, Wm, Whitmire, OK, 42; 16504, Jennie, W, 34; Joe, S, 19; Catcher, S, 11; Rebecca, D, 6

[THOMPSON, Wm. See #12912]
[THOMPSON, Gracie. See #12912]   *(Note: entries separate*
[THOMPSON, Katie. See #12912]   *from other family groups)*

 5491 THOMPSON, Wm D, Kilgore, TX, 51;   Eula Lee, D, 17; Thos. W, S, 11

CHEROKEE DESCENDANTS RESIDING WEST OF MISSISSIPPI RIVER.
VOLUME III (N – Z)

Key: Guion Miller Application Number; Name; Address, Relation (to Head); Age in 1906

27496 THOMPSON, Wm. E, Valeda, KS, 29; Albert T, S, 5; Mamie E, D, 2; Elsie P, D, 1/6
 9466 THOMPSON, Wm J, Edna, KS, 23
 3768 THOMPSON, Wm Presley, Vinita, OK, 40; 31309, Elizabeth C, W, 34; Sadie P, D, 11; Elizabeth C, D, 8
26578 THOMPSON, Wm W, Tahlequah, OK, 27
 4606 THORNBURGH, Hortensa, Coffeyville, KS, 50
25741 THORNE, Caleb, Tahlequah, OK, 22
11284 THORNE, Elias C, Tahlequah, OK, 29; Lula, D, 2; Oplala, D, 1
11961 THORNE, Jacob H, Tahlequah, OK, 19; Walter, Bro, 18; By Wm P. Thorne, Gdn.
33394 THORNE, Julia A, Tahlequah, OK, 48; 33395, Jennette, D, 19; John, S, 17; Crill, S, 16; Willie, S, 13; Thorne, Arthur, S, 10; Oscar, S, 10; Cherokee, D, 4
27112 THORNE, Lucy A, Wagoner, OK, 24
12508 THORNE, Maggie, Muskogee, OK, 30; Georgia E, D, 1
34730 THORNE, Maud E, Tahlequah, OK, 30; Clifford, S, 9; Anna M, D, 7; Edith I, D, 3
24437 THORNTON, Alice, Southwest City, MO, 27
14265 THORNTON, Arch, Vian, OK, 18; By Sallie Thornton, Gdn.
26847 THORNTON, Archie A, Centralia, OK, 29
14266 THORNTON, Eliza, Vian, OK, 21
15918 THORNTON, Flora A, Ft. Gibson, OK,45; 7906, Owen, S, 17
 1119 THORNTON, George W, Welch, OK, R.F.D. #1, 52; Nellie E, D, 17; Mary M, D, 15; Nora V, D, 12; Lucy G, D, 1; George R, S, 9; Blanche E, D, 5; Wilbur J, S, 3; Susie J, D, 1
19086 THORNTON, Henry J, Skiatook, OK, 18; By Luther Allen Dunn, Gdn.
24318 THORNTON, James, Baron, OK, 40; Jesse, S, 9; Rogers, S, 3; Nick, S, 1
26795 THORNTON, Joe Ellis, Vian, OK, 25

[THORNTON, Johnson. See #1782] *(Note: entry separate from other family groups)*

 896 THORNTON, Joseph, Wauhillau, OK, 56; 936, Peggie, W, 56; Jesse, S, 19; Wyly, S, 17; Willie, S, 15
26649 THORNTON, Lila May, Wauhillau, OK, 23

[THORNTON, Mary. See #40793] *(Note: entry separate from other family groups)*

14040 THORNTON, Murrell, Pryor Creek, OK, 12; Gladys, Sis, 9; By Mollie Hosey, Gdn.
26846 THORNTON, Orville E, Centralia, OK, 30
36273 THORNTON, Percy M, Bluejacket, OK, 27; Vivian, D, 3; Dwight H, S, 1
 2214 THORNTON, Reese, Chance, OK, 29; 23188, Mike, W, 29; Walter, S, 6; May, D, 3; Fannie, D, 1
 382 THORNTON, Sallie, Vian, OK, 54
 1965 THORNTON, Smith, Vian, OK, 56; William, S, 18

CHEROKEE DESCENDANTS RESIDING WEST OF MISSISSIPPI RIVER.
VOLUME III (N – Z)

Key: Guion Miller Application Number; Name; Address, Relation (to Head); Age in 1906

24155 THORNTON, Susan E, Baron, OK, 17
12723 THORNTON, Thomas J, Muskogee, OK, 52
 1962 THORNTON, Wallace, Vian, OK, 54; 8353, Minnie E, W, 44; John K, S, 11
25991 THORNTON, Wallace, Jr, Vian, OK, 26
29590 THORNTON, Walter, Vian, OK, 22
19735 THORNTON, William II, Wauhillau, OK, 28
  561 THORNTON, William I, Southwest City, MO, 59; 559, Amanda M, W, 57
11647 THRASHER, Lillie E, Childers, OK, 29; Ella, D, ¼

[THREEKILLER, Jennie. See #23238] *(Note: entry separate from other family groups)*

[THREEKILLER, Joseph. See #6594] *(Note: entry separate from other family groups)*

 6596 THREEKILLER, Tom, Christie, OK, 35
11276 THROWER, Charles, Bunch, OK, 56; Nancy, D, 9
13123 THROWER, Diane, Bunch, OK, 11;   By Jennie Bunch, Gdn.
12545 THURMAN, Ada, Foyil, OK, 29; Elizabeth M, D, 5; William E, S, 3; Samia, S, 1
 5013 THURMAN, Mary E, Westville, OK, 43; Lillie, D, 14; Salina, D, 13; Finis, S, 6
28376 TIBBS, Ida T, Kansas, OK, 24; George R, S, 3; Effie A, D, 1
 4512 TIC-KAH-NEE-SKEE, Anderson, Baron, OK, 54; 4513, Rachel, W, 50; 26715, Nancy, D, 19; Robert E, S, 16; Lena, D, 14; Elmira, D, 9
 5237 TIC-KAH-NEE-SKEE, Jefferson, Stilwell, OK, 62; John, S, 16; Joe, S, 14; Katie, D, 11; Ollie, S, 7; Claude, S, 4; Maude, D, 4; Noah, S, 2
15971 TIDMORE, Emma, Maple, OK, 27; Loy H, S, 8; Laura May, D, 6; Andrew, S, 4; Ruby Lee, D, 3
 7730 TIEASKIE, George, Baron, OK, 44; 3925, Elizabeth, W, 52; Annie, D, 17; Elias, S, 15

[TIE-SKY, Du-del-da-nah. See #15962] *(Note: entry separate from other family groups)*

 6519 TIGER, Eugene, Ketchum, OK, 25

[TIGER, George. See #10084]
[TIGER, Mary. See #10084]   *(Note: entries separate from other family groups)*
[TIGER, Lillie. See #10084]

10647 TIGER, John, Spavinaw, OK, 28; 10638, Emma, W, 29; Olie, S, 5; Jinnie, D, 1
 5908 TIGER, Rachel, Maysville, AR, 68
 8792 TIGER, Rebecca R, Vinita, OK, 3;   By Mollie E. Tiger, Gdn.
13402 TIGER, Thomas T, Kansas City, MO, 2911 Wabash Ave. 27
  913 TILDEN, Daniel, Locust Grove, OK, 30
 1934 TILDEN, Tyler, Locust Grove, OK, 34; 3170, Eliza, W, 26; Tarnie, D, 3; John H, S, 1/12
 2460 TIMBERLAKE, Jennie W, Vinita, OK, 49

CHEROKEE DESCENDANTS RESIDING WEST OF MISSISSIPPI RIVER.
VOLUME III (N – Z)

Key: Guion Miller Application Number; Name; Address, Relation (to Head); Age in 1906

16102 TIMBERLAKE, John A, Muskogee, 318 North K St, OK, 48; Florence N, D, 11; John Dick, S, 1
15603 TIMBERLAKE, William R, Muskogee, 606 South C. St. OK, 37; Cuscia A, D, 1
24228 TIMMONS, Elizabeth, Claremore, OK, 28; Viola, D, 7; Dot, D, 6
38770 TIMPSON, John, Ft. Gibson, OK, 41; Maud, D, 12; John, S, 9
 3820 TIMPSON, Katie, Estella, OK, 12;   By Eliza Buzzard, Gdn.
 4149 TIMPSON, Nancy, Vinita, OK, 19
 3819 TIMPSON, Samuel, Estella, OK, 21

[TIMSON, Agnes. See #29484]   *(Note: entry separate from other family groups)*

24998 TINCHER, Lulia, Gideon, OK, 20
 8634 TINCUP, Henry, Pryor Creek, OK, 24; Jesse Lee, S, 4; Sidney, S, 1
 8643 TINCUP, James, Pryor Creek, OK, 59; Edmon, S, 16; Austin, S, 16; 32981, Florence, D, 20
 1843 Randolph, Joel, Pryor Creek, OK, GS, 15
30852 TINCUP, James Y, Pryor Creek, OK, 21
31318 TINCUP, William W, Pryor Creek, OK, 29; Ethel May, D, 7; Joseph E, S, 6; Jesse W, S, 4; Gracie M, D, 2; Cyrus R, S, ¼
29242 TINDALL, Lucy, Tahlequah, OK, 25; Wagon, Fred, S, 5; Tindall, Arnom T, S, 2
33396 TINDELL, Sarah, Parkhill, OK, 27
12224 TINDLE, Annie, Stilwell, OK, 34; Henry C, S, 15; Alexander, S, 13; Jensie, D, 10; Jeff, S, 5; Nancy Ellen, D, 3
27410 TINER, William J, Hulbert, OK, 25; William C, S, 5; Eva M, D, 2
25394 TINNEY, Ludia, Warner, OK, 25; Benge, Tuglee, D, 8; Tinney, Laura M, D, 5; Nathan F, S, 2
23982 TINNIN, Gonia L, Benton, AR, 24; Lucile Brown, D, 2
27785 TINNIN, Lola, Claremore, OK, 23
22859 TIPTON, Albert M, Tahlequah, OK, 22
22855 TIPTON, Cora A, Tahlequah, OK, 18
22854 TIPTON, Eugene E, Tahlequah, OK, 38; John H, S, 16; Minerva J, D, 14; Myrtle, D, 11; Laura, D, 10; Samuel, S, 7; Jesse, S, 3
22857 TIPTON, George L, Tahlequah, OK, 24
22856 TIPTON, John L, Tahlequah, OK, 30; Cora A, D, 8; Lonie, D, 4; Andrew, S, 1
  206 TIPTON, Fannie or Frankie, Leach, OK, 57

[TIPTON, Rufus. See #23479]   *(Note: entry separate from other family groups)*

22858 TIPTON, William L, Tahlequah, OK, 36; Robert W, S, 16; Fannie, D, 14; William, S, 12; Oscar, S, 10; Frank, S, 8; Annie, D, 6
 5072 TIPPATT, Dora, Big Cabin, OK, 19
40551 TITSWORTH, Nannie, Warner, OK, 25; Reeves S, S, 4; Mary E, D, 3
 4062 TITTLE, Alice, Ft. Gibson, OK, 25
10701 TITTLE, Lizzie, Gritts, OK, 34; Goldie M, D, 17; Clyde L, S, 14; Omer A, S, 12; Bessie, D, 9; Lelia, D, 6; Willie V, S, 4; Thelma, D, 2

CHEROKEE DESCENDANTS RESIDING WEST OF MISSISSIPPI RIVER.
VOLUME III   (N – Z)

Key: Guion Miller Application Number; Name; Address, Relation (to Head); Age in 1906

[TJADEN, Laura. See #3220]   *(Note: entry separate from other family groups)*

[TOBACCO, Aggie White. See #17182]
   (Note: entry separate from other family groups)

24367 TODD, Beatrix R, Chelsea, OK, 25; Waldimer, S, 1
11658 TOLAN, Rachel, Braggs, OK, 57; 11659, Wilson, Watt, S, 16
12506 TOLBERT, Annie, Claremore, OK, 31; Roscoe, S, 11; Otto, S, 8; Jennie, D, 6; Hazel A, D, 2; Fay Leona, D, 1
24275 TONEY, Calvin, Porum, OK, 24; 17249, Leona D, W, 20
5774 TONEY, Eli, Rose, OK, 35
17550 TONEY, George, Campbell, OK, 9;   By Ida Bryan, Gdn.
17551 TONEY, Jennie, Campbell, OK, 9;   By Ida Bryan, Gdn.
17512 TONEY, John, Campbell, OK, 16
12918 TONEY, John, Porum, OK, 52; Mary, D, 16; George, S, 14; Jesse, S, 12; Famous, S, 8; Lela, D, 3
1722 TONEY, Lee, Webbers Falls, OK, 25; 26506, Malinda, W, 28; Annie, D, 2; Lucy, D, 1/3
12917 TONEY, Levi, Porum, OK, 46; 12579, Susie, W, 41; Cicero, S, 19; Betty, D, 14; Kate, D, 11; Sallie, D, 11
3940 TONEY, Mary, Red Rock, NM, 52; Maud Elsie, D, 17
14665 TONEY, Thomas, Webbers Falls OK, 22
27379 TONEY, William Toliver, Red Rock, NM, 33; Lloyd T, S, 11; Gladys V, D, 9; Leona M, D, 6; Delbert W, S, 4; Ellis R, S, 2

[TOOLATE, Oolaweut. See #9903]
[TOOLATE, Davis. See #9903]
[TOOLATE, Buck. See #9903]
[TOOLATE, Nelson. See #9903]
   (Note: entries separate from other family groups)

[TOOLATE, Ally, See #9905]   *(Note: entry separate from other family groups)*

[TOOLATE, Worcester. See #17091]   *(Note: entry separate from other family groups)*

4077 TOOMBS, Lizzie, Muskogee, OK, 631 Market St, 28; Williams, Blanche, D, 9; Robert, S, 7; Clara, D, 5
29109 TOON, Eliza, Mineral Wells, TX, 29; Troy, S, 5
202 TOOTLE, Rachel, Marble City, OK, 51; Harry, S, 16; Charley, S, 10
5917 TORBETT, Walter S, Vinita, OK, 25
5916 TORBETT, William G, Vinita, OK, 28
2899 TOVEY, Anna M, Hudson, OK, 46; Frank L, S, 17; Hoolie B, S, 15; Novel J, S, 9; Ruby D, D, 9; 31650, Anna L, D, 20
32438 TOVEY, Thomas W, Welch, OK, R.F.D. #1, 25; Mamie L, D, 3
42611 TOWER, Isaac, Foyil, OK, 20
15590 TOWERS, Clem R, Longmont, CO, 22

CHEROKEE DESCENDANTS RESIDING WEST OF MISSISSIPPI RIVER.
VOLUME III (N – Z)

Key: Guion Miller Application Number; Name; Address, Relation (to Head); Age in 1906

16726 TOWERS, Maud L, Pryor Creek, OK, 17; James E, Bro, 12; By John Z. Hogan, Gdn.
13558 TOWIE, Jane, Tahlequah, OK, 26
12676 TOWIE, Jeff, Tahlequah, OK, 41; 11971, Pollie, W, 59
12674 TOWIE, Lincoln, Tahlequah, OK, 43; 8144, Martha, W, 37; Jessie, D, 12; Mariah, D, 9; Davidson, S, 1
 4442 TOWIE, Sally, Tahlequah, OK, 66

[TOWIE, Samuel. See #6036]   *(Note: entry separate from other family groups)*

12675 TOWIE, Wilson, Tahlequah, OK, 37
   52 TOWNSEND, Charlotte, Pryor Creek, OK, 53; Sears, Joel M, S, 18; Townsend, Charlotte, D, 10
11417 TOWNSEND, George, Proctor, OK, 35; 11416, Laura, W, 27; Adda, D, 10; Walter, S, 8; Jesse, S, 3; Tommie, S, 1
25950 TOWNSEND, Jennie, Choska, OK, 33
22754 TOWNSEND, Jesse, Lenapah, OK, 30
  990 TOWSER, Charles, Claremore, OK, 47; 1720, Sarah, D, 4; Walker, Susannah, D, 4
23555 TRAHERN, Jessie Mae Hall, Vinita, OK, 35 c/o J. Eugene Hall
22206 TRAINOR, John T, Muskogee, OK, 11;   By Nevermore Prentice, Gdn.
  741 TRAINOR, Leonard E, Chelsea, OK, 27; Clifford R, S, 8; Emmett H, S, 5; Lydia L, D, 2
 1838 TRAINOR, Nevermore, Muskogee, OK, 22
 2405 TRAINOR, Walter E, Amarillo, TX, 25
27476 TRAMMEL, Annie, Roland, OK, 44; 27473, Rossie I, D, 18; Earle Elmo, S, 17; Lizzie W, D, 14; Dennis W, S, 12; Elba T, S, 10; Teddy R, S, 6; Wendell V, S, 3; Corrie M, D, 1/12
26575 TRAPP, Mary S, Tahlequah, OK, 22; William R, S, 2

[TREAGUE, Myrtle. See #17684]   *(Note: entry separate from other family groups)*

 4298 TREASURE, Alex, Locust Grove, OK, 27
10652 TREASURE, Clem, Choteau, OK, 23
 4299 TREASURE, Cornelius, Locust Grove, OK, 31
 4931 TREASURE, Nancy, Locust Grove, OK, 18
24426 TRENARY, Mary, Big Cabin, OK, 21
24306 TREASURER, Rosa, Choteau, OK, 15
10345 TRENT, Jefferson, Pawhuska, OK, 20
37566 TRENT, Martin E, Amarillo, TX, 24
 3148 TRENT, Mollie K, Tahlequah, OK, 47; Thomas B, S, 19
25454 TRENT, Rich. O, Amarillo, TX, 26
25929 TRENTHAM, Sarah Jane, Uniontown, AR, 18
 4213 TREPPARD, James R, Ft. Gibson, OK, 32; James R, Jr, S, 1
 6041 TRICKEY, Mary, Chelsea, OK, 28

CHEROKEE DESCENDANTS RESIDING WEST OF MISSISSIPPI RIVER.
VOLUME III (N – Z)

Key: Guion Miller Application Number; Name; Address, Relation (to Head); Age in 1906

3278 TRIMBLE, Elizabeth, Muskogee, OK, 37
33397 TRIPLET, Daniel, Tahlequah, OK, 23
33390 TRIPLET, Everett, Tahlequah, OK, 21; 21679, Ella, W, 17
33398 TRIPLET, Ollie, Tahlequah, OK, 28
5649 TRIPLETT, Edward D, Collinsville, OK, 34; Lucy E, D, 11; Mary P, D, 10
15085 TRIPLETT, Mary Elizabeth, Tahlequah, OK, 33
24494 TRIPLETT, Mintie B, Centralia, OK, 27
6043 TRIPLETT, William, Tahlequah, OK, 60; Charlotte, W, 50; William, Jr, S, 17; Cobb, S, 13; Susie, D, 10
2702 TRITTHART, Minerva, Wimer, OK, 28; Henry, S, 7; James, S, 5; Robert Roy, S, 3; George W, S, 1/3
9404 TROGLIN, Louisa, Claremore, OK, 33; Rider, Emily, D, 15; Caroline, D, 13; Stand W, S, 3
10949 TROGLIN, Louisa, Claremore, OK, 23; Wesley T, S, 6; Thomas J, S, 3
16415 TROGLIN, Louisa, Claremore, OK, 32; James R, S, 1
27809 TROTH, Susan E, Canon City, CO, 31; Hart, Maggie I, D, 16; Troth, Mary M, D, 12; Buena V, D, 9; Vera L, D, 7; Viola E, D, 4; Mabel E, D, 2
16495 TROTT, Clarence E, Porum, OK, 13; By William E. Titsworth, Gdn.
27970 TROTT, Dot Fay, Vinita, OK, 22
30535 TROTT, Eugene H, Vinita, OK, 33
11798 TROTT, Harden H, Vinita, OK, 18; Belle, Sis, 16; By W. L. Trott, Gdn.
1858 TROTT, James C, Vinita, OK, 67; 4332, Madora, W, 55
31092 TROTT, William H, Vinita, OK, 28; Henry M, S, 3
8618 TROTT, William L, Vinita, OK, 62
31140 TROTTER, Louella, Hanson, OK, 26; Bessie L, D, 6; Fannie E, D, 2
24547 TROTTER, Minnie Bell, White Oak, OK, 29; Lula Bell, D, 11; Harden H, S, 10; Sarah May, D, 6
510 TROTTINGWOLF, Lincoln, Bartlesville, OK, 40; 508, Susan, W, 33; Nelson, S, 12; Sequoyah, S, 10; Clarence, S, 7; Nelly, D, 4
2974 TROUT, Andrew M, Spavinaw, OK, 51; Ethel, D, 14; Newton, S, 13; Wiley B, S, 6; Thomas, S, 4
3043 TROUT, George W, Big Cabin, OK, 59; 24622, Martha, W, 51; Henry W, S, 20; Isaac, S, 18; Georgianna, D, 17; Creed Balex, S, 15
25194 TROUT, James, Spavinaw, OK, 26
23032 TROUT, James M, Big Cabin, OK, 23
23101 TROUT, Logan, Big Cabin, OK, 30; George W, S, 10; Buford L, S, 9; Edith M, D, 5; Thomas L, S, 3
27849 TROUT, Samuel, Big Cabin, OK, 29; 5579, Cornelia, W, 27; Velera V, D, 7; Mary I, D, 5; Jessie V, D, 2
25195 TROUT, William, Spavinaw, OK, 23
11910 TRUEMAN, Mary F, Cherokee City, AR, 59; Samuel O, S, 14; Benjamin O, S, 15
24524 TRUSLER, Elizabeth, Narcissa, OK, 18
6914 TSU-NOO-BEH-HUH-SKEE, Sally, Tahlequah, OK, 61
33760 TUBBS, Ella, Chilocco, OK, 25

CHEROKEE DESCENDANTS RESIDING WEST OF MISSISSIPPI RIVER.
VOLUME III (N – Z)

Key: Guion Miller Application Number; Name; Address, Relation (to Head); Age in 1906

33758 TUBBS, Texie, Leesville, LA, 22
33757 TUBBS, Tobitha[sic] A, Leesville, LA, 47; Laura, D, 16
3995 TUCK, Ellen, Vinita, OK, 18
22546 TUCKER, Adolphus L, Stilwell, OK, 26; 22574, Sarah C, W, 22; Edith M, D, 2
3696 TUCKER, Betsy, Moodys, OK, 34
21090 TUCKER, Charley, Melvin, OK, 50; 21153, Betsey, W, 56; Thompson, S, 15; Coon, S, 12; Keller, Willie W, S of W, 18
4671 TUCKER, Daniel, Catale, OK, 46
9415 TUCKER, David, Choteau, OK, 33; 9416, Susie, W, 48; George, S, 12
26156 TUCKER, Dora, Stilwell, OK, 20
43430 TUCKER, Eliza, Peggs, OK, 60; Lucinda, D, 19
11815 TUCKER, Gus, Oologah, OK, 26
11520 TUCKER, Isaac, Moodys, OK, 34; 12633, Mary, W, 23; Cora, D, 12; Sallie, D, 1
3469 TUCKER, Jennie, Moodys, OK, 58
13171 TUCKER, Jennie, Melvin, OK, 42; Annie, D, 17
22852 TUCKER, John, Hulbert, OK, 33
28530 TUCKER, Johnson, Melvin, OK, 25
22853 TUCKER, Levi, Hulbert, OK, 36; 5538, Annie, W, 30; William, S, 11; Ollie, D, 10; Susie, D, 6; Sallie, D, 4; Eliza, D, 2

[TUCKER, Lizzie. See #9257]   *(Note: entry separate from other family groups)*

15976 TUCKER, Maggie, Westville, OK, 24
1540 TUCKER, Marcus L, Stilwell, OK, 52; 22547, Liver C, S, 18; Felix A, S, 14; Luther C, S, 9; Ethel G, D, 6
24873 TUCKER, Martha, Afton, OK, 32; Cornelia B, D, 15; Edith M, D, 12; Inez L, D, 10; Ozbourn, S, 1; Beulah F, D, 7

[TUCKER, Mary. See #6770]   *(Note: entry separate from other family groups)*

22544 TUCKER, Newel F, Stilwell, OK, 22
6069 TUCKER, Sallie, Melvin, OK, 50; 13172, Cockrum, Lizzie, D, 18; Ned, S, 16

[TUCKER, Thomas. See #17963]   *(Note: entry separate from other family groups)*

[TUCKER, Rachel. See #8136]   *(Note: entry separate from other family groups)*

795 TUCKER, Thomas F, Ramona, OK, 21
792 TUCKER, Walter W, Ramona, OK, 19; Nellie, Sis, 17; Hilliard M, Bro, 15; Viola, Sis, 13; Esther, Sis, 11;   By Jacob D. Newport, Gdn.
30034 TUCKER, William, Spavinaw, OK, 40; George C, S, 6; Lillie M, D, 4; Stella V, D, 2
14063 TUCKER, Zeke, Locust Grove, OK, 67; 9257, Lizzie, W, 53; Lucinda, D, 17; Kingfisher, James, AdS, 12
14212 TUGGLE, Akey, Sallisaw, OK, 18

CHEROKEE DESCENDANTS RESIDING WEST OF MISSISSIPPI RIVER.
VOLUME III (N – Z)
Key: Guion Miller Application Number; Name; Address, Relation (to Head); Age in 1906

13460 TULLY, John, Porum, OK, 47; Morris C, S, 11; Bettie M, D, 7; George E, S, 3
 4872 TUMBLEBUG, Gobat, Southwest City, MO, 49; 4871, Ca-ho-ker, W, 63
25470 TUNNELL, Cora, Oologah, OK, 26
12617 TURN, Henry, Baron, OK, 34; 12618, Sallie, W, 29; Alec, S, 4; Jennie Ann, D, 1
12616 TURN, William, Baron, OK, 30; 12619, Lizzie, W, 23; Downing, Charles, S of W, 6; Pumpkin, S of W, 1
23036 TURNER, Addie, Dodge, OK, 30; Walker, Bessie M, D, 10

[TURNER, Annie. See #10380]   *(Note: entry separate from other family groups)*

 5125 TURNER, Annie, Welling, OK, 45; Anna L, D, 16
14144 TURNER, Louisa, Hulbert, OK, 17
12533 TURNER, Marion Lowrey, Muskogee, OK, 1; By Susie Lowrey, Gdn.
13401 TURNER, Nancy, Peggs, OK, 12; John, Bro, 15;   By Lewis Pann, Gdn.
11461 TURNER, Susan, Tahlequah, OK, 16;   By J. T. Parks, Gdn.
 5987 TURNER, William, Maysville, AR, 34; 5943, Nellie, W, 49; Sam, S, 19; Daniel, S, 12; Iva, D, 11; Isaac, S, 7
 7510 TURNHAM, Jennie, Muldrow, OK, 41; Ira K, S, 18; Della G, D, 16; Ira Geneva, D, 9; Harrold H, S, 7; Clinton, S, 2
16642 TURNOVER, Margarette, Texanna, OK, 46; Van, Fred, S, 19; Nancy, D, 16; Simms, Hannah, D, 13; Hilderbrand, Nettie, D, 11
 5662 TURTLE, Arch, Oaks, OK, 57; 9163, Fanny, W, 49; Adam, S, 19; William, S, 16; Emmie, D, 14; Joe, S, 12
43211 TURTLE, Charley, Oaks, OK, 23; 28228, Lyndia, W, 18; Florence, D, 1
 5811 TURTLE, Peggy, Kansas, OK, 55
17222 TURTLE, William, Kansas, OK, 36; 14257, Sallie, W, 35; Charley, S, 13; Susan, D, 11; Callie, D, 9; Kate, D, 5; Wesley, S, 3; Young, S, 1

[TWEEDLE, Florence. See #16749] *(Note: entry separate from other family groups)*

11467 TWEEDLE, Francis Susan, Davis, OK, 12;   By William Tweedle, Gdn.
24862 TWIST, Albert W, Dutch Mills, AR, 29
17087 TWIST, Ella, Locust Grove, OK, 25; Maggie, D, 3; Sallie, D, 1
14258 TWIST, George, Vian, OK, 24
25001 TWIST, Isaac, Dutch Mills, AR, 28
 6241 TWIST, Jennie, Dutch Mills, AR, 28
 1418 TWIST, John, Dutch Mills, AR, 71
28698 TWIST, John W, Lowery, OK, 45; Felix A, S, 14; Ethel T, D, 12; Gracie B, D, 9; Katie E, D, 7; Darius G, S, 3; Dollie M, D, 1
16989 TWIST, Levi, Oaks, OK, 29
23541 TWIST, Noah A, Hanson, OK, 47; Jesse C, S, 18; Robert E. L, S, 16; Noah F, S, 14; 23544, Doveler, D, 12
 1391 TWIST, Tah-you-ne-See, Dutch Mills, AR, 73; 4598, Sarah C, W, 70
25280 TWIST, Teecie, Gritts, OK, 14; By Wilson Girty, Gdn.

CHEROKEE DESCENDANTS RESIDING WEST OF MISSISSIPPI RIVER.
VOLUME III   (N – Z)

Key: Guion Miller Application Number; Name; Address, Relation (to Head); Age in 1906

27850 TWIST, William G, Tulsa, OK, 46; Albert T, S, 10; Jessie L, D, 8; Edward C, S, 6; Kuroki, S, 3
27888 TWIST, William J, Tulsa, OK, 35
10002 TWITTY, Ludia, Foyil, OK, 54
23786 TYLER, Clara E, Bluejacket, OK, R.F.D. #1, 24
 2153 TYLER, Ruth Ann, Bluejacket, OK, 45; William O, S, 20; Charles Nelson, S, 17; Fred E, S, 12; George Howard, S, 9; Essie Mildred, D, 5
27753 TYNER, Charles, Campbell, OK, 25
40290 TYNER, Edward B, Miles, OK, 39; Ida, D, 14; Lee, S, 12; Conrad, S, 7; Ruby, D, 4
16761 TYNER, George, Ochelata, OK, 31
26322 TYNER, George M, Miles, OK, 23
26320 TYNER, James, Miles, OK, 21
 3918 TYNER, James B, Muskogee, OK, 52; Luther, S, 9; Myrtle, D, 3
40289 TYNER, Jefferson K, Miles, OK, 49; 3719, Nancy, W, 49; 26321, Jananna, D, 20; Frank, S, 18; Alice, D, 14; Carrie, D, 13; Luella, D, 10
27752 TYNER, Joe F, Campbell, OK, 35; 27755, Canzada, W, 31; Cora May, D, 3; William Walker, S, ½
21836 TYNER, John W, Campbell, OK, 59; John W, Jr, S, 17; Ella E, D, 12
16817 TYNER, Laura A, Ochelata, OK, 22
16818 TYNER, Leonard P, Ochelata, OK, 27
27759 TYNER, Lewis, Campbell, OK, 41; 27757, Martha, W, 40; Robert Lee, S, 18; Sarah Delilah, D, 16; Mattie Emarline, D, 8; John Lewis, S, 8; Ben Lafayette, S, 6; Clara Bell, D, 4; Myrtle Irene, D, 2
16760 TYNER, Lula M, Ochelata, OK, 18
26319 TYNER, Mary B, Miles, OK 25
29075 TYNER Maud, Prairie view, AR, 25
16875 TYNER, Robert J, Webbers Falls, OK, 54; 13317, Willie Ann, D, 6; Oscar, S, 4; Zeno, D, 1; Lydia, W, 36; Lillie M, D, 14; Mary e, D, 13; Hugh, S, 9
16759 TYNER, Weaver, Ochelata, OK, 24

[TYNER, Willie Ann. See #26701]   *(Note: entry separate from other family groups)*

 3238 TYNON, Ava, Cleora, OK, 47; 26145, John, S, 20; Thomas C, S, 17; Rufus, S, 15; Joe, S, 12; Ora, S, 9; Lillie B, D, 4
26146 TYNON, William, Cleora, OK, 26; Willa F, D, 5/12

 5213 UHIS, Ruby, Pryor Creek, OK, 7;   By Clem Vann, Gdn.

[UMMERTESKEE. See #13082]   *(Note: entry separate from other family groups)*

25301 UNDERWOOD, Luster, Wauhillau, OK, 25
35348 UNDERWOOD, Margaret, Grove, OK, 22; 25757, Ora Almer, D, 3; Cherokee May, D, 1/12; Job Underwood, Father & Gdn. of two children.
 6610 UNDERWOOD, Martha, Wauhillau, OK, 52

CHEROKEE DESCENDANTS RESIDING WEST OF MISSISSIPPI RIVER.
VOLUME III   (N – Z)

Key: Guion Miller Application Number; Name; Address, Relation (to Head); Age in 1906

21142 USSERY, Sam, Marble City, OK, 28
14823 USSERY, Sam, Sallisaw, OK, 23; 3640, Margaret A. E, W, 33; Claudie, S, 17; Nellie Elsie, D, 1
22023 USSRY, Ezekiel, Vian, OK, 26
28332 UTO, Maggie, Chaffee, OK, 25; Pearlie B, D, 3; Claud, S, 1

30379 VAN ANTWERP, Avis, Ft. Gibson, OK, 36
2470 VANCUREN, Carrie, Chelsea, OK, 27;   [For children. See #17585]
24083 VANDERGRIFF, Alice M, Grove, OK, 22; Tokio, S, 2
1038 VANDEVER, Martha Jane, Centralia, OK, 37
25725 VAN HOEFEN, Minnie M, St. Louis, MO, 22; Harry S, S, 1
5302 VANN, Aggie, Stilwell, OK, 56; 43150,   Nancy, D, 19
28577 VAN MATRE, Alice, Red Bluff, CA, 39; Warren J, S, 19; Vernon V, S, 17; Vivian H, D, 12; Wilda, D, 10
9389 VANN, Alice, Evansville, AR, 59; Scott, S, 16
11859 VANN, Alice, Neodesha, OK, 47
13983 VANN, Alice C, Pryor Creek, OK, 20
13658 VANN, Allen, Bunch, OK, 52
8264 VANN, Amos, Muldrow, OK, 32
41280 VANN, Andrew, Bunch, OK, 27

[VANN, Arcene. See #8098]   *(Note: entry separate from other family groups)*

16553 VANN, Arch, Porum, OK, 52; Ada, D, 6
42184 VANN, Bertha A. L, Pryor Creek, OK, 11; Oscar T, Bro, 9; Jessie J, Sis, 4; Lula M, Sis, 8; Ivy J, Sis, 6; James T, Bro, 2;   By Cornelia F. Vann, Gdn.
30827 VANN, Betsy, Evansville, AR, 47; Sawney, Robert, S, 17; Roy, S, 14; Vann, Doary, D, 11
30482 VANN, Carrie M, Estella, OK, 20
4643 VANN, Charles, Whitmire, OK, 31; 8427,Carolina, W, 33
9157 VANN, Charles E, Webbers Falls, OK, 43; 22701, Ada, W, 34; John S, S, 14
5215 VANN, Clement I, Pryor Creek, OK, 36; 5214, Emma, W, 30; Carrie B, D, 11; Martha E, D, 8; Clement M, D, 6; Alberta Sarah, D, 3; Joseph C, S, 1
17246 VANN, Cornelius, Uniontown, AR, 23; 28520, Ada, W, 25; Nannie Ruth, D, 4; Rachel, D, 1

[VANN, Cornelius. See #1288]   *(Note: entries separate*
[VANN, Ezekiel. See #1288]   *from other family groups)*

[VANN, Daisy. See #24361]   *(Note: entry separate from other family groups)*

2183 VANN, David, Ft. Gibson, OK, 73
2287 VANN, David W, Fairland, OK, 49; Martha Opal, D, 9; Fay, D, 11; Floy E, D, 13; Fannie M, D, 15; John H, S, 16; Pearl R, D, 18
13982 VANN, David W, Pryor Creek, OK, 23; 13550, Mary B, W, 20

CHEROKEE DESCENDANTS RESIDING WEST OF MISSISSIPPI RIVER.
VOLUME III (N – Z)

Key: Guion Miller Application Number; Name; Address, Relation (to Head); Age in 1906

13758 VANN, Dirt Thrower, Bunch, OK, 56; 13397, Mary, W, 54; Patsie, D, 16
11720 VANN, Emma, Pryor Creek, OK, 16; By Jess H. Vann, Gdn.
7923 VANN, Ephriam M, Brushy, OK, 36; Benge, Emmett, AdS, 11
408 VANN, Fisher, Locust Grove, OK, 40?
28369 VANN, Frank J, Webbers Falls, OK, 23

[VANN, Fred, See #16642]   *(Note: entries separate*
[VANN, Nancy. See #16642]   *from other family groups)*

33150 VANN, French, Peggs, OK, 26; 17006, Nannie, W, 31; Joe, S, 5; Arch, S, 4; Jack, S, 1
2722 VANN, George, Melvin, OK, 54; 2829, Sallie, W, 46; Palone, Nancy, D of W, 14; Vann, Walter, S, 7
5935 VANN, George, Vian, OK, 32; 9119, Ellen, W, 31; Rachel, D, 8; George Byers, S, 4
5303 VANN, Heavy, Stilwell, OK, 51; 13208, Nancy, W, 64
8783 VANN, Henry C, Maple, OK, 33; 24910, Susie, W, 30; Harris, Joseph A, S of W, 12
13706 VANN, Herman J, Porum, OK, 54; 13705, Elizabeth, W, 50; Nora, D, 16; Daisy, D, 10
42183 VANN, Hickory, Bunch, OK, 27; Jess, S, 2; Lizzie, D, 1
5911 VANN, Hunter, Marble City, OK, 32; 5957, Linda, W, 32; Frank, S, 9; Elias, S, 3; Martha, D, 1; McCoy, Charley, S of W, 12

[VANN, Ida. See #4400]   *(Note: entry separate from other family groups)*

5668 VANN, Ida, Ft. Gibson, OK, 36
16695 VANN, James, Vian, OK, 25
12384 VANN, James W, Porum, OK, 34; 12389, Florence, W, 29; Mary E, D, 8; Charlotte A, D, 5; Lester D, S, 4
6236 VANN, Jess, Bunch, OK, 54; 6234, Liza, W, 55; Josiah, W, 18
6528 VANN, Jesse, Locust Grove, OK, 24
7413 VANN, Jesse, Stilwell, OK, 22
5202 VANN, Jesse H, Pryor Creek, OK, 36
42096 VANN, Jim, Bunch, OK, 22
24640 VANN, Joanna, Catale, OK, 26
523 VANN, Joe, Locust Grove, OK, 56; 2043, Nancy, W, 50; Sara, D, 15; William, S, 13
4444 VANN, Joe, Tiawah, OK, 47
34242 VAN[sic], Joe B, Webbers Falls, OK, 26
3858 VANN, John C, Bartlesville, OK, 23
4811 VANN, John E, Fairland, OK, 57; 4812, Louisa, W, 57?; Florence, D, 19; Walter, S, 17; Minnie, D, 15; James C, S, 13; Nancy, D, 11; Manila, D, 8
10703 VANN, John F, Ft. Gibson, OK, 31

CHEROKEE DESCENDANTS RESIDING WEST OF MISSISSIPPI RIVER.
VOLUME III (N – Z)

Key: Guion Miller Application Number; Name; Address, Relation (to Head); Age in 1906

1903 VANN, John R, Uniontown, AR, 40; 7001, Mary, W, 27; Julia, Niece, 16; James W, Neph, 10; Flora, D, 10; John Franklin, S, 2
25196 VANN, Johnson, Peggs, OK, 23
1373 VANN, Joseph, Tahlequah, OK, 57; 1375, Cynthia, W, 56; Gid, S, 13
11517 VANN, Joseph C, Freeman, OK, 47
31718 VANN, Joseph J, Porum, OK, 25
11716 VANN, Katy, Leach, OK, 32; Oo-kil-lie, S, 7; George, S, 5
13497 VANN, Keener, Cookson, OK, 31; 13495, Sallie, W, 45

[VANN, Lee. See #9264]   *(Note: entry separate from other family groups)*

13757 VANN, Lila, Uniontown, AR, 19; Bird, John, S, 2

[VANN, Lillie. See #13681]   *(Note: entry separate from other family groups)*

13268 VANN, Lizzie D, Tiahwah, OK, 24 [Died 9-1906]; Clem N, S, 7; Vann, Jessie E, D, 5; William W, S, 2;   By Joe Vann, Gdn.
1281 VANN, Lucullas, Locust Grove, OK, 32;   By William L. Mayes, Gdn.
42182 VANN, Mack, Bunch, OK, 32
9481 VANN, Maggie, Vian, OK, 49
6940 VANN, Mandy, Vian, OK, 56
1708 VANN, Martha, Brushy, OK, 73
14064 VANN, Mary, Locust Grove, OK, 76
33207 VANN, Nannie, Webbers Falls, OK, 28; Gibson, Clausine, S, 4
3936 VANN, Napoleon B, Bartlesville, OK, 21
4185 VANN, Nellie, Locust Grove, OK, 60
16883 VANN, Nelson, Whitmire, OK, 25
5331 VANN, Noname, Stilwell, OK, 47; White, S, 6; Billy, S, 3
23231 VANN, Rachel, Lenapah, OK, 40; Pennington, Malissa, D, 9; Rachel, Jr, D, 7
29682 VANN, Ralph J, Vinita, OK, 25
9261 VANN, Richard, Vian, OK, 38; 17012, Jennie, W, 23
8756 VANN, Robert P, Webbers Falls, OK, 49; 8755, Ermina C, W, 46; Ned F, S, 17; Robert P, Jr, S, 14; Lizzie F, D, 12; Connie G, S, 6
5910 VANN, Samuel, Sallisaw, OK, 36
18428 VANN, Sarah, Whitmire, OK, 60
1280 VANN, Skelley, Locust Grove, OK, 48; 1282, Rachel, W, 56; 25197, Katie, D, 20; Lilah, D, 20; Dick, S, 17; Jess, S, 15
31719 VANN, Sophia, Porum, OK, 20
8805 VANN, Steve, Moodys, OK, 46; 1865, Sarah, W, 53; Tip, S, 48; Harris, S, 17; Thomas, S, 14; Betsy, D, 10; Jodie, D, 8
30171 VANN, Taylor, Vian, OK, 27; 9263, Kizzie, W, 41; Houseberg, Lydia, D of W, 17; Dora, D of W, 12; Jack, S of W, 9; Vann, Maggie, D, 3
4928 VANN, Thomas, Choteau, OK, 25; Thomas, Jr, S, ¼
16909 VANN, Thomas, Peggs, OK, 32; 6036, Jennie, W, 35; Chewie, William, S of W, 12; Towie, Samuel, S of W, 8; Vann, Ida, D, 4; Rosella, D, 2

CHEROKEE DESCENDANTS RESIDING WEST OF MISSISSIPPI RIVER.
VOLUME III   (N – Z)

Key: Guion Miller Application Number; Name; Address, Relation (to Head); Age in 1906

29869 VANN, Wade H, Porum, OK, 29
 2237 VANN, Webster M, Pryor Creek, OK, 61; 13548, William C, S, 18; 13549, Ermina, D, 17
 2182 VANN, William, Ft. Gibson, OK, 34
 7980 VANN, William, Sallisaw, OK, 28
31717 VANN, William H, Porum, OK, 23
27407 VANN, William W, Tulsa, OK, 23
19293 VANN, Youngwolf, Bunch, OK, 50
26122 VAUGHN, Abba, Echo, OK, 24; Lillian V, D, 1

[VAUGHN, Charles. See #2857]   *(Note: entry separate from other family groups)*

 3906 VAUGHN, John W, Plumerville, AR, 49; Emma, D, 19; Millie, D, 16; Elbert, S, 14; Daniel, S, 10; Ethel, S, 4
27712 VAUGHN, Nora, Hay Fork, CA, 19
39462 VAUGHN, Sarah L, Cove, OK, 28; Thelma Lucile, D, 2
11738 VAUGHN, William, Chatsworth, CA, 44
27246 VAUGHT, Junie, Webbers Falls, OK, 25
  160 VAUGHT, Lucinda, Webbers Falls, OK, 53; Joseph, S, 19; John, S, 14; Johanna, D, 10
19485 VICE, Lillie, Muskogee, OK, 24; Margueritte Thelma, D, 3
24350 VICKARY[sic], John, Collinsville, OK, 50; Nancy, D, 19; Tinsey, D, 17; Samuel, S, 15; Charley, S, 13; Susie, D, 11; Annie, D, 7; Andrew, S, 9; Donnie, S, 6
26549 VICKERY, Charles, Uniontown, AR, 28
26574 VICKERY, Cora, Uniontown, AR, 21
26572 VICKERY, Florence, Uniontown, AR, 22
 6244 VICKERY, Frank, Dutch Mills, AR, 49; 27067, Maggie, D, 20; 35019, Sophronia M, D, 15; Callie D, D, 13; Leona, D, 11; Odie B, D, 10
 8759 VICKERY, James N, Remy, OK, 56; 28348, Martha E, W, 27; Mary Ann, D, 14; Mattie Alice, D, 13; Charlotte M, D, 12; Charles, S, 10; William Penn, S, 7; Florine, D, 3; Grant L, S, 1
 4074 VICKERY, John, Uniontown, AR, 65; Richard, S, 18; Ruthie, D, 16
 8679 VICKERY, John W, Muskogee, OK, 32; Edgar Fay, S, 1
26570 VICKERY, Sarah, Uniontown, AR, 25
27261 VICKERY, William, Uniontown, AR, 26
13565 VICTORY, Henry, Collinsville, OK, 24
13564 VICTORY, Samuel, Collinsville, OK, 19; Charles, Bro, 17; Susan, Sis, 15; Andrew, Bro, 13; Anna A, Sis, 10; Donney, Sis, 9;   By John Victory, Gdn.
13567 VICTORY, Tensy, Collinsville, OK, 20
10670 VINCENT, Malderine E, Foyil, OK, 30; Clausine R, S, 3; Robert B, S, 2
18469 VINYARD, Frances E, Wauhillau, OK, 26; John, S, 9; Chelsea, S, 7; Gus, S, 4
 9717 VORE, Frank, Webbers Falls, OK, 53; Charlie Fowler, S, 16; Frank Hutton, S, 14; Mary E, D, 9
10199 VOWELL, Lena C, Porum, OK, 28; Howell Carlile, S, 2

CHEROKEE DESCENDANTS RESIDING WEST OF MISSISSIPPI RIVER.
VOLUME III (N – Z)

Key: Guion Miller Application Number; Name; Address, Relation (to Head); Age in 1906

[VOWELL, Eva C. See #13999]   *(Note: entry separate from other family groups)*

   20 WADE, Berenice[sic] M, Ft. Gibson, OK, 65
22518 WADE, James M, Muskogee, OK, 28; Raymond J, S, 5; Meigs, S, 2
25311 WAGNER, Flossie V, Needmore, OK, 17

[WAGON, Fred. See #29242]   *(Note: entry separate from other family groups)*

28128 WAGNON, James F, Westville, OK, 25; Lola M, D, 1/6
28129 WAGNON, Marshall J, Westville, OK, 33; 36557, Martha E, W, 24; Julian M, S, 5
 4707 WAGNON, Thomas F, Westville, OK, 56; 4712, Lucinda, W, 53; 24858, Maud, D, 19; Thomas J, S, 16; Ada, D, 13; Millard A, S, 11
14319 WAINE, Bill, Evansville, AR, 17
14318 WAINE, Ice, Evansville, AR, 19
33211 WAKEMAN, Vilenia K, Big Cabin, OK, 26; Esther P, D, 1
  100 WALDEN, Minnie, Pryor Creek, OK, 37; James, S, 20; Nora, D, 18; Thomas, S, 15
  167 WALDEN, Nancy, Childers, OK, 51; Melton, James, S, 19; Hartgraves, William, S, 16; Walden, Samuel, S, 11; Elzie E, D, 6
 6062 WALKABOUT, Henry, Tahlequah, OK, 23; John, S, 17
 4285 WALKABOUT, Mary, Tahlequah, OK, 23; Jennie, D, 1
24738 WALKER, Anna, Dodge, OK, 29; Beulah, D, 8; Claudina, D, 5; Sibble, D, 3; Forest, S, 1/12
17208 WALKER, Annie, Wauhillau, OK, 21

[WALKER, Bessie N. See 23036]   *(Note: entry separate from other family groups)*

 9164 WALKER, Betsy, Chance, OK, 54
22527 WALKER, Daniel H, Welch, OK, 35; John F, S, 14; Lucy L, D, 12; Eunice Ruth, D, 2
14191 WALKER, Dick, Locust Grove, OK, 22; 10424, Ka-yor-he, W, 26; Bettie, D, 1
  788 WALKER, Edith H, Ft. Gibson, OK, 50
26073 WALKER, Edmond, Braggs, OK, 29; 12581, Daisy M, W, 22
11871 WALKER, Edward A, Braggs, OK, 50; 11870, Kate, W, 46; John H, S, 16; Jennie, D, 12; Jack O, S, 11; Susie, D, 9
 1118 WALKER, Eliza, Welling, OK, 36
 2179 WALKER, Elizabeth, Ft. Gibson, OK, 81
34573 WALKER, Emlin, Hulbert, OK, 17
11813 WALKER, Evelyn, Oologah, OK, 23
 9232 WALKER, Frederick L, Tahlequah, OK, 30; 3801, India O, W, 25; Lillie E, D, 7; Inez J, D, 4; Cornelius C, S, 1
  363 WALKER, George W, Welch, OK, 76
 9666 WALKER, Henry, Leach, OK, 25
11999 WALKER, Henry, Welling, OK, 26

CHEROKEE DESCENDANTS RESIDING WEST OF MISSISSIPPI RIVER.
VOLUME III (N – Z)

Key: Guion Miller Application Number; Name; Address, Relation (to Head); Age in 1906

22526 WALKER, Henry, Welch, OK, 23; Hazel J, D, 3; Velma N, D, 2/3
29988 WALKER, Henry C, Ft. Gibson, OK, 22
25190 WALKER, Ida T, Welch, OK, 28; James L, S, 10; Goldia E, D, 8; John E, S, 4; Robert C, S, 2
31120 WALKER, Itaska, Coffeyville, KS, 19; By Shelly Keys, Gdn.
2180 WALKER, Jack, Ft. Gibson, OK, 59; 1656, Susan A, W, 60

[WALKER, Jack. See #17057]   *(Note: entry separate from other family groups)*

5730 WALKER, James, Oaks, OK, 64; 18621, Lizzie, D, 5
17527 WALKER, James, Vian, OK, 12;   By Lydia Walker, Gdn.
34845 WALKER, James F, Welch, OK, 30; Arminta L, D, 10; Arreta J, D, 8; Ettie E, D, Ray, S, 4; Ruby V, D, 1
15987 WALKER, James L, Dewey, OK, 41; 27933, Lillie A, W, 37; Lelia E, D, 18; Esther J, D, 16; Grover H, S, 14; Minerva C, D, 12; Josie V, D, 9; Lillian L, D, 3; Clover B, D, 1
3693 WALKER, Joe White, Locust Grove, OK, 25; 10216, Mollie, W, 26; Laura, D of W, 10
16752 WALKER, Katie, Estella, OK, 24
24977 WALKER, Lewis, Kinnison, OK, 24; Esther, D, 2
21095 WALKER, Lizzie, Edna, KS, 52; McDonald, Theodore, GS, 6
30363 WALKER, Lizzie, Copan, OK, 33; Harder, Williard H, S, 14; Walker, James, S, 9; Robert, S, 2
29223 WALKER, Lutitia, Texanna, OK, 19
6932 WALKER, Lydia, Vian, OK, 68
31792 WALKER, Mary, Uniontown, AR, 29
25871 WALKER, Mary E, Cove, OK, 17; Arthur J, S, 5/12
23037 WALKER, Mary S, Grove, OK, 36; Alma W, D, 16; Martha J, D, 15; James E, S, 7
1603 WALKER, Nannie E, Chloeta, OK, 34; Jennie M, D, 17; James T, S, 15; John A, S, 13; Leonard A, S, 11; William J, S, 9; Anna L, D, 6; Opal, D, 1
702 WALKER, Nellie, Kansas, OK, 69
471 WALKER, Ollie, Coffeyville, KS, 15; Nellie, Sis, 14; William T, Bro, 12; Jessie, Sis, 10; Ernest, Bro, 7;   By Geo. L. Walker, Gdn.
86 WALKER, Rachel, Locust Grove, OK, 76
7911 WALKER, Rosa L, Edna, KS, 22
5205 WALKER, Rose E, Peggs, OK, 17
12505 WALKER, Sissie, Vinita, OK, 6;   By James Horsefly, Gdn.

[WALKER, Susanna. See #1720]   *(Note: entry separate from other family groups)*

[WALKER, Susanna. See #10894]   *(Note: entry separate from other family groups)*

5211 WALKER, Susan B, Gans, OK, 25; Myrtle May, D, 6
16859 WALKER, Susie, Braggs, OK, 24; Tehee, Elmira, D, 7; Dora, D, 5

CHEROKEE DESCENDANTS RESIDING WEST OF MISSISSIPPI RIVER.
VOLUME III (N – Z)

Key: Guion Miller Application Number; Name; Address, Relation (to Head); Age in 1906

26097 WALKER, Timothy M, Ft. Gibson, OK, 26
23311 WALKER, Tulla, Kiefer, OK, 19; Mann, Bessie, D, 2
16558 WALKER, Watt, Locust Grove, OK, 21
12646 WALKER, William, Wauhillau, OK, 50; 12663, Mary, W, 45
7646 WALKER, William H, Tahlequah, OK, 40; 27942, Rachel, W, 23; Robert W, S, 17; Frank L, S, 15; John W, S, 12; Bluie G, D, ¼

[WALKER, Willard L. See #26127] *(Note: entry separate from other family groups)*

6721 WALKINGSTICK, Ben, Baron, OK, 26; 1921, Jane, W, 25; Frances, D, 4
12802 WALKINGSTICK, Ben, Baron, OK, 33; Lydia, D, 9
26132 WALKINGSTICK, Calvin, Baron, OK, 22
26131 WALKINGSTICK, Cecil, Baron, OK, 31
4048 WALKINGSTICK, Chas, Marble City, OK, 66; 4051, Betsey, W, 65 [Died 1-1907]; Ellis, Minnie, GD, 2
16345 WALKINGSTICK, Daniel, Proctor, OK, 26; 6915, Rosey, W, 19
6938 WALKINGSTICK, Edward, Baron, OK, 57

[WALKINGSTICK, Ezekiel. See #4911]
(Note: entry separate from other family groups)

15628 WALKINGSTICK, John R, Baron, OK, 19
15629 WALKINGSTICK, Henry, Baron, OK, 36; 2226, Betsy, W, 35; Charlotte, D, 13; Isaac, S, 3
8010 WALKINGSTICK, Huey M, Baron, OK, 27; Alice, D, 2/3
8639 WALKINGSTICK, James M, Stilwell, OK, 32; 8650, Ethel, W, 32; Irene, D, 4; Sallie, D, 2; May, D, 1/12; Whitmire, Maud, D of W, 13
9893 WALKINGSTICK, Jennie, Baron, OK, 16
9921 WALKINGSTICK, Jesse, Baron, OK, 16
5795 WALKINGSTICK, Leona, Tahlequah, OK, 33; Christina, D, 8
4805 WALKINGSTICK, Lewis D, Marble City, OK, 25
30438 WALKINGSTICK, Lucinda, Marble City, OK, 32
30439 WALKINGSTICK, Mack, Marble City, OK, 25
4509 WALKINGSTICK, Mary J, Marble City, OK, 63
3679 WALKINGSTICK, Nancy C, Stilwell, OK, 32; John C, S, 17; Ada J, D, 16; Dora C, D, 12; Mary T, D, 10; Thomas L, S, 8; Rosa A, D, 2; James W, S, 5; Mattie E, D, 3
7688 WALKINGSTICK, Simon, Tahlequah, OK, 38; 26925, Rebecca C, W, 23; Ada S, D, 11; Celeter, D, 9; Bruce, S, 7; Benjamin T, S, 1
4050 WALKINGSTICK, Steven, Marble City, OK, 31; 11018, Sallie, W, 24
7034 WALKINGSTICK, Susa[sic], Stilwell, OK, 95
5535 WALKINGSTICK, Susie E, Tahlequah, OK, 39; Nina M, D, 13; Bettie C, D, 10; Callie L, D, 8
21134 WALKLEY, George, Claremore, OK, 38; Mary A, D, 17; Ruby L, D, 12; William S, S, 10

CHEROKEE DESCENDANTS RESIDING WEST OF MISSISSIPPI RIVER.
VOLUME III (N – Z)

Key: Guion Miller Application Number; Name; Address, Relation (to Head); Age in 1906

26233 WALKLEY, Henry C, Tulsa, OK, 31
26396 WALL, John M, Ocean Park, CA, 22; Cyril L, D, 4; Eva Booth, D, 5/12
21055 WALL, Thomas, Byars, OK, 41; Hiram T, S, 14; Bessie L, D, 10; Robert E, S, 3; Eunice E, D, 1/12
27016 WALLACE, Emma, Collinsville, OK, 27; Floyd C, S, 7; Glen O, S, 4; Lucile, D, 2
25426 WALLACE, Grace, Tahlequah, OK, 22
25020 WALLACE, Jennie, Muskogee, OK, 18
1378 WALLACE, Julia A, Tahlequah, OK, 58; Julius M, S, 18; Alice E, D, 13
25424 WALLACE, Lula, Tahlequah, OK, 25
34729 WALLACE, Martin Dewitt, Tahlequah, OK, 29; 25422, Mollie J, W, 25
29990 WALLACE, Richard N, Pryor Creek, OK, 34; Clarence A, S, 10; Bertha A, D, 8; Jeney[sic] W, D, 7; Florence E, D, 5; Austin H, S, 3; Myrtle B, D, 1
27958 WALLACE, Thos. C, Collinsville, OK, 35; Marion, S, 4
30169 WALLACE, William B, Jr, Oglesby, OK, 13; Ruby, Sis, 11; By W. B. Wallace, Gdn.
24868 WALLEN, Rosanna, Afton, OK, 29; Stuvie, D, 11; Clyde, S, 9; Alta F, D, 8; Jewell, S, 4; Marie, D, 1/12
7444 WALLER, Susie L, Chelsea, OK, 27; Cole B, S, 10; Goldie J, D, 9; William T. H, S, 7; Bertha M, D, 5; Bessie O. W, D, 1
43896 WALLS, Lizzie, Peggs, OK, 6; By J. H. Willyard, Gdn.
4063 WALTERMIRE, Etta, Ft. Gibson, OK, 22

[WALTERS, James. See #5750]   *(Note: entry separate from other family groups)*

24714 WALTERS, Johnnie H, Stilwell, OK, 20; Robert C, S, 4; Mamie R, D, 2
12539 WALTERS, Sarah, Afton, OK, 28; Simson [Simerson], John, S, 6; Walters, Wilbur, S, 1; Glee, S, 1/12
6296 WALTON, Cynthia A, Muldrow, OK, 21; Clara Lee, D, 4; Ethel E, D, 1
7642 WALTON, Judie, Ketchum, OK, 22
25910 WALTRIP, Elmira, Southwest City, MO, 22; James J, S, 7; Rachel, D, 6; James W, S, 4; Cecil, D, 1
27503 WALTRIP, Sarah, Proctor, OK, 21; Briggs, Purdie, D, 2; Georgie, S, 1
34943 WANN, Rosa L, Claremore, OK, 40; Opal, D, 17; Willie, S, 14; Jessie, D, 12; John, S, 10; Maggie, D, 7; Robert L, S, 4
37130 WARD, Amos F, Claremore, OK, 26; 5141, Beatrice, W, 21; Leatrice L, D, 1
8695 WARD, Carrie B. S, Dewey, OK, 18
29204 WARD, Cornelia J. W, Maysville, AR, 20
3072 WARD, Darius E, Lowrey, OK, 52; Sidney R, S, 18; Gertrude I, D, 17; Ruth E, D, 13; Sarah Ruby, S, 10; Martha A, D, 8; Hinman H, S, 20 [Died 6-13-1906]
29683 WARD, Florence A, Foyil, OK, 37; 29684, Minnie L, D, 17; Clem A, S, 15; Lena E, D, 13; Finis, S, 8
34244 WARD, Francis A, Kansas, OK, 45; George D, S, 20; Mary E, D, 16; John R, S, 14; James A, S, 12; Myrtle B, D, 7; Marvin J, S, 5
23942 WARD, George, Whiting, MO, 27; Rosa, D, 3

CHEROKEE DESCENDANTS RESIDING WEST OF MISSISSIPPI RIVER.
VOLUME III (N – Z)

Key: Guion Miller Application Number; Name; Address, Relation (to Head); Age in 1906

- **11767** WARD, George D, Afton, OK, 59
- **2146** WARD, George M, Grove, OK, 64; 2145, Martha J, W, 49
- **23718** WARD, Geo. W, Hollow, OK, 4; George Nathaniel, S, 18; Florence Pearl, D, 14
- **1005** WARD, Geo. Washington, Whiting, MO, 62; John, S, 19; Charley, S, 16; Sam, S, 13; Martin, S, 11; Harry, S, 7
- **23867** WARD, Henry H, Miami, OK, R.F.D. #4 Box 9, 20
- **643** WARD, Henry Julian, Muskogee, OK, 44; Samuel J, S, 20; Ethel M, D, 14
- **15663** WARD, Hugh T, Caney, KS, 24; John S, S, 3
- **33828** WARD, Jas. D, Collinsville, OK, 26; Dortha L, D, 1
- **23717** WARD, James L, Hollow, OK, 30; Jas V, S, 3; Bertha A, D, 2; Lucile E, D, 1
- **23267** WARD, James O, Afton, OK, 33; Lee O, S, 1
- **33827** WARD, Jay H, Collinsville, OK, 27; George H, S, 2
- **9** WARD, Joe L, Maysville, AR, 61; Louisa, D, 20
- **22738** WARD, John E, Afton, OK, 30; 22739, Minnie, W, 27; Paul H, S, 4; Daphne A, D, 1
- **2410** WARD, John L, Maysville, AR, 46; Winnie D, D, 15; Addie D, D, 12; John D, S, 8
- **23943** WARD, Joseph, Whiting, MO, 21
- **13433** WARD, Joseph M, Wann, OK, 28 [Non. Comp.]; Delena, Sis, 14; Beulah, Sis, 16; By Eli Williams, Gdn.
- **35595** WARD, Laura E, Kansas City, MO, 1733 Belview Ave, 20; Bonne[sic] Jean, D, 1/12
- **24139** WARD, Lillie, Hulbert, OK, 20
- **15667** WARD, Lillie D, Wann, OK, 19

[WARD, Louella. See #965]   *(Note: entry separate from other family groups)*

- **24857** WARD, Lucinda, Chance, OK, 29
- **4846** WARD, Margaret, Siloam Springs, AR, 74
- **30047** WARD, Marion W. S, Siloam Springs, AR, 21
- **1832** WARD, Mary Ann, Hollow, OK, 60
- **9703** WARD, Minnie, Foyil, OK, 27
- **754** WARD, Vann, Grove, OK, 73
- **9702** WARD, William R, Foyil, OK, 19; Ellis B, Bro, 17; Charles R, Bro, 14;   By Joel B. C. Ward, Gdn
- **37131** WARD, William R. Claremore, OK, 24; William L, S, 1
- **3559** WARD, William W, Claremore, OK, 52; Alta J, D, 15; Maud M, D, 10
- **4669** WARD, William W, Chelsea, OK, 50; Walter M, S, 14; Minerva E, D, 12; Tennie, D, 10; Effie E, D, 8; Leona, D, 5; Willie, S, 2; Clarence, S, 1/12
- **25265** WARE, Ada A, Muskogee, OK, 230 North 8th St, 27
- **25076** WARE, Hattie A, Miles, OK, 37; Prather, Richard L, S, 18; Ware, Goldie A, D, 10; Beulah T, D, 8; Edward I, S, 4; Mary M, D, 1
- **28336** WARE, Mary J, Collinsville, OK, 32; George F, S, 11; Josephine M, D, 9; Thelma, D, 1
- **29199** WARFIELD, Myrtle I, Sapulpa, OK, 29

CHEROKEE DESCENDANTS RESIDING WEST OF MISSISSIPPI RIVER.
VOLUME III   (N – Z)

Key: Guion Miller Application Number; Name; Address, Relation (to Head); Age in 1906

2389 WARNEKE, Annie, Blackgum, OK, 44; Katie, D, 14; Mary, D, 14; Edward, S, 12; Maudie, D, 10; Irene, D, 4; Elizabeth, D, 2; Louis, S, 1
3045 WARREN, Arthur, Adair, OK, 23

[WARREN, John H. See #14774]   *(Note: entries separate*
[WARREN, Willie D, See #14774]   *from other family groups)*

33756 WARREN, Lula I, Mimosa, AR, 21
  638 WARREN, Viola G, Wagoner, OK, 21; Canup, Harry T, S, 6
 7674 WARSEAT, David, Cookson, OK, 26
13685 WARSEAT, Isaac, Cookson, OK, 30; Gracie, D, 2
13684 WARSEAT, Levi, Cookson, OK, 21
13682 WARSEAT, Lucinda, Cookson, OK, 29
 3497 WARSEAT, Lucy T, Cookson, OK, 53; 13683, Ellis, S, 17
27431 WARTHAN, Flora, Siloam Springs, AR, 21
32085 WARWICK, Elbert S, Texanna, OK, 21
35603 WARWICK, Geo. F, Porum, OK, 23
10200 WARWICK, Jacob M, Porum, OK, 44; William L, S, 19; Alice C, D, 17; Francis M, S, 14; Le Roy, S, 6; Lena, D, 1/12
 4373 WARWICK, Thomas A, Checotah, OK, 36
10084 WASHAM, Lizzie, Pryor Creek, OK, 54; Tiger, George, S, 19; Mary, D, 16; Lillie, D, 13
 9963 WASHAM, Mary A, Pryor Creek, OK, 31; Rufus O, S, 12; Robert E, S, 6; Garrett H, S, 3
29775 WASHBOURNE, Bert, Eucha, OK, 32; Sequoyah, S, 1/12
 6458 WASHBOURNE, Claude L, Nowata, OK, 49; Joy L, D, 17; Rollin R, S, 14
 5566 WASHBOURNE, Ed. N, Eucha, OK, 36; 5939, Caroline, W, 39; Clyde, S, 12; Ruth, D, 11
28847 WASHBOURNE, Myra M, Eucha, OK, 23
 5565 WASHBOURNE, Percy H, Southwest City, MO, 60; Noble P, S, 18; Percy H, Jr, S, 16; Bryan W. J, S, 10
29372 WASHBOURNE, Roscoe C, Eucha, OK, 21
28846 WASHBOURNE, Washington A, Eucha, OK, 30
16852 WASHINGTON, Betsy, Braggs, OK, 23
11195 WASHINGTON, George, Cookson, OK, 59; 10282,Lizzie, W, 50; Red, S, 17; Blue, S, 13; Leach, S, 11; Neque, D, 10
13680 WASHINGTON, Jennie, Cookson, OK, 17; William, S, 1
21107 WASHINGTON, John, Cookson, OK, 29; 5593, Mary, W, 30; Bettie, D, 9; Emmett, S, 6; William, S, 4; John, S, 1
10282 WASHINGTON, Lizzie, Oktaha, OK, 39
11210 WASHINGTON, Lizzie, Braggs, OK, 50
41506 WASHINGTON, Peggy, Cookson, OK, 21
  794 WASHINGTON, Vauda L, (?), 17
24138 WASSOM[sic], Maggie M, Wagoner, OK, 34; Blaine W, S, 15; Mattie, D, 12; John, S, 10; George W, S, 3

CHEROKEE DESCENDANTS RESIDING WEST OF MISSISSIPPI RIVER.
VOLUME III (N – Z)

Key: Guion Miller Application Number; Name; Address, Relation (to Head); Age in 1906

2111 WASSON, Catherine I, Welch, OK, 51
26825 WASSON, Lizzie M, Muldrow, OK, 23
22516 WASSON, Myrtle C, Muskogee, OK, 24
22517 WASSON, Nettie May, Muskogee, OK, 22

[WATERDOWN, Joe. See #13129] *(Note: entry separate from other family groups)*

[WATERDOWN, Ellis. See #13128] *(Note: entry separate from other family groups)*

[WATERDOWN, Steve. See #13127] *(Note: entry separate from other family groups)*

6258 WATERDOWN, Lynch, Bunch, OK, 32; 13296, Lizzie, W, 33; Susie, D, 8; Bettie, D, 6; Robert or Bow, S, 2
7870 WATERFALLEN, James, Tahlequah, OK, 40; 9248, Wilda, W, 40; Eli, S, 15; Annie, D, 9 [Died 5-1908]; Bessie, D, 5; John, S, 2
9247 WATERFALLEN, Nancy, Gideon, OK, 21
7871 WATERFALLEN, Sarah, Tahlequah, OK, 17; Lee, Bro, 15; Lillie, Sis, 13; By James Waterfallen, Gdn.
17323 WATERFALLING, Rachel, Kansas, OK, 5; By John Beamer, Gdn.
3219 WATERKILLER, Ellis, Ft. Gibson, OK, 37

[WATERMELON. See #11434] *(Note: entry separate from other family groups)*

11426 WATERMELLON, Charlie, Southwest City, MO, 44; 11431, Katie, W, 23; 11427, Bird, S, 6; 11407, Winnie, D, 16; 11426, Lee, S, 1/12
11974 WATERMELLON, John, Southwest City, MO, 26; 11975, Laura E, W, 34; Kate, D, 1; Peak, Lillie M, D of W, 13
27741 WATERS, Annie, Warner, OK, 26; Dobbs, William R, S, 6
9580 WATERS, Charles, Long, OK, 46; Richard, S, 19; Lucy, D, 1; Mike, S, 13; Jennie, D, 11; Annie, D, 10; Charlie, S, 7; William, S, 4
12238 WATERS, Dick, Blackgum, OK, 66
11541 WATERS, Dick, Jr, Marble City, OK, 12; By Dave Bird, Gdn.
28190 WATERS, George, Long, OK, 29; George McK, S, 4; Alpha E, D, 3; Clara M, D, 1
17058 WATERS, George, Jr, Vian, OK, 32; Georgia, D, 1
895 WATERS, George, Sr, Vian, OK, 58; 2118, Mary C, W, 48; Gertrude, D, 13; Eulala, D, 11
27444 WATERS, Grover, Vian, OK, 21
40049 WATERS, James, Long, OK, 22
8337 WATERS, John, Vian, OK, 33 [Died 3-1907]; Florence, D, 13; John, Jr, S, 10; Saphrona, D, 8; Samuel, S, 5
11478 WATERS, Johnson, Braggs, OK, 57
10933 WATERS, Josiah, Braggs, OK, 27; 11188, Hattie, W, 25; Richard, S, 3; Anderson, S, 2; Smith, John, S of W, 6
41514 WATERS, Lillie, Vian, OK, 32; Zack, S, 14; Zeff, S, 12; Pearl, D, 10; Harry, S, 6

CHEROKEE DESCENDANTS RESIDING WEST OF MISSISSIPPI RIVER.
VOLUME III (N – Z)

Key: Guion Miller Application Number; Name; Address, Relation (to Head); Age in 1906

1902 WATERS, Lydia, Uniontown, AR, 29; Welch, Thomas S, S, 6; Waters, Arthur, S, 1
11477 WATERS, Lydia, Braggs, OK, 5;   By Johnson Waters, Father.
4038 WATERS, Mary, Long, OK, 67; Belle, GD, 11; Ella, GD, 7; Okla, GD, 2
27742 WATERS, Mary, Warner, OK, 29; Annie, D, 10; Sarah, D, 6; Lydia, D, 4
22760 WATERS, Maudie, Westville, OK, 28; Cora May, D, 5; Eva, D, 4; John W, S, 2; Berlia, D, 1/3
27434 WATERS, Mose, Vian, OK, 26
11480 WATERS, Nellie, Braggs, OK, 14
26336 WATERS, Susie, Blackgum, OK, 28; 17073, Dick, S, 7; 17074, Ee-gar-dah-gee, S, 2
28189 WATERS, Sylvester, Long, OK, 33; William, S, 14; Mary A, D, 12; Andrew, S, 9
11479 WATERS, Tom, Braggs, OK, 16
24928 WATERS, Vina E, Lenapah, OK, 39; 29636, Gertrude A, D, 19; Eva M, D, 17; Florence W, D, 13; Julia S, D, 1
18992 WATKINS, Alex, Oaks, OK, 16
29101 WATKINS, Allie, Nubia, TX, 28; Effie, D, 8
35459 WATKINS, Amanda E, Foyil, OK, 30; Myrtle, D, 9; Arlie, D, 6; Flora, D, 3; Beulah, D, 1/12
10403 WATKINS, Fannie, Catoosa, OK, 16;   By Cyrus A. Watkins, Gdn.
4517 WATKINS, Lydia S. M, Pryor Creek, OK, 32; Mary G, D, 16; John F, S, 13; William P, S, 12; George A, S, 10; Joel, S, 7; De Witt T, S, 5; Goldie M, D, 2
25496 WATKINS, Lillie C, Pryor Creek, OK, 30; Bertha May, D, 16; William G, S, 14; Elizabeth E, D, 12; Jessie L, D, 10; Berley W, S, 8; Henry A, S, 5; Dallas R, S, 1/12
10402 WATKINS, Minnie M, Catoosa, OK, 25
1644 WATKINS, Nancy, Dodge, OK, 24; Bud, S, 1
28885 WATKINS, Sallie, Sallisaw, OK, 22; Callie, D, 2
18991 WATKINS, Samuel, Oaks, OK, 15
28826 WATKINS, Samuel, McLain, OK, 46; Grover Lee, S, 6; Omie Gertrude, D, 4; Clarence Newton, S, 2
30372 WATKINS, Sarah J, Centralia, OK, 32; Gideon M, S, 16; Dallas R, S 14; Franklin S, S, 12; Bessie M, D, 10; Mary E, D, 9; Ollie L, D, 7; Clyde O, S, 5; Effie G, D, ¾
10405 WATKINS, William, Catoosa, OK, 14;   By Cyrus A. Watkins, Gdn.
5007 WATSON, Addie C, Muskogee, OK, 46; Drucilla, D, 16; Nathaniel, S, 13; Bessie, D, 9; Jessie, D, 9
8306 WATSON, Chas W, Grove, OK, 15; Claud, Bro, 13; Frank, Bro, 11; Floyd, Bro, 9;   By William B. Watson, Gdn.
45570 WATSON, Emma F, Blackgum, OK, 16
16375 WATT, Agen, Stilwell, OK, 32
16464 WATT, Callie, Westville, OK, 13;   By Henry Watt, Gdn.
2390 WATT, Chas. T, Cookson, OK: 28; 13370, Nellie, W, 24
4108 WATT, Elizabeth, Baron, OK, 38; 9186, Terrell, Charles, S, 16; William, S, 15; Dennis, S, 13; Lucinda, D, 10; Watt, Jeannette, D, 5; Ada, D, 1

CHEROKEE DESCENDANTS RESIDING WEST OF MISSISSIPPI RIVER.
VOLUME III (N – Z)

Key: Guion Miller Application Number; Name; Address, Relation (to Head); Age in 1906

16462 WATT, Henry, Westville, OK, 47
8944 WATT, Jackson, Westville, OK, 54; 8943, Emily, W, 95
5853 WATT, John, Westville, OK, 25; 8956, Nannie, W, 20
11536 WATT, Johnson, Dutch Mills, AR, 59
5854 WATT, Jonah, Westville, OK, 36; 10375, Maud, W, 25; Lila, D, 1
16458 WATT, Lidia[sic], Westville, OK, 10; By Henry Watt, Father.
16461 WATT, Louisa, Westville, OK, 24
16502 WATT, Mary, Westville, OK, 10; By Henry Watt, Father.
17263 WATT, Mush, Baron, OK, 54; 17262, Ella, W, 50
5706 WATT, Steve, Westville, OK, 35; 15637, Linnie, W, 21
12623 WATT, William, Baron, OK, 26; 12622, Jennie, W, 25; Peggie, D, 1
8293 WAT-TI-HU, John, Cherokee City, AR, 60; 8292, Susie, W, 31; Parchmeal, James, S, 14; Joe, S, 11; Walker, S, 9; Betsey, D, 5
25108 WATTS, Cleopatra, Tyler, TX, 19
27418 WATTS, Ella N, Coffax, CA, 28; Pearl, D, 11; Lavern, S, 8; Cyril, S, 6; Henry, S, 4; Evelyn, D, 2
3457 WATTS, Jacob, Muskogee, OK, 53; Richard, S, 12; Minnie, D, 10
17236 WATTS, John, Muskogee, OK, 20; By Jacob Watts, Gdn.

[WATTS, Lizzie. See #11197] *(Note: entry separate from other family groups)*

29169 WATTS, Martha E. E, Catoosa, OK, 23; Hannah E, D, 2
17235 WATTS, Mary, Muskogee, OK, 23
6718 WATTS, Tom, Texanna, OK, 87
7420 WATTS, Walter, Stilwell, OK, 26

[WATTS, Watt. See #11197] *(Note: entry separate from other family groups)*

28469 WATTS, Will T, Texanna, OK, 31
8017 WATTS, Young Beaver, Stilwell, OK, 25; Nannie, D, 5; Nancy, D, 2; Arthur, S, 1
6909 WATTS, Zoe A, Muldrow, OK, 27; Mildred W, D, 4; Mary A, D, 3
4628 WATY, Nancy, Stilwell, OK, 54; 9938,Polly, D, 19; Mary, D, 10; 9937, Sallie, D, 14; 9936, Johnson, S, 13
10483 WAYBOURN, Edna A, Collinsville, OK, 6; By Georgia A. Waybourn, Gdn.
23304 WAYBOURN, John T, Pryor Creek, OK, 22
9953 WAYBOURN, Lawson T, Pryor Creek, OK, 17; Eva, D, 1
9961 WAYBOURN, Levi W, Pryor Creek, OK, 41; David L, S, 11; Liddy, D, 6; Sarah F, D, 3½
9960 WEYBOURN[sic], Robert L, Pryor Creek, OK, 49; Oscar, S, 14; Reana, D, 12; Henry, S, 6; John, S, 3
9967 WAYBOURN, William D, Pryor Creek, OK, 51; Levi, S, 6; Sallie A, D, 5; Ada A, D, 2; Hulet M, S, 10; Earl C, S, 12; Arthur C, S, 15
9954 WEYBOURN [sic], Wm D, Jr, Pryor Creek, OK, 19; Alton, Bro, 14; By Jacksie Waybourn, Gdn.

CHEROKEE DESCENDANTS RESIDING WEST OF MISSISSIPPI RIVER.
VOLUME III (N – Z)

Key: Guion Miller Application Number; Name; Address, Relation (to Head); Age in 1906

27488 WEATHERFORD, Julia, Metory, OK, 18
9712 WEAVEL, Miller, Bunch, OK, 35; 9711, Caroline, W, 40; Nancy, D, 15; Betsy, D, 13; Albert, S, 11; Noah, S, 8

[WEAVER, Nannie. See #2269]   *(Note: entry separate from other family groups)*

2275 WEAVEL, Oodahye, Stilwell, OK, 59; Rattler, Sar-da-gah, GS, 10
3296 WEAVEL, William, Stilwell, OK, 30; 29666, Tawney, W, 27; Lizzie, D, 27; Least, D, 3; Polly, D, 4; Che-sta-chee, D, 1/12
161 WEAVER, Florence D, Briartown, OK, 45; Laura, D, 18; Fannie, D, 15; Maud, D, 13; Pearl, D, 9
23125 WEAVER, Herman, Briartown, OK, 24
2686 WEAVER, Hettie, Proctor, OK, 53; Tommie, S, 16
1224 WEAVER, Jessie A, Denver, CO, 3117 Stern St, 21
3209 WEAVER, Joe, Maple, OK, 66
24046 WEAVER, Katie, Proctor, OK, 20
16496 WEAVER, Mary Jane, Muldrow, OK, 54
23692 WEAVER, Nellie, Rose, OK, 26; Luge, D, 7; Margaret, D, 5; Jim, S, 4; Nancy, D, 3
3873 WEAVER, Riley, Bunch, OK, 27; 4402, Nancy, W, 32; Hooper, Rabbit, S of W, 9; Weaver, Levi, S, 3
23675 WEAVER, Samantha, Rose, OK, 26; Robert L, S, 5; Florence, D, 3; Minnie, S, 2
1239 WEBB, Bascum, Tahlequah, OK, 7; By Col. J. Harris, Gdn.
1243 WEBB, Clarence, Tahlequah, OK, 18; By Col. J. Harris, Gdn.

[WEBB, Emma P. See #28830]   *(Note: entry separate from other family groups)*

29374 WEBB, Jennie D, Adair, OK, 30; Georgia, D, 3
1209 WEBB, Jessie, Tahlequah, OK, 18; By Col. J. Harris, Gdn.
11681 WEBB, Johanna, Muskogee, OK, 18
1491 WEBB, Karl, Muskogee, OK, 22
1242 WEBB, Mary, Tahlequah, OK, 11; By Col. J. Harris, Gdn.
1238 WEBB, Maud, Tahlequah, OK, 16; By Col. J. Harris, Gdn.
1240 WEBB, Olin, Tahlequah, OK, 13; By Col. J. Harris, Gdn.
1241 WEBB, Paul, Tahlequah, OK, (?); By Col. J. Harris, Gdn.
14992 WEBBER, Charlie, Campbell, OK, 30; 14991, Oo-da-yee, W, 32; 14992, Adam, S, 5
14813 WEBBER, John, Campbell, OK, 22; 12989, Nancy, W, 17
16181 WEBBER, Mollie, Campbell, OK, 16; By William Webber, Gdn.
8686 WEBBER, Richard, Sequoyah, OK, 27; Clinton N, S, 4
16164 WEBBER, Sallie, Campbell, OK, 27; Smith, Jim, S, 9; Webber, Squirrel, S, 7; Wah-leah, D, 5
5767 WEBSTER, Arthur, Siloam Springs, AR, 15; Charles, Bro, 14; Silas, Bro, 13; Henry, Bro, 12; Hubbard, Bro, 10;   By Bird Webster, Gdn.

CHEROKEE DESCENDANTS RESIDING WEST OF MISSISSIPPI RIVER.
VOLUME III (N – Z)

Key: Guion Miller Application Number; Name; Address, Relation (to Head); Age in 1906

28827 WEBSTER, Galer Brite, Tahlequah, OK, 35; Ralph, S, 11; Bonnie, D, 10; Harry, S, 8; Walter, S, 6; Florence, D, 4; Edith, D, 2

35107 WEDDELS, Mary E, Muskogee, OK, 30; George N, S, 8; Beulah, D, 5; Ora Ethel, D, 2

21108 WEELEY, William, Welling, OK, 48; 21109, Queh-lee-coo, W, 47

2745 WEEMS, Jennie, Tahlequah, OK, 36

2836 WEINBERGER, Rachel A, Big Cabin, OK, 47; Katherine, D, 12; Henry S, S, 11; Susan F, D, 4

43303 WEIR, John W, Sacramento, CA, 1116 14th St, 33; Lillie May, D, 10

24502 WEIR, Nathaniel B, Fairland, OK, 15; Mary P, D, 8; Ruth A, D, 12; Chas. S, S, 19

24503 WEIR, Rex J, Fairland, OK, 21; Frances E, D, 1

26467 WEIR, Samuel K, Tulsa, OK, 506 South Elgin St, 36; Earl F, S, 14; William D, S, 8; Vinita F, D, 1

1353 WEIR, Webster W, Sacramento, CA, 1116 14th St, 61; Joseph, S, 16

22762 WEISS, Rebecca J, McAleester[sic], OK, 22; Alfred B, S, 1

10727 WELCH, Alex, Muldrow, OK, 34; 10728,Victory, W, 29; Maggie, D, 12; Chandler, Richard, S of W, 13

5929 WELCH, Alfred G, Sallisaw, OK, 36; 38528, Mary A, W, 27

1703 WELCH, Anna, Eucha, OK, 20

5323 WELCH, Annie, Tahlequah, OK, 41

11606 WELCH, Bettie, Chilocco, OK, 24

2350 WELCH, Bruce, Ballard, OK, 16;   By John Welch, Gdn.

7561 WELCH, Cella, Southwest City, MO, 23

32732 WELCH, Charley, Stilwell, OK, 22

31999 WELCH, David V, Uniontown, AR, 48; 1994, Sallie, W, 47; Ned, S, 17; Downing, Susie Bell, D of W 16; Lucy, D of W, 13; Welch, Looney, S, 13

7019 WELCH, Edw, Southwest City, MO, 39

2808 WELCH, Eva A, Needmore, OK, 12; Veda E, Sis, 14;   By Randolph Ballard, Gdn.

17526 WELCH, Francis B, Tip, OK, 44

5936 WELCH, George, Sallisaw, OK, 46; John B, S, 17; Carrie, D, 13; Frank, S, 10; Emma, D, 7; Cherokee, D, 7; Sadie, D, 3

8369 WELCH, Geo. T, Stilwell, OK, 31

7018 WELCH, Hester, Southwest City, MO, 58

27805 WELCH, Hester A, Oaks, OK, 27; Susie, D, 9; Jesse, S, 6; Mary, D, 2

11259 WELCH, James, Miami, OK, 38; 939, Cynthia A, W, 47; McLaughlin, William, S of W, 16; Welch, Maud, D, 8

15771 WELCH, James B, Browning, MT, 33

5713 WELCH, James Mack, Chance, OK, 40; 5714, Cleo J, W, 36

9795 WELCH, John, Melvin, OK, 35; 31559, Maggie, W, 20; 9794, Luke, S, 9; 9795, Cornelius, S, 5; Simon, S, 4; Cobb, S, 3; Bessie, D, 1/6

17094 WELCH, John, Ballard, OK, 37; 37504, Dovie, W, 25; 17094, Frank, S, 14; Iva, S, 12; Robert, S, 10; Harry, S, 5; Roy D, S, 3; Irra[sic] C, D, ¼

CHEROKEE DESCENDANTS RESIDING WEST OF MISSISSIPPI RIVER.
VOLUME III (N – Z)

Key: Guion Miller Application Number; Name; Address, Relation (to Head); Age in 1906

6017 WELCH, John Cobb, Grove, OK, 57; 3003, Elsie, W, 50; 43505, Sam S, Neph, 16; 3003, Ausley, S, 15

8250 WELCH, John D, Edna, KS, 33; Virgel[sic] L, S, 8; Cherokee R, D, 5; Maud M, D, 3; Fred F, S, 1/6

9773 WELCH, John E, Bartlesville, OK, 62; Jessie, D, 17; Jos V, S, 9; Hoolie, S, 4; Esther M, D, 2

4361 WELCH, John P, Grove, OK, 43 [Died 7-1906]; By J. C. Welch, Admr.

17092 WELCH, Mack, Ballard, OK, 35; Esther, D, 10; Myrtle, D, 8; Georgie, D, 6; Ethel, D, 4; Cecil, S, 1

24688 WELCH, Mack E, Edna, KS, 28; 9749, Annie, W, 23; Phoebe Irene, D, 5; Lorene, D, 3

11613 WELCH, Mary, Sallisaw, OK, 21

14183 WELCH, Mary, Locust Grove, OK, 8; By Thomas Bluejacket, Gdn.

2349 WELCH, Moses, Siloam Springs, AR, 24

[WELCH, Nancy. See #9276]   *(Note: entry separate from other family groups)*

14160 WELCH, May, Ballard, OK, 49; John, S, 14; Minnie C, D, 12; May Emma, D, 10; Link W, S, 8; Hattie A, D, 5; Nettie, D, 3; George S, 1

17036 WELCH, Nenahwe, Eucha, OK, 14; 17038, John Davis, Bro, 13; 17037, Maline, Sis, 10; 17039, Standingdeer, Bro, 5;   By Eve Wolfe, Gdn.

8157 WELCH, Richard L, Edna, KS, 25; 9383, Polly, W, 25; Leroy, S, 6; Thos D, S, 4; Emmett, S, 3

11611 WELCH, Robt. G, Sallisaw, OK, 18; Jos, Bro, 14;   By A. G. Welch, Gdn.

6805 WELCH, Sarah, Melvin, OK, 28

11669 WELCH, Scott, Dragger, OK, 47; Elizabeth D, 17;   Mary, D, 14; Charlotte, D, 12; John, S, 10; George, S, 4; Ollie, D, 2

5731 WELCH, Thomas J, Ballard, OK, 47; 8243, Fannie, W, 40; Samuel, B, S, 18; Thos. R, S, 15; John, S, 11; Loice, D, 8; Efel, D, 1/12

[WELCH, Thomas S. See #1902]   *(Note: entry separate from other family groups)*

23209 WELCH, Tom, Stilwell, OK, 20
43359 WELEY, Joe, Etta, OK, 29
43358 WELEY, Mary Jane, Etta, OK, 26; Pigeon, Sam, S, 2
43360 WELEY, Nelson, Etta, OK, 60; 43357, Nancy, W, 59; Jay C, S, 17 [Died 1-1907]
5210 WELLBAUM, Susan, Cookson, OK, 49
11748 WELLS, Arch L, Inola, OK, 22
25029 WELLS, Laura A, Chetopa, KS, 24; William, S, 5; Samuel B, S, 4; Janie M, D, 1/6
1237 WELLS, Lucy Jane, Grove, OK, 27; Milo C, S, 6
11750 WELLS, N. L, Inola, OK, 15; Burl, Bro, 12; Emma, Sis, 10; By Volney E. Wells, Gdn.
24241 WELLS, Nannie B, Wagoner, OK, 29; Thomas D, S, 8; Anna R, D, 5; Daisy B, D, 4; William E, Jr, S, 1

CHEROKEE DESCENDANTS RESIDING WEST OF MISSISSIPPI RIVER.
VOLUME III   (N – Z)

Key: Guion Miller Application Number; Name; Address, Relation (to Head); Age in 1906

- **26167** WELLS, Nellie, Ahniwake, OK, 19
- **11657** WESSON, Catherine, McKey, OK, 27
- **11655** WESSON, David, McKey, OK, 12;   By W. S. Wesson, Gdn.
- **4435** WEST, Clifton, Ft. Gibson, OK, 28; 27556, Nannie, W, 20; Pearl W, D, 7; Ethel, D, 5; Rosa, D, 4; Jesse, S, 1
- **23814** WEST, Culliciah D, Spavinaw, OK, 24
- **16688** WEST, Dolly, Tahlequah, OK, 24
- **26534** WEST, Ellis C, Porum, OK, 37; Vera, D, 8; Robbie L, S, 5; Henry L, S, 3
- **31777** WEST, Frank I, Okmulgee, OK, 25; Francis M, S, 4
- **10888** WEST, George H, Checotah, OK, 40; Bertha May, D, 5; Laura Annie, D, 3
- **4434** WEST, Geo. M, Ft. Gibson, OK, 22
- **4432** WEST, Henry, Ft. Gibson, OK: 18; Charley, Bro, 16; Morgan, Bro, 15;   By D. B. West, Gdn.
- **6431** WEST, James P, Texanna, OK, 27; Claude o, S, ¼
- **5870** WEST, Jeff, Texanna, OK, 17; John, Bro, 19;   By A. J. Williams, Gdn.
- **10193** WEST, John B, Briartown, OK, 31; Dora, D, 3
- **7987** WEST, John C, Muskogee, OK, 64; 8677, Margaret, W, 59
- **26737** WEST, John Henry, Vian, OK, 40
- **2906** WEST, Josephine, Spavinaw, OK, 47; Joseph, S, 18; Calvin C, S, 15; Josephine D, D, 9
- **30680** WEST, Laura B, Bushyhead, OK, 16   c/o Tom West
- **7022** WEST, Lizzie, Tahlequah, OK, 36
- **35715** WEST, Lizzie V, Tahlequah, OK, 36; LeRoy, S, 16; Minnie, D, 13
- **16077** WEST, Ray R, Edna, KS, 5; Cyrel C, Bro, 3;   By Grace Gray, Gdn.
- **10195** WEST, Richard, Briartown, OK, 27; Lucie E, D, 2
- **27657** WEST, Richard F, Checotah, OK, 34; Dubert E, S, 11; John A, S, 4
- **10419** WEST, Robert E, Warner, OK, 35; William E, S, 13; Walter T, S, 11; Martin L, S, 9; Elizabeth D, D, 7; Valeria E, D, 5; Robert I, S, 3; Richard E, S, ¼
- **4433** WEST, Rufus B, Ft. Gibson, OK, 24
- **23968** WEST, Sallie, Westville, OK, 31; Alice P, D, 10; Bettie V, D, 7; William J. B, S, 2
- **16687** WEST, Sandy, Tahlequah, OK, 22
- **23815** WEST, Sequoyah B, Spavinaw, OK, 22
- **10800** WEST, Thomas C, Briartown, OK, 38; Tecumseh, D, 5; William C, S, 1/3
- **7016** WEST, Tiney, Spavinaw, OK, 33; Mahala M, D, 14; Nola A, D, 12; Tooker B, D, 10; Willie J, S, 7; Bertha J, D, 4; Emma E, D, 1; Emmet S, S, 1
- **6430** WEST, William, Texanna, OK, 24
- **5217** WEST, William D, Lynch, OK, 41; 3619, Leona C, W, 30; Walter A, S, 5; Sallie E, D, 1
- **14196** WEST, William Horest, Campbell, OK, 3;   By Daniel Cripple, Gdn.
- **24786** WESTENHAVEN, Flora, Chelsea, OK, 30; Bertha M, D, 11; George B, S, 4; Henry R, S, 2
- **23485** WESTOVER, Lelia E, Wann, OK, 18
- **23588** WESTOVER, Thomas H, Wann, OK, 21

CHEROKEE DESCENDANTS RESIDING WEST OF MISSISSIPPI RIVER.
VOLUME III   (N – Z)

Key: Guion Miller Application Number; Name; Address, Relation (to Head); Age in 1906

[WESTOVER, Warren. See #23487]   *(Note: entry separate from other family groups)*

23596   WESTOVER, Willard W, Tahlequah, OK, 24
11769   WETZEL, Martha C, Maysville, AR, 65; Claud C, GS, 19; Ida May, GD, 17; Eddie, GS, 12; Oliver, GS, 16
16084   WHALER, Akie, Tahlequah, OK, 24
 9808   WHALER, Daniel, Tahlequah, OK, 28; 17125, Mary, W, 59
 9805   WHALER, Henry, Proctor, OK, 54; 9806, Wahleesee, W, 56; Eli, S, 18; Spears, Walter, GS, 6
17070   WHALER, Jennie, Tahlequah, OK, 19
17124   WHALER, Levi, Tahlequah, OK, 14; Lydia, Sis, 12;   By Daniel Whaler, Brother.
16078   WHALER, Maggie, Tahlequah, OK, 21
13351   WHEELER, Nancy, Sallisaw, OK, 34; John P, S, 2
26201   WHELCHEL, Mary E, Westville, OK, 40; Stella, D, 11; Fanny, D, 9; James O, S, 7; Frances E, D, 4; Mary B, D, 3; 26202, Louella, D, 17
10263   WHIRLWIND, Ketcher, Spavinaw, OK, 45; Mollie, D, 17; Lizie[sic], D, 13
 5104   WHIRLWIND, Lewis, Foyil, OK, 42; 24167, Susie L, W, 30; Lola A, D, 7; Rosa A, D, 4; Lewis E, S, 1/6
27334   WHITAKER, Austin, Pryor Creek, OK, 30; Virgil O, S, 11; Eldie E, S, 8
 4522   WHITAKER, Edgar, Pryor Creek, OK, 11;   By Rosa Whitaker, Gdn.
27335   WHITAKER, Victor, Philippine Islands, Co. K, 2d Inft., 27
23754   WHITAKER, William J, Pryor Creek, OK, 23
23755   WHITAKER, William T, Pryor Creek, OK, 52; Charley, S, 18; Ella O, D, 16; Claud C, S, 11; Clarence, S, 9; Edna May, D, 5

[WHITE, Alice. See #5992] } *(Note: entries separate*
[WHITE, Okah. See #5992] } *from other family groups)*

32299   WHITE, Florence, Ft. Gibson, OK, 40; Edgar, S, 13; Flossie E, D, 11; Lillian, D, 10
11857   WHITE, Hattie, Braggs, OK, 17
 1619   WHITE, Helen D, Oologah, OK, 32; Beuna Vista, D, 15

[WHITE, James. See #9330]   *(Note: entry separate from other family groups)*

 6969   WHITE, James, Stilwell, OK, 49; 5899,Jennie, W, 33; Tom, S, 25; Sunday, S, 13; Annie, D, 9; George, S, 7; Watt, S, 3; Luna, D, ½

[WHITE, Lee. See #5947]   *(Note: entry separate from other family groups)*

33130   WHITE, Louvenia, Warner, OK, 23; Burgess, Garnet M, D, 3

[WHITE, Lucinda. See #5441]   *(Note: entry separate from other family groups)*

CHEROKEE DESCENDANTS RESIDING WEST OF MISSISSIPPI RIVER.
VOLUME III (N – Z)

Key: Guion Miller Application Number; Name; Address, Relation (to Head); Age in 1906

25152 WHITE, Maggie, Cookson, OK, 19; Eva M, D, 1   [Died 10-1906]
1647 WHITE, Mary, Southwest City, MO, 28
17213 WHITE, Nancy J, Lenapah, OK, 34; Mary M, D, 9; Ruth E, D, 7; Fabean V, S, 4; Charles H, S, 1; Mamie F. J, D, 1/12
623 WHITE, Nancy J. F, San Bernardino, CA, 71
10941 WHITE, Sager, Maysville, AR, S of #5002, 14;   By Ben O. Fields, Gdn.
32432 WHITE, Sarah M, Collinsville, OK, 31; Ida M, D, 8; Clarence S, S, 4; Tennie, D, 1
3250 WHITE, Tom, Stilwell, OK, 76; 1286, Aka, W, 66
8663 WHITEDAY, Mariah F, Salina, OK, 20; Morris B, S, 2; Francis D, S, 7/13
6052 WHITEKILLER, Buffalo, Melvin, OK, 55; 6063, Eliza, W, 27; Amers, S, 9; Willie, S, 2; Alice, D, 1/3
11856 WHITEKILLER, Carrie, Rex, OK, 18
4060 WHITEKILLER, David, Ft. Gibson, OK, 49; Charles, S, 17

[WHITEKILLER. Willie W. See #21153]
   (Note: entry separate from other family groups)

17182 WHITE, Tobacco Aggie, Campbell, OK, 20; Eli, S, 3; Polly, D, 1/6

[WHITEWALKER, Joe. See #3693]   *(Note: entry separate from other family groups)*

[WHITEWALKER, Ka-yor-he. See #10424]
   (Note: entry separate from other family groups)

[WHITEWALKER, Geo. See #13635]
   (Note: entry separate from other family groups)

12414 WHITEWALKER, Ellen, Cookson, OK, 51; Sally, D, 17; Mary, D, 14
12367 WHITEWATER, Famous, Braggs, OK, 34; 13790, Betsy,W, 24; Lizzie, D,2; Ross, S, 1
4177 WHITEWATER, Willie, Collinsville, OK, 5;   By James R, Stout, Gdn.
1389 WHITFIELD, Benjamin, Wauhillau, OK, 23
9016 WHITFIELD, Hulda, Wauhillau, OK, 54; John D, S, 12
1390 WHITFIELD, Luke, Wauhillau, OK, 26; 15951, Lovey, W, 24; Ray, S, 1
26234 WHITMIRE, Andy, Proctor, OK, 26
2420 WHITMIRE, Charles, Proctor, OK, 57; Jack, S, 18; William, S, 14
1593 WHITMIRE, Charlotte, Baron, OK, 36; Hoskin, Mary Ann, D, 14; Capps, Lillie May, D, 11
5647 WHITMIRE, Dennis, Westville, OK, 22
1847 WHITMIRE, Eli H, Westville, OK, 48; 3910, George C, S, 19
362 WHITMIRE, George, Hayden, OK, 29
4619 WHITMIRE, George, Whitmire, OK, 36
4692 WHITMIRE, George G, Baron, OK, 35; 6480, Lydia, W, 29; George V, S, 6; Goldie E, D, 3

CHEROKEE DESCENDANTS RESIDING WEST OF MISSISSIPPI RIVER.
VOLUME III   (N – Z)

Key: Guion Miller Application Number; Name; Address, Relation (to Head); Age in 1906

- **5708** WHITMIRE, James, Westville, OK, 26
- **24683** WHITMIRE, James W, Proctor, OK, 23
- **4618** WHITMIRE, Johnson, Whitmire, OK, 32
- **8909** WHITMIRE, Mary L, Christie, OK, 18

[WHITEMIRE[sic], Maud. See #8650]   *(Note: entry separate from other family groups)*

- **28171** WHITMIRE, Noah, Pryor Creek, OK, 20
- **25182** WHITMIRE, Ruth, Ketchum, OK, 19; Mamie, D, 5
- **4595** WHITMIRE, Sarah A, Hulbert, OK, 28
- **5648** WHITMIRE, Watt S, Westville, OK, 54; Thomas, S, 16; Johnson, S, 14; Nellie, D, 11
- **4863** WHITMIRE, White, Westville, OK, 46; 1592, Anna, W, 41; William, S, 16; Walter, S, 13; Joseph, S, 11; Stephen, S, 8; John, S, 6; White, S, 3
- **2462** WHITMIRE, William W, Westville, OK, 31
- **11164** WHITNEY, Louella E, Adair, OK, 38; Ethel, D, 17; Bertha J, D, 6
- **3487** WHITTINGTON, Cornelius, Leach, OK, 49; Jessie, D, 18; John, S, 16; James, S, 14; Annie, D, 11; George L, S, 6; Cornelius, S, 3; Eli, S, 1

[WHOOPER, Charlie. See #16591]   *(Note: entry separate from other family groups)*

[WICKLIFF, Sam. See #4409]   *(Note: entry separate from other family groups)*

- **25106** WICKED, Annie Lee, Checotah, OK, 6;   By Lemuel Wicked, Gdn.
- **691** WICKED, James P, Akin, OK, 35; Docie M, D, 6; Oma L, D, 4
- **3749** WICKED, Jessie, Warner, OK, 16;   By Newton Wicked, Gdn.
- **3746** WICKED, Johnnie, Warner, OK, 14;   By Newton Wicked, Gdn.
- **3745** WICKED, Lemuel, Warner, OK, 57; Alpha OK, D, 17
- **25105** WICKED, Lemuel, Checotah, OK, 5;   By Lemuel Wicked, Gdn.
- **1322** WICKED, Maria, Evansville, AR, 76
- **3747** WICKED, Newton, Warner, OK, 34; Mary Florence, D, 10; Nettie G, D, 8; Ola, D, 5; Clide[sic] Virgil, S, 1; Charles Claud, S, 1
- **319** WICKED, Vaden, Bartlesville, OK, 29
- **10958** WICKET, Chas, Cookson, OK, 36
- **10307** WICKET, Emily, Cookson, OK, 35
- **16010** WICKET, Jesse, Webbers Falls, OK, 26; Stella, D, 1

[WICKET, Lillie. See #3748]   *(Note: entry separate from other family groups)*

- **10407** WICKETT, Mary E, Muskogee, OK, 50
- **22539** WICKETT, Richard, Zena, OK, 25
- **7577** WICKETT, Submit, Park Hill, OK, 27; John M, S, 4
- **16445** WICKETT, Webb, Southwest City, MO,   43; 1564, Sarah, W, 41; Laurena, D, 14; Lucy, D, 5; Lottie, D, 18

CHEROKEE DESCENDANTS RESIDING WEST OF MISSISSIPPI RIVER.
VOLUME III (N – Z)

Key: Guion Miller Application Number; Name; Address, Relation (to Head); Age in 1906

5547 WICKLIFFE, Charles, Lowrey, OK, 32; 8849, Charlotte, W, 35; James F, S, 10; William B, S, 2

5596 WICKLIFFE, James, Locust Grove, OK, 58; 5597, Annie, W, 68

5544 WICKLIFFE, John, Lowrey, OK, 58

10427 WICKLIFFE, John, Spavinaw, OK, 62; 10626, Nellie, W, 35; 14179, Tiger, Hattie, D, 13

5595 WICKLIFFE, Lewis, Locust Grove, OK, 47; 24699,Nellie, W, 39; Annie, D, 16; Alsie, D, 14; Joe, S, 10; Susan, D, 8; Daykie, D, 6; Ben, S, 3; Charlie, S, 1/3; Tom, S, 1/3   [Died 8-12-1906]

5546 WICKLIFFE, Thomas, Lowrey, OK, 24

13953 WICKS, George A, Braggs, OK, 20; John, Bro, 18; Nancy Jane, Sis, 16; By J. A. Wicks, Gdn.

[WICKS, Joseph. See #5219]   *(Note: entries separate*
[WICKS, Benjamin. See #5219]   *from other family groups)*

14794 WILDCAT, Ben, Campbell, OK, 15;   By Walker Wildcat, Gdn.

14803 WILDCAT, Cole-See-nee, Campbell, OK, 12;   By Charlie Webber, Gdn.

8338 WILDCAT, Goround, Campbell, OK, 37; 14783, Jor-wa-yu-ger,W, 18; Yah-ho-lah, S, 1

26369 WILDCAT, Joseph, Campbell, OK, 30

22110 WILDCAT, Rachel, Melvin, OK, 30

14802 WILDCAT, Spade, Campbell, OK, 17;   By Charlie Webber, Gdn.

8339 WILDCAT, Walker, Campbell, OK, 51

6696 WILDCAT, William, Campbell, OK, 45; 6697, Annie, W, 50; Gee-yah-ha, S, 19; Gar-ler-gi or French, S, 16; Alex, S, 14; Charlotte [Solard], D, 12; Charlie-tee-hee [Charldee], S, 10

9672 WILEY, Davison, Marble City, OK, 57; 9671, Nancy, W, 42

8377 WILEY, George, Cherokee City, AR, 42; 8376, Na-ne, W, 50; John, S, 18; Elijah, S, 16; Frank, S, 9

26940 WILEY, Louvenie, Texanna, OK, 37; Cavalier, Jon, S, 19; Wiley, Bertha D, 2

9296 WILEY, Steel, Cherokee City, AR, 59

17145 WILKERSON, Barney L, Cherokee City, AR, 8;   By Thomas Wilkerson, Father.

29217 WILKERSON, Daniel, Webbers Falls, OK, 20

8673 WILKERSON, Ellen, Webbers Falls, OK, 47; Daniel, S, 18; Ora, D, 13; Lillie, D, 1; Lena, D, 9

1554 WILKERSON, George, Webbers Falls, OK, 19; 16507, Eliza, W, 22

1576 WILKERSON, George W, Peggs, OK, 52; Cora, D, 17; Austin, S, 15; Maggie, D, 12; Maud, D, 10; Jesse, S, 2

1567 WILKERSON, George W, Peggs, OK, 33; Linzie H, S, 11; Lewis E, S, 7; Hattie, D, 4; Addie M, D, 2

1565 WILKERSON, James, Peggs, OK, 36; Leeler, S, 8; Andrew J, S, 5; Mark Ranle[sic], S, 4; Wyly F, S, 2; Virgie Mary, D, 1/12

17142 WILKERSON, Jay Hugh, Cherokee City, AR, 3;   By Thomas Wilkerson, Father

CHEROKEE DESCENDANTS RESIDING WEST OF MISSISSIPPI RIVER.
VOLUME III (N – Z)

Key: Guion Miller Application Number; Name; Address, Relation (to Head); Age in 1906

17144 WILKERSON, John OK, Cherokee City, AR, 16;   By Thomas Wilkerson, Father.
17254 WILKERSON, Leonard W, Porum, OK, 40; Oscar, S, 8; Allen, S, 2 [Died 10-1906]
  987 WILKERSON, Lizzie, Claremore, OK, 45; 2688, Halfbreed, Lucy, D, 18; 8214, Wilkerson, Rachel, D, 13
 8674 WILKERSON, Margaret, Webbers Falls, OK, 51[Died 10-1906]; 29217, Daniel, S, 20; 8574, Lester, S, 19; Margaret, D, 15; Colbert, S, 11;   By Asa Wilkerson, Husband.
17143 WILKERSON, Mattie E, Cherokee City, AR, 6;   By Thomas Wilkerson, Father.
 2136 WILKERSON, Mollie, Locust Grove, OK, 25
12884 WILKERSON, Richard, Dewey, OK, 39; 13053, Annie, W, 35; Ella M, D, 12; Katy, D, 9; Oliver C, S, 7; William, S, 4
13164 WILKERSON, Robert E, Webbers Falls, OK, 28
17141 WILKERSON, Vera May, Cherokee City, AR, 1;   By Tom Wilkerson, Father.
 1566 WILKERSON, William D, Peggs, OK, 20
 2233 WILKES, Kathleen, Tahlequah, OK, 22; Kirkpatrick, Lillian, D, 1/12
22886 WILKIE, David, Westville, OK, 52; John W, S, 19; Ollie L, D, 15; George W, S, 11; David L, S, 5; Jesse H, S, 2
23495 WILKIE, George H, Westville, OK, 29; Myrtle L, D, 2
22616 WILKIE, Jesse W, Westville, OK, 37; John W, S, 10; Samuel D, S, 7; Walter D, S, 4; Lizzie, D, 2
22616½ WILKIE, John W, Westville, OK, 16; Nancy T, Sis, 13; David, Bro, 11; Louisa, Sis, 9; Margaret, Sis, 4;   By Jesse W. Wilkie, Gdn.
23372 WILKIE, John M, Westville, OK, 54; Nancy M, D, 15; Leli[sic] L, D, 11
24164 WILKIE, John W, Westville, OK, 31; Stella, D, 4; Clinton, S, 2; Jessie, D, 1/6
24832 WILKIE, Mary B, Westville, OK, 19
22776 WILKIE, Minnie E, Westville, OK, 28; Hayes, Charles J, S, 12; McClain, Mattie M, D, 10; Mollie A, D, 8; Maudie L, D, 6; Mason T, S, 2
  132 WILKIE, Sidney Elizabeth, Westville, OK, 78
 4699 WILKINS, Fannie, Muskogee, OK, 27; Nannie E, D, 9
11415 WILKINS, George W, Chloeta, OK, 29; Ethel, D, 5; Bertha, D, 2
11988 WILKINS, Sally, Muskogee, OK, 27; Mary, D, 2
33493 WILKINSON, Clara M, Nowata, OK, 22; John F, S, 5; Lucile, D, 3
 5918 WILKINSON, Louisa J, Claremore, OK, 58
22926 WILLARD, Albert Bird, Baxter Springs, KS, 22; Alton Propp, S, 1
22927 WILLARD, Leon L, Baxter Springs, KS, 30
 4391 WILLARD, Lucinda A, Baxter Springs, KS, 66
26942 WILLEY, Chas W, Ft. Gibson, OK, 33; 16422, Jananna, W, 27; Madaline, D, 2
 4014 WILLEY, Mary, Ft. Gibson, OK, 55
26799 WILLEY, Milo J, Ft. Gibson, OK, 27; Myrtle, D, 6; Addie, D, 4; Lena, D, 2; Dora D, D, ¼
21827 WILLIAMS, Addie M, Vinita, OK, 21
 5260 WILLIAMS, Alex, Dewey, OK, 25

CHEROKEE DESCENDANTS RESIDING WEST OF MISSISSIPPI RIVER.
VOLUME III   (N – Z)

Key: Guion Miller Application Number; Name; Address, Relation (to Head); Age in 1906

2742 WILLIAMS, Anna I, Tahlequah, OK, 19; Percy F, S, 1
3732 WILLIAMS, Belle, Catoosa, OK, 15; James S, Bro, 14; Leroy H, Bro, 13;   By James S. Williams, Gdn.

[WILLIAMS, Charley. See #10219]   *(Note: entries separate*
[WILLIAMS, Betsy. See #10219]   *from other family groups)*

16977 WILLIAMS, Clara May, White Oak, OK, 21; Opal N, D, 4; Ruby V, D, 3
30376 WILLIAMS, Cora L, Afton, OK, 20
31990 WILLIAMS, Cornelia J, Fairland, OK, 23
21814 WILLIAMS, David S, Vinita, OK, 16;   By Jane Williams, Gdn.

[WILLIAMS, Delilah. See #3868]   *(Note: entry separate from other family groups)*

4334 WILLIAMS, Elgin M, Chetopa, KS, R.F.D. #6, 31; Ira Edwin, S, 8; Bertha May, D, 2; Hilda Opal, D, ¼
2055 WILLIAMS, Elizabeth, Choteau, OK, 36; Charley, S, 19; Pearl, D, 17; Hattie M, D, 13; Clem, S, 8; John, S, 5; Virdgie[sic], D, 3; Terry, S, 1
6959 WILLIAMS, Eugenia M, Howland, TX, 50
8438 WILLIAMS, Geo. W, Chelsea, OK, 40; Minnie B, D, 16; Andrew N, S, 14; Clarence E, S, 12; Raleigh H, S, 9
10694 WILLIAMS, Harrison, Chelsea, OK, 64; Emma S, D, 8; Harrison, Jr, S, 6; Leonard, S, 3; Amanda P, D, 1
7711 WILLIAMS, Henry C, Ft. Missoula, MT, Co. L, 6th Inft, 27
544 WILLIAMS, Herbert A, Wagoner, OK, 23
8437 WILLIAMS, Jack, Claremore, OK, 44; Guy, S, 12; Joana[sic], D, 9; Jessie Arthur, S, 4; Laura J, D, 1
1103 WILLIAMS, Jennie, Vinita, OK, 66

[WILLIAMS, Jennie. See #1407]   *(Note: entry separate from other family groups)*

12659 WILLIAMS, Jesse, Moodys, OK, 21; 17068, Jennie, W, 22
21829 WILLIAMS, Joel M, Miles, OK, 35; Jennie M, D, 7; Joe F, S, 4; Melvin R, S, 1
4310 WILLIAMS, John, Locust Grove, OK, 70; 4304, Polly, W, 57
1640 WILLIAMS, Joseph L, Chelsea, OK, 40; Nellie Lee, D, 11; Timothy, S, 10; Hazel May, D, 7; Carlos E, S, 5
2733 WILLIAMS, Leonard W, Mark, OK, 50; 10423, Mary, W, 42; Clem, S, 17; Viola, D, 15; Kittie, D, 13; Flora, D, 3
21813 WILLIAMS, Lottie N, Vinita, OK, 19
5011 WILLIAMS, Louisa, Tyro, KS, 55
16419 WILLIAMS, Louisa J, Wann, OK, 55
17192 WILLIAMS, Magdalena, Vian, OK, 13;   By Ben. Williams, Gdn.
24249 WILLIAMS, Maggie, Tisdale, KS, 27; Everett, S, 1
1128 WILLIAMS, Malinda N, Afton, OK, 46; Mayes, S, 19; Charlotte, D, 17; Arthur R, S, 15

CHEROKEE DESCENDANTS RESIDING WEST OF MISSISSIPPI RIVER.
VOLUME III (N – Z)

Key: Guion Miller Application Number; Name; Address, Relation (to Head); Age in 1906

5310 WILLIAMS, Maud L, Echo, OK, 29; Frank E, S, 7; Colbert A, S, 4; Edgar R, S, 1
12121 WILLIAMS, Minnie, Claremore, OK, 37; DeWitt, S, 18; Sue, D, 13; Anna, D, 3
23535 WILLIAMS, Nancy, Kansas, OK, 20; Laura, D, 4; Newton A, S, 3
12244 WILLIAMS, Oma, Westville, OK, 9;   By Robert Williams, Gdn.
 330 WILLIAMS, Paulina, Dodge, OK, 50; Bates, Josephine, D, 16
17190 WILLIAMS, Robert, Vian, OK, 7;   By Ben. Williams, Gdn.
12242 WILLIAMS, Robert, Westville, OK, 11;   By Robert Williams, Gdn.
12889 WILLIAMS, Robt. E, Yuma, AZ, 30, U.S. Constable; 29114, Hattie O, W, 28; Vera F, D, 9
24436 WILLIAMS, Samuel C, Afton, OK, 31; Leona E, D, 8
11761 WILLIAMS, Sue G, Claremore, OK, 38; Sid, S, 1
11464 WILLIAMS, Thos, Metory, OK, 29
12243 WILLIAMS, Thomas, Westville, OK, 6;   By Robert Williams, Gdn.
25225 WILLIAMS, Tuxie, Mark, OK, 23
17191 WILLIAMS, Walter L, Vian, OK, 11;   By Ben. Williams, Gdn.
22054 WILLIAMS, Watie, Ft. Smith, AR, 27; Clarence, S, 5; Rossie E, D, 3
23132 WILLIAMS, William A, Afton, OK, 28

[WILLIAMS, William P. See #21815] *(Note: entry separate from other family groups)*

28036 WILLIAMSON, Nellie M, Welch, OK, 27; Mary Nettie, D, 3; William F, S, 2

22809 WILLIS, Bessie E, Warner, OK, 17; Claudie M, Bro, 19; Armour A, Bro, 15; Walter B, Bro, 13; William W, Bro, 10
24085 WILLIS, Claud C, Westville, OK, 23; E. L, S, 1/12
 5363 WILLIS, Florence A, Wann, OK, 31; Nora M, D, 14; Robert h, S, 13; Oma, D, 9; Hazel M, D, 5; Louise, D, 1
24199 WILLIS, George G, Westville, OK, 26; 24200, Roxie, W, 38; Toin, S of W, 16; Watie, S of W, 14; James, S of W, (?); Charles, S of W, (?)
 5650 WILLIS, Hester, Westville, OK, (?); Thula Alice, D, (?)

[WILLIS, Jerry. See #7006]   *(Note: entry separate from other family groups)*

24032 WILLIS, Jesse R, Westville, OK, 27; Grace, D, 5/12
25384 WILLIS, John W, Woodbury, TX, R.F.D. #2, 32; Hugh W, S, 13; Minnie A, D, 8

[WILLIS, Leander. See #27719]   *(Note: entry separate from other family groups)*

22650 WILLIS, Nathaniel D, Wauhillau, OK, 39; James E, S, 13; Charles, S, 11; Annie M, D, 9; Thomas E, S, 7; Robert L, S, 4
17747 WILLIS, Rogina, Peggs, OK, 30
28491 WILLIS, Thomas J, Welch, OK, 38; Charles, S, 12
29088 WILLIS, William B, Etta, OK, 47; Effie, D, 13
 5510 WILLS, Kate R, White Oak, OK, 51; Clarence R, S, 12; John B, S, 10
25729 WILSON, Albert M, Turley, OK, 24; Ruby F, D, 2

CHEROKEE DESCENDANTS RESIDING WEST OF MISSISSIPPI RIVER.
VOLUME III (N – Z)

Key: Guion Miller Application Number; Name; Address, Relation (to Head); Age in 1906

4553 WILSON, Alice, Talala, OK, 59
25253 WILSON, Arminda, Wauhillau, OK, 29; Floyd, S, 1
4842 WILSON, Benj. F, Tahlequah, OK, 47; 26172, Lowaner, W, 34; Polly M, D, 9; Fay E, D, 3; Percy W, S, 1

[WILSON, Betsy. See #17187] *(Note: entry separate from other family groups)*

[WILSON, Chudahagi. See #16438] *(Note: entry separate from other family groups)*

24140 WILSON, Cora C, Dodge, OK, 21
5653 WILSON, Dorcus, Maysville, AR, 29
2188 WILSON, Eli, Welling, OK, 29; 17187,Dick, Betsy, W, 17; Wilson, Rubbie, S, 2; Bud, S, 1/12
29400 WILSON, Ella, Foyil, OK, 21; Nora, D, 4; John, S, 2
4010 WILSON, Ella M, Tahlequah, OK, 42; Lelia Stapler, D, 17; Clinton Adair, S, 13
5657 WILSON, Enoch, Maysville, AR, 26; 28280, Lula, W, 27; Gooden, William, S of W, 7; Wilson, Nellie, D, 2
8164 WILSON, Finnie, Muldrow, OK, 26; Ella, D, 14; William, S, 13; Oma, S, 11; Finnie, Jr, S, 5; Minnie, D, 5; Emma, D, 1
2189 WILSON, George, Welling, OK, 32; 5848, Annie, W, 33; Lizzie, D, 8
10683 WILSON, James, Whitmire, OK, 39; 41233, Bettie, W, 50; Stealer, S, 16; Will, S, 14; Nancy, D, 10; Lizzie, D, 8
23933 WILSON, James M, Gideon, OK, 21
2382 WILSON, James W, Turley, OK, 52; Robert, S, 16; Sue, D, 11
12908 WILSON, Jessie L, Vian, OK, 27; Chas. A, S, 5; Keener C, S, 1
1885 WILSON, Jim, Locust Grove, OK, 48; 11524, Lydia, W, 22

[WILSON, John. See #1338] *(Note: entry separate from other family groups)*

4841 WILSON, John F, Tahlequah, OK, 36; John M, S, 16; Joe A, S, 4; Fred C, S, 2
41797 WILSON, Josephine, Tahlequah, OK, 36
27129 WILSON, Laura, Dodge, OK, 22
4795 WILSON, Letitia M, Tahlequah, OK, 45
1936 WILSON, Lydia, Row, OK, 26; Edna I, D, 7; Thomas S, S, 3; Mary M, D, 1
10655 WILSON, Martha E, Bluejacket, OK, 50; Elgin D, S, 13; Martha E, D, 12; Clara E, D, 9; Donithan A, D, 6; Wade C, S, ½
4806 WILSON, Martha J, Kansas, OK, 44; Miller, George, S, 18; Christina, D, 16; Wilson, Hettie, D, 14; Myrtle, D, 12; Robert Lee, S, 9; Homes, S, 6
25308 WILSON, Martha J, Sallisaw, OK, 23; Fred B, S, 4; Clyde C, S, 2; Bonnie May, D, 1/12
5655 WILSON, Mary, Maysville, AR, 14; By Rachel Smilin, Mother
24444 WILSON, Mary A, Dodge, OK, 34; Bertha L, D, 13
22615 WILSON, Mary E, Choteau, OK, 21; Ethel, D, 6; Claude Roy, S, 1
23934 WILSON, Mary E, Gideon, OK, 58; Samuel S, S, 17; Eva E, D, 11; William D. L, S, 8

CHEROKEE DESCENDANTS RESIDING WEST OF MISSISSIPPI RIVER.
VOLUME III   (N – Z)

Key: Guion Miller Application Number; Name; Address, Relation (to Head); Age in 1906

- **3161** WILSON, Mattie L, Holly, CO, 30; Butler, Frank L, S, 14; Myrtle A, D, 12; Wilson, Parmelia A, D, 2
- **29282** WILSON, Nancy C, Chelsea, OK, 33; John H, S, 6; Janie B, D, 5; Alta M, D, 2

[WILSON, Nannie. See #2268]   *(Note: entry separate from other family groups)*

[WILSON, Nannie. See #12552]   *(Note: entry separate from other family groups)*

- **6027** WILSON, Nannie E, Chelsea, OK, 31; Miller, Ray F, D, 10
- **26031** WILSON, Ned, Hulbert, OK, 28; 26032, Lilia, W, 29; Selsie, D, 7; Nannie, D, 3
- **26294** WILSON, Nettie A, Centralia, OK, 18; Clemie B, D, 1
- **2737** WILSON, Rebecca Victoria, Phillips, OK, 35; James Robert, S, 16; Cora A, D, 6; Thomas, S, 3; Wilmer W, S, 1
- **10003** WILSON, Rory M, Muldrow, OK, 38; Rory S, S, 4
- **6075** WILSON, Runabout, Melvin, OK, 58
- **27953** WILSON, Sarah S, Sallisaw, OK, 11; Daniel M, Bro, 9; George S, Bro, 5; Oscar, Bro, 3;   By William M. Wilson, Gdn.
- **1755** WILSON, Susan, Tahlequah, OK, 53; 40298, Minervia, D, 20; Elizabeth, D, 16; Susie, D, 15
- **29259** WILSON, Susan E, Tulsa, OK, 34

[WILSON, Watt. See #11659]   *(Note: entry separate from other family groups)*

- **721** WILSON, Youngpigeon, Eucha, OK, 49
- **5198** WIMER, Hallie C. T, Vinita, OK, 33
- **28378** WINDHAM, Emma W, Chelsea, OK, 23; Fleeta Mae, D, 2; Cherokee Eliz, D, 1/3
- **40600** WING, Otis J, Nowata, OK, 22
- **4003** WINGET, Nannie A, Kansas, OK, 38; Chas. M, S, 17; Tudy[sic] M, D, 13; Hannan[sic] P, D, 11; Jesse, S, 6; Myrtle L, D, 4; Nono E, D, 1
- **8648** WISWELL, Susan, Brent, OK, 30; Myrtle F, D, 9; Dee Earnest, S, 7; James Franklin, S, 2; Baldridge, S, 1/12
- **29252** WITHERSPOON, Maggie, Verdigris, OK, 22
- **29281** WITT, Abe, Chelsea, OK, 27
- **31290** WITT, Allie, Okoee, OK, 23
- **17519** WITT, David T, Vinita, OK, 32; Hugh F, S, 4; Maud M, D, 2
- **11247** WITT, Jane I, Okoee, OK, 62
- **30459** WITT, John W, Centralia, OK, 39; Norma, D, 8; Rufus, S, 6; Phillip, S, 1
- **30458** WITT, Michael O, Eckville, Canada, 39
- **29981** WITT, Tipton, Eckville, Canada, 22
- **44280** WITT, Elmer L, Vinita, OK, 15; Della J, Sis, 14; Bert E, Sis(?), 11; Mary E, Sis, 9 [Died 1908]; Monroe W, Bro, 7; Nettie, Sis, 5;   By William F. Witt, Gdn.
- **1808** WOFFORD, Amanda M, Tahlequah, OK, 48
- **27062** WOFFORD, Charley, Cherokee City, AR, 33; Ed Lee, S, 11; Homer H, S, 8; Walter F, S, 3; Arthur D, S, 1/6
- **18468** WOFFORD, Elizabeth E, Vinita, OK, 21

CHEROKEE DESCENDANTS RESIDING WEST OF MISSISSIPPI RIVER.
VOLUME III (N – Z)
Key: Guion Miller Application Number; Name; Address, Relation (to Head); Age in 1906

[WOFFORD, George. See #25634]   *(Note: entry separate from other family groups)*

3205 WOFFORD, George A, Tahlequah, OK, 49; 1810, Sarah J, W, 62
25774 WOFFORD, Geo. N, Tahlequah, OK, 21

[WOFFORD, Jackson E. See #16978]   *(Note: entries separate*
[WOFFORD, Pearl. See #16978]   *from other family groups)*

1191 WOFFORD, Jennie, Stilwell, OK, 89
7012 WOFFORD, Jess, Melvin, OK, 24
26563 WOFFORD, John, Cherokee City, AR, 23; 42619, Nancy, W, 25; Sampson, S, 5; Bob, S, 2
5514 WOFFORD, Josie B, Tahlequah, OK, 46; Jessie, D, 11; Wilson, S, 6
27182 WOFFORD, Louanna, Moodys, OK, 23; Eliza A, D, 1
6695 WOFFORD, Maggie, Sallisaw, OK, 27; Mary Gertrude, D, 4; Ira Eugene, S, 1
3802 WOFFORD, Martha J, Tahlequah, OK, 64
3548 WOFFORD, Nathaniel, Moodys, OK, 55
27061 WOFFORD, Ned, Cherokee City, AR, 25; 42529, Linda, W, 27; 17050, Blue, Martha, D of W, 8; 42529, Wofford, Martha A, D, ¼
1477 WOFFORD, Ruth, Moodys, OK, 46; Alexander, S, 17

[WOFFORD, Susie. See #44311]
[WOFFORD, Annie. See #44311]   *(Note: entries separate*
[WOFFORD, Mary. See #44311]   *from other family groups)*
[WOFFORD, Sarah. See #44311]

8904 WOFFORD, William S, Cherokee City, AR, 65; 8908, Ona, W, 54; State, S, 15; Ben, S, 11; Jim, S, 9
2492 WOLF, Elizabeth, Stilwell, OK, 66
9945 GAR-WA-JI-YU-LAR, Oaks, OK, 15;   By Mary Raven, Gdn.
6926 WOLF, George, Oaks, OK, 21
13718 WOLF, Jack, Cookson, OK, 23
2834 WOLF, Jennie, Proctor, OK, 76
5724 WOLF, John, Flint, OK, 28; 9622, Dora, W, 19; Jessie, D, 1

[WOLF, Katie. See #5710]   *(Note: entry separate from other family groups)*

4906 WOLF, Lewis, Claremore, OK, 51; Lewey, S, 17; Richard, S, 15
21988 WOLF, Linda, Braggs, OK, 29; Fox, Lillie, D, 9
14180 WOLF, Lossie P, Spavinaw, OK, 40; Arch, S, 20; Ella, D, 18; Betsy, D, 16; Medicine, S, 12
13671 WOLF, Nannie, Wauhillau, OK, 57
5770 WOLF, Pick-up, Rose, OK, 45; 5784, Eliza, W, 30; Lewis, Polly, D of W, 13; 5770, Wolf, Dick, S, 3; Dave, S, 1
12641 WOLF, Quaitsy, Christie, OK, 36

CHEROKEE DESCENDANTS RESIDING WEST OF MISSISSIPPI RIVER.
VOLUME III (N – Z)

Key: Guion Miller Application Number; Name; Address, Relation (to Head); Age in 1906

12639 WOLF, Richard, Christie, OK, 23; 33148, Nannie, W, 24; Hider, S, 4; Riley, S, 1
6927 WOLF, Stopp, Oaks, OK, 17
3206 WOLF, Susan E, Proctor, OK, 52
16933 WOLF, Tom, Oaks, OK, 47; 10648, Nannie, W, 52; 16935, Chuwee, Sam, S of W, 17
13970 WOLF, William, Stilwell, OK, 46; 13368, Betsy, W, 56; Nancy, D, 16; Ah-ley, S, 15; Cealie, D, 10; Ezekiel, S, 10
16625 WOLF, William N, Childers, OK, 38
5269 WOLF, E, Arch, Wauhillau, OK, 33 [Non Comp.]; By Charles Young, Gdn.
5349 WOLFE, Arch, Locust Grove, OK, 21
5907 WOLFE, Ben, Maysville, AR, 23; 5654, Charlotte, W, 25; Clabe[sic], S, 1
2394 WOLFE, Chas, Stilwell, OK, 23
12638 WOLFE, Cynthia, Christie, OK, 18
6435 WOLFE, David, Proctor, OK, 47; 12640, Mary, W, 33; 18102, Hugh, S, 18; Monroe, S, 16; Redcloud, S, 13; Henry, S, 11
4907 WOLFE, Eli, Claremore, OK, 47; 1424, Caroline, W, 37; Henry, S, 14; Richard, S, 12; Jinnie, D, 6; Doney[sic], S, 4; Ollie, D, 1/12

[WOLFE, Ethel May. See #24573] *(Note: entry separate from other family groups)*

1561 WOLFE, Eve, Eucha, OK, 55
8006 WOLFE, Foster L, Centralia, OK, 35; Samuel W, S, 5; Addie L, D, 9; Lewis A, S, 1
12642 WOLFE, Hummingbird, Christie, OK, 14; By Katy Wolfe, Gdn.
8947 WOLFE, Jackson T, Tahlequah, OK, 26; 37070, Jennie, W, 20
19822 WOLFE, James, Stilwell, OK, 37; 22534, Betsy, W, 28; 19823, Fannie, D, 2
3155 WOLFE, Jane, Spavinaw, OK, 60
15952 WOLFE, John, Stilwell, OK, 57
5096 WOLFE, Joseph, Baron, OK, 32; Wolfe, William, S, 7
1850 WOLFE, Katie, Stilwell, OK, 65; Wah-lo-lah, S, 14
2036 WOLFE, Katie, Oaks, OK, 16; By Minnie Israel, Gdn.
22017 WOLFE, Lila, Eucha, OK, 5; By Eve Wolfe, Gdn.
11162 WOLFE, Lincoln, Stilwell, OK, 30; 22525, Lizzie, W, 30; 10272, Hider, Rachel, D of W, 9; 22525, HORN, George, S of W, 6; Wolfe, Ophelia, D, 2; Lincoln, S, 1
2461 WOLFE, Martha C, Vinita, OK, 45; Paul, S, 16; Ralph, S, 11; Gordon, S, 8; Louise M, D, 6; Catherine, D, ½
23496 WOLFE, Mary, Proctor, OK, 28
29041 WOLFE, Mitchel W, Proctor, OK, 31; 28465, Daisy D, W, 27
2841 WOLFE, Nannie, Locust Grove, OK, 31; Hasting, S, 1
4385 WOLFE, Peter, Locust Grove, OK, 30; 4855, Annie, W, 28; Cull, S, 3; Susie, D, 1
1706 WOLFE, Peter Eucha, OK, 34
3467 WOLFE, Richard M, Tahlequah, OK, 57
5621 WOLFE, Richard M, Jr, Tahlequah, OK, 20
23548 WOLFE, Richard T, Proctor, OK, 23

CHEROKEE DESCENDANTS RESIDING WEST OF MISSISSIPPI RIVER.
VOLUME III (N – Z)
Key: Guion Miller Application Number; Name; Address, Relation (to Head); Age in 1906

23251 WOLFE, Sallie, Claremore, OK, 20; Oo-wa-lu-ki, S, 5/6
12643 WOLFE, Sarah, Stilwell, OK, 24
5121 WOLFE, Susan, Proctor, OK, 22
5949 WOLFE, William, Maysville, AR, 58; Tom, S, 18
1733 WOLFE, William Riley, Ruby, OK, 28; Avola M, D, 5; Mattie J, D, 4
24667 WOOD, Columbia, Zena, OK, 21; Bernard, S, 2
1999 WOOD, Francis M, Zena, OK, 27; Ernest, S, 10; Roy, S, 9
1996 WOOD, Henry P, Zena, OK, 42; Timpie, D, 14; Sherman, S, 12; Minnie, D, 9; Hemp, S, 7
2000 WOOD, James F, Zena, OK, 46; Bennie V, S, 16; Frankie O, S, 12; Bessie M, D, 9; Magdaline, D, 4
27513 WOOD, James M, Zena, OK, 23
36599 WOOD, Jno, Ft. Baker, CA, 22
31366 WOOD, Lewis E, Vinita, OK, 25; Leroy, S, 1
31293 WOOD, Lucy B, Chillicothe, TX, 21; Buster Brown, S, 2
31432 WOOD, Martin C, Chetopa, KS, 29; Grace E, D, 7; Artie Evert, S, 2
24178 WOOD, Mary, Lynch, OK, 21; McRay, S, 2

[WOOD, Rollin M. See #1745]   *(Note: entry separate from other family groups)*

23638 WOOD, Roxie M, Chelsea, OK, 28; Ansalem Tillman, S, 10; Freddie T, S, 8; Donas Oland, S, 5; Barnett Rogers, S, 3; Theo E, S, 1/6
16861 WOODS, Sarah, Uniontown, AR, 18; Joe, S, 1
30701 WOOD, Sarah B, Needmore, OK, 24
2932 WOOD, William H, Miles, OK, 53; Lila J, D, 2;   Howard K, S, 1/12
24666 WOOD, William H. C, Fredonia, OK, 28; Lee E, S, 1
23782 WOOD, William O, Zena, OK, 17; Maude May, Sis, 14; Bertha E, Sis, 11;   By Acenith Pallock, Gdn
10147 WOODALL, Amanda, Wimer, OK, 20
10286 WOODALL, Anna, Wimer, OK, 24; Gray, Thomas J, S, 6; Aimes, Myrtle, D, 1
2984 WOODALL, Bettie, Vinita, OK, 53; Ose, S, 18

[WOODALL, Beuna V. See #23211] *(Note: entry separate from other family groups)*

11296 WOODALL, Caty, Melvin, OK, 21
2929 WOODALL, Clara, Baron, OK, 58
4848 WOODALL, George, Locust Grove, OK, 30; 32738, Maggie, W, 26; Beulah, D, 6; Ellen, D, 4; Susie, D, 2
33588 WOODALL, George R, Tahlequah, OK, 27
1612 WOODALL, Henry H, Hulbert, OK, 24; 1611, Alcie, W, 28
5004 WOODALL, Hiram, Melvin, OK, 32
27017 WOODALL, Ira, Welch, OK, 26; Effie B, D, 4; Annie, D, 3; Ruby E, D, 1
32108 WOODALL, Isaac, Welch, OK, 23
21152 WOODALL, James, Melvin, OK, 21; James, Jr, S, 2
28468 WOODALL, James, Welch, OK, 21

CHEROKEE DESCENDANTS RESIDING WEST OF MISSISSIPPI RIVER.
VOLUME III   (N – Z)

Key: Guion Miller Application Number; Name; Address, Relation (to Head); Age in 1906

 3807 WOODALL, James B, McIntosh, NM, 46; 4136, Anna M, W, 46; Frank F, S, 2?; Jefferson A, S, ?; Benjamin J, S, ?; Mary E, D, ?; Lucy A, D, ?; Alee A, D, ?
33589 WOODALL, John, Tahlequah, OK, ?
38354 WOODALL, John D, Grove, OK, ?
23759 WOODALL, Leander, Vinita, OK, 30

[WOODALL, Looney. See #31813]   *(Note: entry separate from other family groups)*

23758 WOODALL, Louis, Vinita, OK, 28
 909 WOODALL, Lucien B, Wimer, OK, 51
38353 WOODALL, Lucy Anna, Grove, OK, 27
33591 WOODALL, Maggie F, Tahlequah, OK, 30
 869 WOODALL, Nancy, Metory, OK, 60; Albert D, S, 18; Cora Emma, D, 13

[WOODALL, Nancy. See #2143]   *(Note: entry separate from other family groups)*

33590 WOODALL, Oscar D, Tahlequah, OK, 24; 8244, Della, W, 19
33587 WOODALL, Robert, Tahlequah, OK, 33; Bertha E, D, 7; Bert Vance, S, 2; Maggie May, D, 1/12
 5952 WOODALL, Stand W, Bartlesville, OK, 32; Mary D, D, ¼
 4324 WOODALL, Susan, Grove, OK, 51?; Nancy L, D, 13
 8737 WOODALL, Thomas, Locust Grove, OK, 27; 3642, Polly, W, 38; 8737, Richard, S, 10; 16919, Raven, Mary, D of W, 14; 3642, Panther, Josiah, S of W, 10; Lydia, D of W, 7
 4547 WOODALL, Thomas F, Warner, OK, 46; 26313, Emma V, W, 36; Mamie, D, 12; Mary, D, 6; Lola, D, 4; Caroline, D, 1
36388 WOODALL, Walter, Vinita, OK, 32
 5348 WOODALL, William, Locust Grove, OK, 56
 4395 WOODALL, William B, Wimer, OK, 29
 3810 WOODALL, William C, Jr, Vinita, OK, 36; Lida W, D, 11; Stand W, S, 9; Vera M, D, 6; Charles W, S, 4

[WOODARD. See also WOODWARD.]

[WOODARD, Albert. See #23044]   *(Note: entries separate*
[WOODARD, Bert. See #23044]   *from other family groups)*

17466 WOODARD, Ann Eliza, Tahlequah, OK, 65
23313 WOODARD, Annie, McLain, OK, 41?
23301 WOODARD, Bettie [Cowesta], McLain, OK, 26
 3145 WOODARD, Bunch, Tahlequah, OK, 19; Nannie, Sis, 16; Daniel, Bro, 14; Allen, Bro, 12; Looney, Bro, 10; Minnie, Sis, 8; Della, Sis, 5; Yula, Sis, 1; By Joseph Woodard, Gdn
18995 WOODARD, David, Tahlequah, OK, 6;   By John S. Woodard, Gdn.
 3139 WOODARD, George, Braggs, OK, 54; Edwin, S, 14; Mary, D, 5; Joeellar, D, 2

CHEROKEE DESCENDANTS RESIDING WEST OF MISSISSIPPI RIVER.
VOLUME III (N – Z)

Key: Guion Miller Application Number; Name; Address, Relation (to Head); Age in 1906

- **3150** WOODARD, Jack, Tahlequah, OK, 23
- **8238** WOODARD, James O, Centralia, OK, 24; Erna Lee, D, 2; Lay Mabel, D, 1
- **94** WOODARD, John, McLain, OK, 30
- **4482** WOODARD, John S, Tahlequah, OK, 46
- **4479** WOODARD, Joseph, Tahlequah, OK, 58
- **269** WOODARD, Martha, McLain, OK, 52; Eliza, D, 20
- **29592** WOODARD, Mary A, Newsome, TX, 20
- **17233** WOODARD, Mary J. L, Honolulu, HA, 46
- **23302** WOODARD, Ollie, McLain, OK, 38?
- **23303** WOODARD, Sarah, McLain, OK, 46?
- **8239** WOODARD, Zack, Centralia, OK, 22
- **33733** WOODCOOK, Julia A, Jenks, OK, 29; David W, S, 2; Thelma M, D, 1
- **11742** WOODS, Alice A, Westville, OK, 20
- **3558** WOODS, Charles W, Zena, OK, 35; James M, S, 18; Louis E, S, 16; William P, S, 14; Mamie E, D, 12; Elbert B, S, 9; Charles A, S, 8; John H, S, 3
- **24411** WOODS, Clara L, Zena, OK, 6; Walter, Bro, 4;   By Augustus Dover, Gdn.
- **467** WOODS, Gertrude B, Table Mounds, OK, 22; Ruth V, D, 2
- **7551** WOODS, Lizzie, Claremore, OK, 31; Georgia A, D, 13; Annie E, D, 11; Mary, D, 7; Beulah, D, 5; Emma, D, 1; Gordon, S, 1/12
- **1459** WOODS, Nannie, Sallisaw, OK, 25; Christie, Angie M, D, 6; May C, D, 1
- **43525** WOODS, Vinnie May, Portland, OR, 23; Eugenie V, D, 3

[WOODWARD. See also WOODARD.]

- **3138** WOODWARD, Henry, Tahlequah, OK, 25; Ethel, D, 2; Clyde, S, ½
- **29313** WOODWARD, Janie, Muldrow, OK, 24; Edwin H, S, 5
- **14788** WOOL, Jim, Sallisaw, OK, 39; 14789, George, S, 10; 14787, Ben, S, 8
- **10278** WOOLEY, Minerva, Muldrow, OK, 20; Joseph E, S, 2
- **1085** WORK, Charles, Honey Creek, OK, 56; 1102, Eliza, W, 56; Will, S, 14
- **5738** WORK, Jesse, Afton, OK, 22
- **24972** WORK, John, Afton, OK, 24; Ruby, S, 1; Ludie, S, 1

[WORKER. See WORK.]

- **24611** WRIGHT, Alex. D, Summers, AR, 28
- **24701** WRIGHT, Annie, Rose, OK, 25; William R, S, 6; Ellis, S, 5; Bessie, D, 3; Andy, S, 2
- **31643** WRIGHT, Belle, Wauhillau, OK, 26; Willie E, S, 7; Julia A, D, 5; Caleb P, S, 2; Gertrude F, D, 1/3
- **23732** WRIGHT, Betsy, Westville, OK, 30; Curtis, S, 2
- **1848** WRIGHT, Charlotte, Christie, OK, 59; Sallie W, D, 19
- **10604** WRIGHT, Cornelius E, Christie, OK, 30; Jack, S, 4; Claude, S, 1
- **24609** WRIGHT, Eli, Summers, AR, 26

[WRIGHT, Ellis. See #24700]   *(Note: entry separate from other family groups)*

CHEROKEE DESCENDANTS RESIDING WEST OF MISSISSIPPI RIVER.
VOLUME III (N – Z)

Key: Guion Miller Application Number; Name; Address, Relation (to Head); Age in 1906

[WRIGHT, Ella W. See #24700]   *(Note: entry separate from other family groups)*

 5801 WRIGHT, Ethel J, Rose, OK, 5;   By Joe I. Wilson, Gdn.
22045 WRIGHT, George, Blackgum, OK, 20; Grace, Sis, 5;   By William C. Wright, Gdn.
10487 WRIGHT, George W, Christie, OK, 33
 6681 WRIGHT, Jack, Christie, OK, 21
24559 WRIGHT, Jackson, Southwest City, MO, 26; Lucinda, D, 6
 1737 WRIGHT, James, Southwest City, MO, 59; Thomas, S, 13; Josie, D, 11; Annie, D, 10; Lizzie, D, 8
15979 WRIGHT, Jesse E, Pryor Creek, OK, 35; 15980, Mary E, W, 31; Willia C, D, 8; Sallie U, D, 3
24610 WRIGHT, Jesse J, Summers, AR, 24
 2911 WRIGHT, Jesse V, Baron, OK, 58; John H, S, 12; Myrtle D, D, 6
11907 WRIGHT, Johnathan R, Christie, OK, 25
11707 WRIGHT, Kate, Coffeyville, KS, 32; Shelley K, S, 6; William J, S, 4
 9370 WRIGHT, Lydia C, Hanson, OK, 27; Frank J, S, 2
 8234 WRIGHT, Maggie E, Vinita, OK, 36; 27766, Mabel, D, 17; Dora, D, 16; Benge, S, 14; Willie E, S, 13; Toney M, S, 11; Pauline, S, 7; Buster B, S, 2
29137 WRIGHT, Mollie J, Baker City, OR, 28; Fannie May, S, 9; Samuel D, S, 9; Gertrude, D, 5; Bessie R, D, 3
22143 WRIGHT, Nettie, Evansville, AR, 18
 6659 WRIGHT, Tillmon R, Ramona, OK, 39; 8751, Malinda, W, 30
13901 WRIGHT, William C, Blackgum, OK, 26, Edgar I, S, 3; William S, S, 1
11010 WRIGHT, William W, Baron, OK, 38; 6620, Mollie, W, 34; Jesse, S, 12; Colbert, S, 10; William C, S, 8; Ada, D, 5
13364 WYCHE, John W, Claremore, OK, 38; Willie May, D, 6; Thomas G, S, 2
 4288 WYCHE, Robert D, Muskogee, OK, 44; 4297, Jessie C, D, 8; Bernice M, D, 6
27855 WYETT, Helen Eiffert, Warner, OK, 21
 8788 WYLY, Albert S, Tahlequah, OK, 35; 9250, Lillian A, W, 26
 5947 WYLY, Annie, Maysville, AR, 23; White, Lee, S, 1
 5946 WYLY, Lydia, Maysville, AR, 29; Tehee, Susie, D, 8
 5942 WYLY, Lynnie, Maysville, AR, 14;   By Rachel Tiger, Gdn.
 5977 WYLY, Mouse, Maysville, AR, 23
10920 WYLY, Nancy, Maysville, AR, 20
 3501 WYLY, Oliver Lynch, Tahlequah, OK, 54; 25251, Keziah or Betsey, W, 31
 5261 WYLY, Percy, Tahlequah, OK, 45; James Robert, S 20; Thurman, S, 15
 4601 WYLY, Robert L, Tahlequah, OK, 44
 5259 WYLY, William B, Tahlequah, OK, 32; 5712, Cora, W, 28; Lucien B, S, 4

[WYLY, Wilson. See #5514]   *(Note: entry separate from other family groups)*

14814 WYLY, Worcester, Caney, KS, 48; Rachel, D, 8
12813 YAHOLA, Heavy, Braggs, OK, 21; Joanna, D, 2

CHEROKEE DESCENDANTS RESIDING WEST OF MISSISSIPPI RIVER.
VOLUME III (N – Z)

Key: Guion Miller Application Number; Name; Address, Relation (to Head); Age in 1906

[YAHOLA, Nellie. See #9374] ⎱ *(Note: entries separate*
[YAHOLA, Kahoga. See #9374] ⎰ *from other family groups)*

15721 YAHOLA, Sul-le-coo-ke [or Johnson], Braggs, OK, 61
16730 YAHOLA, Alexander, Vian, OK, 21
 8066 YAHOLAH[sic], Daniel, Braggs, OK, 28
 9789 YAHOLA, Dave, Vian, OK, 50; 16729, Lydia, W, 41; 16728, Wah-yor-he [Rock], S, 15; Na-ya-he, S, 14; Jack, S, 9; Charlotte, D, 2; Sam, S, 5
 9785 YAHOLAH[sic], Jennie, Vian, OK, 30
16663 YAHOLA, John, Vian, OK, 24
11488 YAHOLAH[sic], Johnson, Braggs, OK, 55; 11493, Polly, W, 51
23731 YARBOROUGH, Lizzie, Ft. Gibson, OK, 32
37741 YARBOROUGH, Minerva W, Reeds, MO, 35; Samuel A R, S, 12; Minerva, D, 9; Bessie, D, 7; Roy, S, 5
 4242 YATES, Ellen, Ft. Gibson, OK, 53; Edith, D, 12
23491 YEARGAIN, Joseph D, Southwest City, MO, 37
23490 YEARGAIN, Turner A, Southwest City, MO, 21
 1972 YEARGAIN, Mary J, Maysville, AR, 60; Robert P, S, 16
23489 YEARGAIN, Scott A, Maysville, AR, 34; Marjorie Clair, D, 9
 1343 YEARGAR, Claud W, Maysville, AR, 23
16382 YELLOWBIRD, (No other name given), Vian, OK, 58
16924 YELLOWBIRD, Sallie, Marble City, OK, 32; Young, Rufus, S, 3

[YOCUM, John V. See #3522]   *(Note: entry separate from other family groups)*

25498 YOCUM, Susie, Grove, OK, 25

[YOK-SA. See #9608]   *(Note: entry separate from other family groups)*

24965 YORK, Lillie B, Adair, OK, 24; Vera M, D, 4; Mary I, D, 1
 7654 YORTUCK, Nannie, Stilwell, OK, 27; Jennie, D, 15; Mary, D, 9; John, S, 2
35346 YOUNG, Annie, Braggs, OK, 26; Foreman, Juanita, D, 7; Young, Willie, S, 4; Evaline, D, 3; Johnie, S, 1
1831½ YOUNG, Callie, Wauhillau, OK, 25; Smith, Charley, S, 2
 6599 YOUNG, Carrie E, Choteau, OK, 53
 1831 YOUNG, Charlie, Wauhillau, OK, 51; 1829, Betsy, W, 51; Silas, S, 19
36573 YOUNG, Daniel, Jr, Rex, OK, 23; Mary, D, 3
43147 YOUNG, Eli, Marble City, OK, 25; Louella, D, 1
12239 YOUNG, Eva, Blackgum, OK, 35; James, S, 10

[YOUNG, George. See #9706]   *(Note: entry separate from other family groups)*

23315 YOUNG, Jack, Vian, OK, 27

[YOUNG, James. See #11191]   *(Note: entry separate from other family groups)*

CHEROKEE DESCENDANTS RESIDING WEST OF MISSISSIPPI RIVER.
VOLUME III (N – Z)

Key: Guion Miller Application Number; Name; Address, Relation (to Head); Age in 1906

1968 YOUNG, Joe, Vian, OK, 29; 13219, Jennie, W, 27
10673 YOUNG, John, Marble City, OK, 20
23204 YOUNG, John W, Vian, OK, 31; Fannie, D, 2
  525 YOUNG, Josiah, Locust Grove, OK, 46 [Died 12-21-1906]; 17084, Young, Dick, S, 17;   By William Young, Gdn.
10907 YOUNG, Houston, Marble City, OK, 24
23316 YOUNG, Lewis, Vian, OK, 38; 3645, Mary, W, 37; Alice, D, 13; Simon, S, 12; Viola, D, 5; Johnson R, S, 1
16396 YOUNG, Louisa M, Rex, OK, 58

[YOUNG, Lydia. See #13276]   *(Note: entry separate from other family groups)*

25740 YOUNG, Mary, Tahlequah, OK, 48; Mike, S, 19; Dick, S, 17; Robert, S, 12; Eva, D, 10; Dewey, S, 8
 8750 YOUNG, Ned, Locust Grove, OK, 21; 8732, Peggie, W, 16
23925 YOUNG, Pressha S, Ahniwake, OK, 37; Grace B, D, 15; Ocean P, D, 13; Ollie M, D, 8; Mary, D, 5; George A, S, 4; Neoma B, D, 2; William J, S, 7   [Died 8-25-1906]
1830½ YOUNG, Roach, Wauhillau, OK, 27
 3979 YOUNG, Roach, Vian, OK, 74 [Died 6-10-1907]; 3697, Naney, W, 63; Richard, S, 18

[YOUNG, Rufus. See #16924]   *(Note: entry separate from other family groups)*

26554 YOUNG, Samantha J, Ahniwake, OK, 25; Nellie M, D, 10; Bessie B, D, 6; Ella M, D, 3; Johnie C, S, 1
 8740 YOUNG, Tassel, Locust Grove, OK, 78
36572 YOUNG, Thomas F, Rex, OK, 36; Lillietta, D, 10; Commillious, D, 9; Camie, D, 5
 6675 YOUNG, Tom, Braggs, OK, 33; 30855, Cynthia, W, 32; William, S, 4
16595 YOUNG, Tom, Marble City, OK, 26; 11764, Elsie, W, 28
 1253 YOUNG, William, Locust Grove, OK, 32; Conseen, S, ½; Oo-yas-tah, D, 4
 1460 YOUNG, William, Marble City, OK, 71; Lillie, D, 8

[YOUNG BEAVER, Katie. See #9619]
                        (Note: entry separate from other family groups)

10641 YOUNGBIRD, Andy, Lometa, OK, 60; 10645, Sallie, W, 46; Nakie, S, 19; Elsie, D, 17; William, S, 16; Lossie, D, 15; Jack, S, 13
 1198 YOUNGBIRD, Isaac, Kansas, OK, 66; 1197, Nancy, W, 56; James, S, 19; Lucy, D, 15

[YOUNGBIRD, James. See #9620]   *(Note: entry separate from other family groups)*

43404 YOUNGBIRD, Nellie, Kansas, OK, 20; Davis, Mary, D, 4; Johnson, S, 1

CHEROKEE DESCENDANTS RESIDING WEST OF MISSISSIPPI RIVER.
VOLUME III   (N – Z)

Key: Guion Miller Application Number; Name; Address, Relation (to Head); Age in 1906

43405 YOUNGBIRD, Sam, Kansas, OK, 20
34081 YOUNGBIRD, Nakie, Lometa, OK, 18; Johnson, Ross, S, 3
6621 YOUNGBIRD, White, Kansas, OK, 37; 11231,Ella, W, 28; Ina, D, 10; Tillie, D, 3
5810 YOUNGBIRD, William, Kansas, OK, 40; 12611, Lora, W, 36; Maggie, D, 16; Sallie, S, 14; Ida, D, 6; Sarah, D, 4; Annie, D, 2
24745 YOUNGBLOOD, Emma, Long, OK, 20

[YOUNGDEER, Reuben. See #1190]   *(Note: entry separate from other family groups)*

1189 YOUNGDEER, *(No other name given)*, Oaks, OK, 76; 1423, Che-ka-yoo-ee, W, 83
16931 YOUNG DUCK, Mollie, Kansas, OK, 6; (Daughter of #16932.)
665 YOUNG DUCK, Sallie, Cherokee City, AR, 13; By Lizzie Ju-lo-dah-deh-gy [or Cornshucker] Gdn.

30362 YOUNGER, Linnie F, Hulbert, OK, 21; Daisy E, D, 3; Mattie A, D, 1; Spade, Emma, AdD, 5
22278 YOUNG PIG, Arch, Tahlequah, OK, 33
7681 YOUNG PIG, French, Tahlequah, OK, 33 [Died 1-1907]

[YOUNGPUPPY, John. See #22014]*(Note: entry separate from other family groups)*

[YOUNGPUPPY, Sallie. See #22015]   *(Note: entry separate from other family groups)*

5025 YOUNGWOLF, Dave, Christie, OK, 56
5718 YOUNGWOLF, Eliza, Oaks, OK, 42
23238 YOUNGWOLF, Jennie, Christie, OK, 24; Lucy, D, 1
2224 YOUNGWOLF, Walter, Proctor, OK, 24; 2693, Lucinda, W, 25; Jesse, S, 3; Nan, D, 1
3718 YOUNT, Effie Ethel, Vinita, OK, 46
25969 ZENO, Maud B, Spavinaw, OK, 25

[ZINN, Beulah. See #16135]   *(Note: entry separate from other family groups)*

27514 ZINN, Melvina J, Zena, OK, 26; William H. F, S, 5
32967 ZUFALL, George E, Jr, Muskogee, OK, 708 S. Cherokee St, 30
31419 ZUFALL, Louis, Muskogee, OK, 32; Raymon, S, 9; Elva, D, 5; Dorothy, D, 1
5064 ZUFALL, Margaret, Muskogee, OK, 5?; Herbert, S, ?; Grace, D, ?
28929 ZUFALL, Magaret, Muskogee, OK, 708 S. Cherokee St, ?
28928 ZUFALL, Pearl E, Muskogee, OK, 708 S. Cherokee St, ?

THE EASTERN CHEROKEES *vs* THE UNITED STATES

No. 23,214

Supplemental Roll of Eastern Cherokees

JANUARY 5, 1910

List of names to be added to and stricken from the original roll Eastern Cherokees as reported on May 28, 1909, as recommended by Guion Miller, Special Commissioner, in his supplemental report of January 5, 1910, together with certain clerical corrections to be made in the original roll.

SUPPLEMENTAL ROLL of
EASTERN CHEROKEES RESIDING WEST OF MISSISSIPPI RIVER.

Key: Guion Miller Application Number, Name, Address, Relation (to Head), Age in 1906.

      ADAIR, Mintie, Nowata, OK, 21
      ADAMS, Arthur T, Vinita, OK, 20
24238 ADKINSON, Ora B, Catoosa, OK, 22; Ella M, D, 1
      AGENT, Sallie, Oaks, OK, 22

[ALBERTY, Allen. See Roll #30726]   *(Note: Application number not given..)*

      ALEXANDER, Lewis, Tahlequah, OK, 14   By Ross Daniels, Gdn.

[ALLEN, Clarence. See #21014]

43347 ANDERSON, John F, Eureka, OK, 25
      ANDOE, Nellie C, Collinsville, OK, 17
5220 ARCHER, Anna B, Vinita, OK, 28; Ina, D, 8; Otto B, S, 6; Fannie B, D, 4; Thomas B, Jr, S, 3; Abram, S, 1

      BAILEY, Josie, Christie, OK, 21
      BARBER, Peggie, Porum, OK, 60
10887 BARNETT, Bertha M, Flint, OK, 2   By Sarah F. Barnett, Mother and Gdn.
33091 BARNEY, Cordelia, Plateau, CA, 23
32271 BARRY, Billie B, Adair, OK, 15; 32272, Stella M, (Prob. Sis), 13   By Kidder S. Barry, Father
36074 BASSETT, Henry, Cottonwood, CA, 26
21014 BASSETT, Nancy C, Cottonwood, CA, 56; Enos, Carrie, D, 18; Allen, Clarence, GS, 4
      BATT, Akie, Stilwell, OK, 44
      BATT, Lizzie, Campbell, OK, 76 [Deceased.]   By Joseph Batt, Son.
1785 BEAN, Susan, Baron, OK, 56
6468 BECK, Daniel S, Needmore, OK, 19; Sut R, Bro, 16; Grace P, Sis, 9;   By Arthur W. Beck, Brother and Gdn.
13365 BELL, Mattie M, Oolagah, OK, 41; Daniel H, S, 16; James E, Jr, S, 10; Pearl, D, 7; Mark R, S, 5; Irene, D, 3
      BENGE, Young or Dooley, Sand Point, ID, 34; Young, Lawrence, S, 5; Arthur, S, 2
      BIGHAM, James M, Lewiston, ID, ?
14396 BIGHAM, Tolithia E, Redding, CA, 46; Pearl, D, 16; Edith, D, 14; Earl, S, 9
      BIGHEART, Alice, Bigheart, OK, 34
44118 BISHOP, Fannie, Miles, OK, 36
      BLACKBEAR, Nancy, Locust Grove, OK, 20
25814 BLAIR, Thomas W, Cookson, OK, 1   By Jesse T. Blair, Parent and Gdn.
      BLOSSOM, Betsy, Locust Grove, OK, 26
8366 BOWERS, Ida, Tallahassee, OK, 45; Paul W, S, 5
      BRYSON, Mary J, Stilwell, OK, 15; Williametta, Sis, 14   By Martha Duncan, Grandmother.
      BURKS, Elmer H, Vinita, OK, 22

SUPPLEMENTAL ROLL of
EASTERN CHEROKEES RESIDING WEST OF MISSISSIPPI RIVER.

Key: Guion Miller Application Number, Name, Address, Relation (to Head), Age in 1906.

      BURROWS, Annie E, Claremore, OK, 16
      BUTCHER, Ollie, Hulbert, OK, 17
11780 BUTLER, Robert E, Muskogee, OK, 40; Willie E, S, 9
      BUTTON, Minnie, Watova, OK, 17; Ruth, D, 1

      CABE, Kate, Proctor, OK, 24; Taylor, Lizzie, S, 9; Cabe, Marvin, S, 6
      CABE, Marvin, S, 6
      CAPS, Sersis, Westville, OK, 19
      CAREY, Sarah A, Grove, OK, 33
      CARR, Mary L, Ramona, OK, 48
      CARR, Vida, Checotah, OK, 25; Lillian May, D, 5; Ollie Ponder, D, 4
      CHAIR, Mary, Whitmire, OK, 8; Jones, Charlie, ½ Bro, 5 By Lohn(sic) Locust, Stepfather.
      CHEWIE, Willie, Campbell, OK, 13   By Nancy Rodgers, Gdn.
      CHRISTIE, Stand, Wauhillau, OK, 16; Rider, Charlotte, ½ Sis, 4; By Sarah Rider, Gdn and Mother.
  900 COCHRAN, Scott, Hulbert, OK, 5   By Nellie David, Grandmother
      COFFMAN, Jesse S, Fairland, OK, 4; Sequichie(sic) E, Bro, 3; Earl S, Bro, 1 By Cornelia J. Williams, Parent and Gdn.
      COLLIER, Richard, Sallisaw, OK, 27
      CORDERY, David S, Manard, OK, 14
44348 COUCH, Jesse T, Alluwee, OK, 37
      CRITTENDEN, James, Baptist, OK, 6; Lacie, Lizzie, Sis, 1 By Betsy Suwake, Grandmother
      CRITTENDEN, Walter S, Claremore, OK, 39
      CRUTCHFIELD, Mary, Muskogee, OK, 21

[DAVID, Lucy and child. See #10194]

      DEGE, Phillip S, Muskogee, OK, 22 907 N F Street
31336 DIXON, Francis M, Miami, OK, 25; Ruby Mae, D, 1
      DOUTHITT, Cora E, Afton, OK, 16
      DOWNING, Mary, Muldrow, OK, 38

      EARLEY, Clara A, Checotah, OK, 26
      EIBING, Marie H, Galena, KS, 26, 803 Short St.; Georgia S, S, 6; Frank A, S, 2; Gertrude M, D, 1
      ELMORE, Mary, Brent, OK, 20

[ENOS, Carrie. See #21014]

      ERCHBACH, Mae Ora, San Bernardino, 665 Arrowhead Ave. CA, ?

      FARMER, William L, Checotah, OK, 24

SUPPLEMENTAL ROLL of
EASTERN CHEROKEES RESIDING WEST OF MISSISSIPPI RIVER.

Key: Guion Miller Application Number, Name, Address, Relation (to Head), Age in 1906.

[FIELDS, Cora W. See #24140]

    FITE, Houston B, Tahlequah, OK, 21
12519 FLYING, Linda A, Oglesby, OK, 10; Jessie J, ?, 8   By Rebecca Minew, Parent and Gdn.

[FREELAND, Martha C. See #2713]

    GENTRY, Kizzie, Tyrone, OK, 25; William F, S, 6; Henry L, S, 3; George D, S, 2
    GETTINGDOWN, Betsy, Stilwell, OK, 30; Holmes Simon, AdS, 13
44946 GILBERT, Dennis B, Muskogee, OK, 24
    GIRTY, Jacob, Porum, OK, 4   By Nancy Toney, Parent and Gdn.
    GOINS, Noble, Vian, OK, 26
24235 GRAVITT, Addie, Catoosa, OK, 17
24236 GRAVITT, Alice, Catoosa, OK, 19
    GRAVITT, Esther D, Catoosa, OK, 10   By Ella Gravitt, Gdn.
24234 GRAVITT, Eula, Catoosa, OK, 13   By Ella Gravitt, Gdn.
24237 GRAVITT, Lillie P, Catoosa, OK, 20
24239 GRAVITT, Luther O, Catoosa, OK, 23
    GREEN, Jennie M, Stilwell, OK, 20
    GRITTS, Daniel, Tahlequah, OK, 19; Charlie, Bro, 17; Cahnundeski, Sis, 15; Teesuyahkee, Sis, 11   By Sarah Gritts, Parent and Gdn.
    GRITTS, Florence, Braggs, OK, 21
    GUINN, Bell, Ahniwake, OK, 17

43630 HARLIN, James R, Quapaw, OK, 23
54588 HARLIN, Lewis S, Quapaw, OK, 30
28342 HARRISON, Susan E, Warner, OK, 28; Edward, S, 1
24285 HARTNESS, Josie, Tahlequah, OK, 14   By Octavia Hartness, Parent and Gdn.
    HEARTLY, Mary, Vian, OK, 30

[HEFLIN, Ada. See #23243]

    HENRY, Benjamin L, Claremore, OK, 18
    HENRY, Florence A, Claremore, OK, 16 [Deceased] By Eddie E. Rector, Adm.
20210 HENSON, Bessie, Vinita, OK, 14
    HIBBS, Maggie M, Estella, OK, 16; Sarah J, Sis, 14; Leona E, Sis, 11   By Mary A. Hibbs, Parent and Gdn.
    HILDEBRAND, Joe, Estella, OK, 26
    HILDEBRAND, Linda, Peggs, OK, 9; Rowe, Alice, Sis, 5   By C. C. Manus, Gdn.

[HILL, Louisa S. See #16432]

SUPPLEMENTAL ROLL of
EASTERN CHEROKEES RESIDING WEST OF MISSISSIPPI RIVER.

Key: Guion Miller Application Number, Name, Address, Relation (to Head), Age in 1906.

      HINES, Frank, Wann, OK, 22
15969 HINMAN, Vinita Frances, Las Animas, CO, D, 4 By Anna B. Hinman, Mother.
      HOGNER, Nancy, Stilwell, OK, 31

[HOLMES, Simon. See Roll #30600]   *(Note: Application number not given.)*

28312 HOOVERMALE, William, Pryor Creek, OK, 19 By Mary A. Hoovermale, Parent and Gdn.
      HORN, Narcie, Vian, OK, 8   By Bettie McCoy, Parent and Gdn.
24697 HOSEA, Tim, Locust Grove, OK, 25
17052 HOWELL, Juliette Smith, Ft. Gibson, OK, 23
23518 HUGHES, Icie V, Stilwell, OK, 1 By Theodocia Hughes, Parent and Gdn.

      ISAACS, Agent, Locust Grove, OK, 16 By Mary Sanders, Parent and Gdn.
      ISBELL, Charles T, Vinita, OK, 6; Harold Cleo, Bro, 3; Clifford LeRoy, Bro, 1 By Morris F. Isbell, Parent and Gdn.
24158 ISRAEL, Philip, Braggs, OK, 14; Mary or Nellie, (S?), 12 [Children of #12814 (John Israel)]

      JERNIGAN, Elde E, Madill, OK, 4 By Drusilla A. Jernigan, Mother and Gdn.

[JOHNSON, Alice R. See #31367]

1379 JOHNSON, Henry, Tahlequah, OK, 18 By Cicero Johnson, Father and Gdn.

22612 JOHNSON, Henry A, Tahlequah, OK, 15; Joseph F, Bro, 13; Charles P, Bro, 10 By Rebecca A. Johnson, Parent and Gdn.

[JONES, Charlie. See Roll #30564]   *(Note: Application number not given.)*

      JORDAN, Fary A, Glydeville, MO, 18
31410 JORDAN, John C, Muskogee, OK, 43; Herbert R, S, 12; Roy C, S, 10

[JOREE. (See) JOEREE and JESSON.]

      KEENER, Lizzie, Hulbert, OK, 26
16160½ KEYS, Levi, Porter, OK, 46; Carrie M, D, 16; Herbert G, S, 11; Carl L, S, 9; Cora E, D, 4
      KIDD, Crecie L, Warner, OK, 30
      KILLER, David, Marble City, OK, 8 By Sallie Walkingstick, Mother and Gdn.
32023 KIRKSEY, James F, Bower Mills, MO, 44; Charles P, S, 17; George W, S, 16; William T, S, 14; Jeffy F, S, 12; Fanny B, D, 10; Beula G, D, 5; Finis W, S, 2; Elton, S, 1
      KLEIN, Mary E, Ft. Smith, AR, 22

SUPPLEMENTAL ROLL of
EASTERN CHEROKEES RESIDING WEST OF MISSISSIPPI RIVER.

Key: Guion Miller Application Number, Name, Address, Relation (to Head), Age in 1906.

KNAPP, Clara E, Camas, WA, 21

[KNIPPENBERG, Mollie. See #11011]

KNOWLES, Ethel A, Tahlequah, OK, 16

[LACIE, Lizzie. See Roll #30576]   *(Note: Application number not given.)*

10748   LATTA, Mary F, Porum, OK, 12; Felix, Bro, 10; Samuel, ½ Bro, 3   By Felix Latte, Parent and Gdn.

[LENOIR, Thomas R. See #13206]

17676   LEPHEW, Charles C, Muskogee, OK, 5   By Robert E. Lephew, Parent and Gdn.
12830   LEWIS, Hettie, Chetopa, KS, 27; Grace E, D, 3; Ira A, D, 1
19190   LIZZARD, Dudie, Gritts, OK, 59
        LOCUST, Maggie, Tulsa, OK, 24
24841   LOVE, John Ella, Chelsea, OK, 23; Samuel Drake, S, 2
        LOWERY, Carrie M, Wann, OK, 25
13523   LYNCH, Ellen, Ft. Gibson, OK, 57

11287   McCAFFREE, Bradley D, Ramona, OK, 5; Barton A, Bro, 3; Laura V, Sis, 1   By Czarina V. McCaffree, Mother and Gdn.

        MANLEY, Minnie W, Claremore, OK, 23; Charles Lawrence, S, 3
11485   MARTIN, Daniel, Sallisaw, OK, 46
        MARTIN, Enos Q, Los Angeles, CA, 34; 1917½ E. 14th St.
43704   MARTIN, Harvey C, Banning, CA, 36
23787   MARTIN, Joysoline, Bluejacket, OK, 6; Mary E, D(sic), 5; Dorothy L, D(sic), 2   By Florence Martin, Parent and Gdn.
11662   MARTIN, Richard, Braggs, OK, 48; Octavia, D, 13; Sanford M, S, 8
11486   MARTIN, Thomas, Sallisaw, OK, 32; Lora, D, 7; Phronia, D, 3
22644   MARTIN, Walter A, Blunt, OK, 24
25594   MARTIN, William A.H, Braggs, OK, 21
44080   MARTIN, William W, San Bernardino, CA, 48
        MAYES, Mary L, Pryor Creek, OK, 29
        MAYFIELD, William W, Muldrow, OK, 14   By D. M. Patton, Gdn.
 5223   MEEK, William A, Vinita, OK, 26
 7580   MEIGS, James R, Park Hill, OK, 21 [Deceased.]   By Return R. Meigs, Parent and Gdn.

[MERCER, Etta M, See #32250]

44793   MILLER, Beatrice, Braggs, OK, 11;   By A. C. Collier, Gdn.

SUPPLEMENTAL ROLL of
EASTERN CHEROKEES RESIDING WEST OF MISSISSIPPI RIVER.

Key: Guion Miller Application Number, Name, Address, Relation (to Head), Age in 1906.

      MILLER, Cornelius B, Needmore, OK, 22
      MOATS, Bertha, Hulbert, OK, 15
      MOORE, Walter F, Pryor Creek, OK, 23
      MULKEY, James D, Warner, OK, 29
      MULKEY, Julia, Warner, OK, 35
13261 MURPHY, Lizzie, Marble, OK, 10   By James L. Murphy, Parent and Gdn.
27254 MURPHY, Thomas, Metory, OK, 43, Sallie, D, 16, Looney, S, 13, Jesse, S, 7, Thomas J, S, 1

      NELSON, Roxie D, Oolagah, OK, 28; Robbins, William O, S, 12; Alberty, Allen, S, 9

      OLDFIELD, Fannie, Kansas, OK, 25

      PALONE, Nona B, Lenapah, OK, 7   By Lacie R. Palone, Parent and Gdn.
25983 PARIS, Sirena, Braggs, OK, 17
24974 PARKS, Jennie B, Vinita, OK, 6   By Samuel F. Parks, Parent and Gdn.
44023 PARRIS, Mose, Rose, OK, 21
      PARTIN, Everett T, Oklahoma City, OK 1415 R. North Broadway, 7 By William T. Partin, Parent and Gdn.
      PAYNE, Valzie E, Lofton, LA, 25

[PENINGTON, Josephine. See #41797]

[PERDUE, Ada E. See Roll #30755]   *(Note: Application number not given.)*

[PERDUE, William H. See #30756]   *(Note: Application number not given.)*

      PHILLIPS, Jessie D, Baxter Springs, KS, 25; Volney, D, 5; Archie, S, 1
      PHILLIPS, Macajah H, Jr, Nowata, OK, 21
      POLSON, Martin, Coffeyville, KS, 9; Mattie, D, 6; Earl S, 5; John W, S, 3; Charley, S, 1   By Kellie Polson, Mother and Gdn.
      PRATHER, Elizabeth, Foyil, OK, 17
      PRATHER, George E, Claremore, OK, 19
      PRATHER, John E, Claremore, OK, 22 [Deceased]   By G. W. Spann, Adm.
      PRICE, Esther L, Uvalde, TX, 7; Bunyon M, Bro, 3 By David W. Price, Parent and Gdn.
      PUMPKIN, Betsy, Tahlequah, OK, 12; Sparrowhawk, Maggie, Sis, 7 By Annie Stopp Standingdeer, Mother

      RAMSEY, Rebecca, Tyrone, OK, 27
3649 RAPER, Harley, Durant, OK, 21 [Incompetent.]   By Berry Raper, Father
      RAPER, Margaret, Pryor Creek, OK, 10   By Vida Raper, Mother and Gdn.

[RIDER, Charlotte. See Roll #30567]   *(Note: Application number not given.)*

SUPPLEMENTAL ROLL of
EASTERN CHEROKEES RESIDING WEST OF MISSISSIPPI RIVER.

Key: Guion Miller Application Number, Name, Address, Relation (to Head), Age in 1906.

      ROACH, Thomas, Muskogee, OK, 27

[ROBBINS, William O. See Roll #30725]   *(Note: Application number not given.)*

      ROBINSON, Etta, Tulsa, OK, 31; Perdue, Ada E, D, 14; William H, S, 13
      RODGERS, Bettie, Braggs, OK, 16
      ROGERS, Charley, Braggs, OK, 18; Cynthia, Sis, 17; Laura, Sis, 16   By Missouri E. Rogers, Parent and Gdn.
15621 ROGERS, Frederic E, Claremore, OK, 22
15620 ROGERS, Iola, Claremore, OK, 41
      ROGERS, Lovely, Campbell, OK, 16   By William Rogers, Father and Gdn.
9178 ROGERS, Walter S, Claremore, OK, 35; Camille, D, 4; Kenneth S, S, 3

[ROOKER (or RUCKER), Josie. See #30655]

      ROSS, Jess, Coffeyville, KS, 26 [Deceased.]   By Maria Ross, Adm.

44945 ROSS, Maud W, Muskogee, OK, 32 438 North 13th St.
      ROSS, Sarah, Locust Grove, OK, 27

[ROWE, Alice. See #30631]   *(Note: Application number not given.)*

4055 RUNYON, Robert C, Ft. Gibson, OK, 3; Thomas J, Bro, 1   By Robert Runyon, Father

      SANDERS, James M, Stilwell, OK, 21
10715 SANDERS, Thomas D, Braggs, OK, 32
      SAWNEY, Columbus, Stilwell, OK, 51
      SCOBEY, Floyd L, Sapulpa, OK, 6
23468 SCOTT, Elizabeth F, Warner, OK, 18
9175 SEABOLT, James, Hanson, OK, 22
      SEABOLT, Sallie, Muldrow, OK, 32
26697 SIX, John W, Southwest City, MO, 16   By William H. Martin, Stepfather
34330 SMITH, Edwin B, Braggs, OK, 28
11424 SMITH, Elizabeth J, Braggs, OK, 51; Junie, S, 14; Jennie, D, 11

[SMITH, Juliette. See Roll #30634]   *(Note: Application number not given.)*

32096 SMITH, Juliette T, Braggs, OK, 24
32088 SMITH, Mae, Braggs, OK, 18

32097 SMITH, Mannie G, Braggs, OK, 21
19605 SMITH, Roach Young, Keefeton, OK, 14; Annie, Sis, 12; Jennie, Sis, 10 By Frank Smith, Gdn.
      SMITH, Samuel, Keefeton, OK, 16

SUPPLEMENTAL ROLL of
EASTERN CHEROKEES RESIDING WEST OF MISSISSIPPI RIVER.

Key: Guion Miller Application Number, Name, Address, Relation (to Head), Age in 1906.

        SMITH, Susan, Keefeton, OK, 16
42288 SMITH, Walter, Braggs, OK, 26
40066 SMITH, Wilson N, Braggs, OK, 22
        SPANN, Josephine, Claremore, OK, 14

[SPARROWHAWK, Maggie. See Roll #30749] *(Note: Application number not given.)*

        SPLITLOG, Myrtle, Grove, OK, 16
        SPRINGWATER, Pollie, Sallisaw, OK, 15

[STANDINGDEER, Annie Stop. See #21029]

        STARR, Lucinda, Grove, OK, 27
        STARR, Saphronia, Stilwell, OK, 43
4727 STEEL, Sarah, Ramona, OK, 23
16967 STEWART, Margaret A, Welch, OK, 31; James Austin, S, 8; John W, S, 6; Nancy J, D, 4; Land, S, 2
        STILL, Edward, Jr, Tahlequah, OK, 21
9762 STILL, Elias, Oktaha, OK, B of #16003 (Martha McDowell), 17   By Jane Still, Mother
20235 STILWELL, Sarah E, Cushing, OK, 25
5069½ STONE, Foster, Oolagah, OK, 19
24838 STRANGE, Mary B, Chelsea, OK, 28; Mary E, D, 12; John D, S, 8; Janie A, D, 6; Ella, D, 5; Lula, E, D, 2
        STROUP, Edward L, Inola, OK, 20
4873 STUDY, Polly, Southwest City, MO, 16
        SUNDAY, George, Porum, OK, 27
        SUNDAY, Izora, Porum, OK, 21
        SUNDAY, James, Porum, OK, 23
        SUWAT, Margaret, Honey Creek, OK, 20

43184 TAFT, Asa S, Roland, OK, 17; Nellie H, Sis, 16; Sherman W, Bro, 14; Stanley B, Bro, 10; Daniel E, Bro, 8   By J. J. Spencer, Gdn.
33484 TAFT, Austin K, Roland, OK, 21
33483 TAFT, Clarence A, Roland, OK, 25
        TALBERT, Arna, Newport, WA, 21
        TANNER, Nancy, Eucha, OK, 11; Peter, Bro, 10   By Leander Vann, Grandmother
        TAYLOR, Clinton Roger, McKay, OK, 3; Sequoyah Gordon, Bro, 2   By John Taylor, Parent and Gdn.

[TAYLOR, Lizzie. See #11780]

27496 THOMPSON, Laura, Valeda, KS, 9   By William E. Thompson, Parent and Gdn.
        THOMPSON, Lois, Taylor, TX, 22

SUPPLEMENTAL ROLL of
EASTERN CHEROKEES RESIDING WEST OF MISSISSIPPI RIVER.

Key: Guion Miller Application Number, Name, Address, Relation (to Head), Age in 1906.

8950½ THORNTON, Polly, Baron, OK, 27; Watt, Edna, D, 7

[TILLEY, Oma. See #27357]

    TONEY, Nancy, Porum, OK, 21

[TOOKAH. See #14099]

    TOONIGE, (No other name), Adair, OK, [Deceased]; 64 By J. E. Smith, Adm.
18540 TYNER, Amy E, St. Joe, AR, 12; Jesse, Bro, 10   By Nancy Tyner Scott, Gdn.
    TYNER, Daniel, N.F.H.C, Vian, OK, 36

    VANN, William, Lofton, LA, 22
    VICTOR, Delilah C, Tahlequah, OK, 37; Octa Lucile, D, 15; Fred Samuel, S, 13; James Y, S, 10; Sadoe, D, 9; Gladys, D, 7

    WAKEFIELD, Iva May, Bishop, CA, 26
34149 WALKABOUT, Henry, Jr, Tahlequah, OK, 23
36158 WALKABOUT, Joseph, Tahlequah, OK, 26
42689 WALKABOUT, Levi, Inola, OK, 20
    WATERS, Albert, Long, OK, 31
16194 WATSON, Homer, Vineyard, TX, 8   By Emma Crutchfield, Gdn.
    WATT, Charley, Baron, OK, 31

[WATT, Edna. See #8950½]

    WATT. Jennie, Baron, OK, 15
  8956 WATT, Rosa, Westville, OK, 2   By Nannie Watt, Gdn.
    WAYNE, John, Stilwell, OK, 25
    WEIR, Brack C, Vinita, OK, 21
11750 WELLS, Effie M, Inola, OK, 32   By Volnie E. Wells, Committee
    WESSON, George N, McKay, OK, 6; Virginia, Sis, 4; Wiley A, Bro, 1   By Catherine Wesson, Mother and Gdn.
    WHALEN, Eliza, Tahlequah, OK, 26
  1847 WHITMIRE, Roy C, Westville, OK, 6; Reginald H, Bro, 2   By Eli H. Whitmire, Father and Gdn.
    WHITNEY, Mack W, Adair, OK, 21
    WITT, Dee, Okoee, OK, 15   By William F. Witt, Gdn.
44280 WITT, William F, Vinita, OK, 37
25984 WOODS, Anna M, Braggs, OK, 24; Amos R, S, 4; Cornelius M. H, S, 1

[WOODS, Laura S. See #7876]

    WOODWARD, Viola, Braggs, OK, 32; Jennie, D ?, 1
    WRIGHT, Annie, Southwest City, MO, 30

SUPPLEMENTAL ROLL of
EASTERN CHEROKEES RESIDING WEST OF MISSISSIPPI RIVER.

Key: Guion Miller Application Number, Name, Address, Relation (to Head), Age in 1906.

[YOUNG, Amy. See #6689]

YOUNGBLOOD, Annie B, Kilgore, R.F.D. #4   TX, 28

THE FOLLOWING NAMES, ORIGINALLY ENROLLED AS ENTITLED TO PARTICIPATE IN THE FUND, ORDERED BY THE COURT OF CLAIMS TO BE STRICKEN FROM THE ROLL OF MAY 28, 1909.

Key: Guion Miller Application Number, Name, Address, Relation (to Head), Age in 1906.

31260 GOBLE, James, Albertville, AL, 21   [Duplicate]

15704 SMITH, Jessie, Cherokee, NC, 14; Mandy, ?, 11; Martha, ?, 10

3721 ADAIR, May E, Stilwell, OK, 17; George W, Bro, 15; Samuel W, Bro, 13; Lula E, Sis, 11; Lilly E, Sis, 8   [Duplicates]

41210 CHANDLER, William P, Tahlequah, OK, 35

28252 JORDAN, Felix R, Collinsville, OK, 17   [Duplicate]
36166 JORDAN, Mollie, Collinsville, OK, 15   [Duplicate]

37062 KRIGBAUM, James A, Coweta, OK, 7   [Duplicate]

12530 LOWERY, Susie, Muskogee, OK, 17; Elsie J, Sis, 14; Andrew, Bro, 12; Henry C, Bro, 7   [Duplicates]
12892 LYNCH, Nancy E, Bunch, OK, 1   [Duplicate]

13701 MABRY, Sallie B, Briertown, OK, 47

40048 RYAN, Emmett, Proctor, OK, 10; Calvin, ?, 8; William, ?, 5   [Duplicates]

34463 SCALES, Mattie, Flint, OK, 38; Grover, S, 17; Joseph, S, 15; Lillie, D, 12; Louisa, D, 10; George, S, 7; Ann L, D, 3; Mary E, D, 5/12
11862 SMITH, Lee, Braggs, OK, 17; Arch, Bro, 14; Mattie, Sis, 11   [Duplicates]
31995 STEWART, Celina K, Grove, OK, 60
31998 STEWART, George W, Bluejacket, OK, 24
31996 STEWART, John H, Bluejacket, OK, 34; Max, S, 6
31997 STEWART, William W, Grove, OK, 31
8233 SWEANEY, John T, Eugene, MO, 32
175 SWIMMER, Louisa, Rose, OK, 17   [Duplicate]

13564 VICTORY, Samuel, Collinsville, OK 19; Charles, Bro, 17; Susan, Sis, 15; Andrew, Bro, 13; Anna A, Sis, 10; Donney, Sis, 9; Tensy, Sis, 20 [Duplicates]

3005 WATERS, Polly, Cleveland, TN, 71
5011 WILLIAMS, Louisa, Tyro, KS, 55   [Duplicate]

Index

ADAIR
  Floyd 63
  Frankie M 95
  George W 157
  Lilly E 157
  Lula E 157
  May E 157
  Mintie 147
  Samuel W 157
ADAMS
  Arthur T 147
  Richard 61
ADKINSON, Ora B 147
AGENT, Sallie 147
AIMES, Myrtle 137
ALBERTY, Allen 147,152
ALEXANDER, Lewis 147
A-LI SE NI DE NEI xiii
ALLEN, Clarence 147
AMOS, Pansy Madeline 9
ANDERSON, John F 147
ANDOE, Nellie C 147
ANN .... xii,xiv
ARCHER
  Abram 147
  Anna B 147
  Fannie B 147
  Ina 147
  Otto B 147
  Thomas B, Jr 147
ARMSTRONG, Mary S 13
BAILEY, Josie 147
BALEW, Jennie 5
BALLARD, Randoloh 123
BARBER, Peggie 147
BARNETT
  Bertha M 147
  Sarah F 147
BARNEY, Cordelia 147
BARRY
  Billie B 147
  Kidder S 147
  Stella M 147
BASSETT
  Henry 147
  Nancy C 147
BATT
  Akie 147

Joseph 147
Lizzie 147
BEAMER, John 119
BEAN, Susan 147
BECK
  Arthur W 147
  Daniel S 147
  Grace P 147
  Sut R 147
BELL
  Charlotte 20
  Daniel H 147
  Irene 147
  James E, Jr 147
  Mark R 147
  Mattie M 147
  Pearl 147
BENDABOUT, Chas 57
BENGE
  Arthur 147
  Dooley 147
  Emmett 110
  Young 147
BETHEL, Clarence W 76
BEVEART, Lucie 38
BIBLE, George 4
BIGHAM
  Earl 147
  Edith 147
  James M 147
  Pearl 147
  Tolithia E 147
BIGHEART, Alice 147
BIRD
  Dave 119
  Eloise 24
  John 111
BISHOP, Fannie 147
BLACK FOX 27
BLACKBEAR, Nancy 147
BLACKBIRD, Wilson 26
BLAIR
  Jesse T 147
  Thomas W 147
BLOSSOM, Betsy 147
BLUE, Martha 135
BLUEBIRD, Elias 88
BLUEJACKET, Thomas 124

Index

BOWERS
   Ida 147
   Paul W 147
BOWLEY, Alton 2
BROWN
   Jesse B 96
   A L 27
BRYAN, Ida 103
BRYSON
   Mary J 147
   Williametta 147
BUNCH
   Eli 87
   Jennie 101
BURGESS, Garnet M 126
BURK, William R 97
BURKS, Elmer H 147
BURNS, Carrie 34
BURROWS, Annie E 148
BUSSEY, Emma B 96
BUSTER
   George 60
   Nellie 65
BUTCHER, Ollie 148
BUTLER
   Frank L 134
   Robert E 148
   Willie E 148
BUTTON
   Minnie 148
   Ruth 148
BUTZ, W B 61
BUZZARD, Eliza 102
BYERS, Annie 99
CABBAGEHEAD, Jennie 43
CABE
   Kate 148
   Marvin 148
CANUP, Harry T 118
CAPPS, Lillie May 127
CAPS, Sersis 148
CAREY
   Frances 11
   Sarah A 148
CARR
   Lillian May 148
   Mary L 148
   Ollie Ponder 148

   Vida 148
CHAIR, Mary 148
CHANDLER, William P 157
CHEWIE
   Lucy 86
   Sarah 40
   William 111
   Willie 148
CHRISTIE
   Angie M 139
   Stand 148
CHUWEE, Sam 136
CLAREMORE, Seabolt 59
CLAY, Henry 65
COBB, Ida 82
COCHRAN
   George 81
   Scott 148
COCKRUM, Lizzie 106
COFFMAN
   Earl S 148
   Jesse S 148
   Sequichie E 148
COLLIER
   A C 151
   Richard 148
COOK
   Henry N 5
   Susan 37
COOPER
   Claud D 17
   Joanna 52,53,54
CORDERY, David S 148
CORNSHUCKER, Lizzie 143
COTNER, John C 62
COUCH, Jesse T 148
COX, William Jerome 28
CRAIG
   Coleman 6
   Julie M 21
CRAMP, Johnson 2
CRAPOE, Lewis 51
CRAYTON, Oliver 3
CRIPPLE, Daniel 125
CRITTENDEN
   James 148
   Mary 148
   Walter S 148

Index

CROMWELL, Zeddie 36
CRUTCHFIELD, Emma 155
CUNNINGHAM, Howard 42
DA GI xii
    Aunt xiv
DA TLE VV SDA xiv
DA TLE VV SDO xii
DA TSV S xiv
DA YA xiii
DA YA NE .... xii,xiv
DANIELS, Ross 147
DAUGHERTY, Money 27
DAVID
    Lucy 148
    Nellie 148
DAVIS
    Mary 142
    W C xv
DEER-IN-WATER, Star 17
DEGE, Phillip S 148
DICK, Betsy 133
DIXON
    Francis M 148
    Ruby Mae 148
DOBBS, William R 119
DOBSON, Bonnie L 33
DOUTHITT, Cora E 148
DOVER, Augustus 139
DOWNING
    Charles 107
    Jesse 93
    Joe 77
    Mary 148
    Susie Bell 123
    Will 52
DUNCAN, Martha 147
DUNN, Luther Allen 100
EAGLE
    Annie 3
    John 3
EARLEY, Clara A 148
EATON, John E 70
EIBING
    Frank A 148
    Georgia S 148
    Gertrude M 148
    Marie H 148
ELLIS, Minnie 115

ELMORE, Mary 148
ENOS, Carrie 147,148
ERCHBACH, Mae Ora 148
EVANS, William A 26
FALLING, Car-na-noo-lis-kie 21
FARMER, William L 148
FENBURG, Alice C 96
FERGUSON, Allie E 51,53
FIELD, Moses D 91
FIELDS
    Ben O 127
    Cora W 149
FISHER, Steve 52
FITE, Houston B 149
FIXING, David 55
FLYING
    Jessie J 149
    Linda A 149
FODDER, Susanna 7
FOGG, Dick 29
FOREMAN
    Reuben 71
    William B 87
FOX, Lillie 135
FREDERICK, Sarah A 61
FREELAND, Martha C 149
FREEMAN, Peggy 35
FULLER, R C 88
GALCATCHER
    Emma 42
    Lilly 88
    Wesley 88
GALLOMORE, N C 39
GAR-WA-JI-YU-LAR 135
GEE KEE, Johnson xiii
GEES KEE, Johnson xii
GENTRY
    George D 149
    Henry L 149
    Kizzie 149
    William F 149
GETTINGDOWN, Betsy 149
GIBSON
    Clausine 111
    James 18
GILBERT, Dennis B 149
GIRTY
    Jacob 149

Index

Wilson 107
GLENN, Franklin 4
GOBLE, James 157
GOINGSLEEP, Nancy 74
GOINS
    Kena 9
    Noble 149
GOODEN, William 133
GOODRICH, Jack 66
GOSS, J C 7
GRAVITT
    Addie 149
    Alice 149
    Ella 149
    Esther D 149
    Eula 149
    Lillie P 149
    Luther O 149
GRAY
    Grace 125
    Thomas J 137
GREEN
    Arthur 66
    Jennie M 149
GRIFFITH, Martha H 26
GRITTS
    Cahnundeski 149
    Charlie 149
    Daniel 149
    Florence 149
    Sarah 149
    Teesuyahkee 149
GUESS, Victoria 64
GUINEYHEAD, Emma 73
GUINN, Bell 149
HALL, Eugene 104
HANEY, Roxie 29
HARDER, Williard H 114
HARDY, Mary A 23
HARLIN
    James R 149
    Lewis S 149
HARRIS
    Col J 122
    Joseph A 110
HARRISON
    Edward 149
    Susan E 149

HARTGRAVES, William 113
HARTNESS
    Josie 149
    Octavia 149
HAWKINS, John 58
HAYES, Charles J 130
HEARTLY, Mary 149
HEFLIN, Ada 149
HENDRICKS, Dave 80
HENRY
    Benjamin L 149
    Florence A 149
HENSON
    Bessie 149
    Lucy 82
HEREFORD, Blanche M 18
HEWING, Ruth 68
HIBBS
    Leona E 149
    Maggie M 149
    Mary A 149
    Sarah J 149
HICK, Walter 72
HIDER, Rachel 136
HILDEBRAND
    Joe 149
    Karlardee 64
    Linda 149
HILDERBRAND
    Na-ke 80
    Nettie 107
HILL, Louisa S 149
HINES, Frank 150
HINMAN
    Anna B 150
    Vinita Frances 150
HITCHER, Wilson 75
HOGAN, John Z 104
HOGNER, Nancy 150
HOGSHOOTER, Charlotte 28
HOLMES, Simon 149,150
HOOD, Susie 19
HOOPER, Rabbit 122
HOOVERMALE
    Mary A 150
    William 150
HOPPER, Martin 13
HORN

Index

Florence 68
George 136
Narcie 150
HORNER, Louis C 48
HORSEFLY, James 114
HOSEA, Tim 150
HOSEY, Mollie 100
HOSKIN, Mary Ann 127
HOUSEBERG, Lydia 111
HOWARD, Frank 78
HOWELL, Juliette Smith 150
HUGHES
    Icie V 150
    Theodocia 150
HULLY
    Jalum 21
    Webster 21
HUSTON, Ola 52
HUTCHINGS, Agnes P 74
HUTCHINS, Agnes 90
I TSU LA LV xii
ISAACS, Agent 150
ISBELL
    Charles T 150
    Clifford LeRoy 150
    Harold Cleo 150
    Morris F 150
ISRAEL
    John 150
    Mary 150
    Minnie 136
    Nellie 150
    Philip 150
JERNIGAN
    Drusilla A 150
    Elde E 150
JESSON 150
JOEREE 150
JOHNSON
    Alice R 150
    Charles P 150
    Cicero 150
    Dick xiv
    Henry 150
    Henry A 150
    Joseph F 150
    Rebecca A 94,150
    Ross 143

JONES, Charlie 148,150
JORDAN
    Fary A 150
    Felix R 157
    Herbert R 150
    John C 150
    Mollie 157
    Roy C 150
JOREE 150
JU-LO-DAH-DEH-GY, Lizzie 143
KEENER, Lizzie 150
KELLER, Willie W 106
KELLEY, Claude 88
KELLY, Edna 34
KEYS
    Carl L 150
    Carrie M 150
    Cora E 150
    Herbert G 150
    Levi 150
    Shelly 114
KIDD, Crecie L 150
KIDDY, George 62
KILLER, David 150
KINGFISHER, James 106
KINSLOW, Sarah 25
KIRKPATRICK, Lillian 130
KIRKSEY
    Beula G 150
    Charles P 150
    Elton 150
    Fanny B 150
    Finis W 150
    George W 150
    James F 150
    Jeffy F 150
    William T 150
KLEIN, Mary E 150
KNAPP, Clara E 151
KNIPPENBERG, Mollie 151
KNOWLES, Ethel A 151
KRIGBAUM, James A 157
LACIE, Lizzie 148,151
LACY, Starr 82
LAMBERT, John 36
LATTA
    Felix 151
    Mary 151

Index

Samuel 151
LATTE, Felix 151
LEACH, Che-arke 17
LEE, Julius P 65
LENOIR, Thomas R 151
LEPHEW
   Charles C 151
   Robert E 151
LEWIS
   Grace E 151
   Hettie 151
   Ira A 151
   Polly 135
   S R 8
LILLARD, Zack 15
LINDSEY, Jennie 93
LIZZARD, Didoe 151
LOCUST
   Lohn 148
   Maggie 151
LOVE
   John Ella 151
   Samuel Drake 151
LOWERY
   Andrew 157
   Carrie M 151
   Elsie J 157
   Henry C 157
   Susie 157
LOWREY, Susie 107
LYNCH
   Ellen 151
   Nancy E 157
MABRY, Sallie B 157
MANAHAN, Emma 68
MANLEY
   Charles Lawrence 151
   Minnie W 151
MANN, Bessie 115
MANUS
   C C 149
   Sallie 26
MARTIN
   Daniel 151
   Dorothy L 151
   Enos Q 151
   Florence 151
   Harvey C 151

Joysoline 151
Lora 151
Maqry E 151
Octavia 151
Phronia 151
Richard 151
Sanford M 151
Thomas 151
Walter A 151
William A H 151
William H 153
William W 151
MATHEWS, Madaline 2
MAYES
   Mary L 151
   William L 111
MAYFIELD
   Oscar H 70
   William W 151
MCCAFFREE
   Barton A 151
   Bradley D 151
   Czarina V 151
   Laura V 151
MCCLAIN, Mattie M 130
MCCLENATHAN, Julia 8
MCCONNELL, Wm E 55
MCCOY
   Alex 5
   Bettie 150
   Charley 110
MCDONALD, Theodore 114
MCDOWELL, Martha 154
MCENERY, Fred B 97
MCGLUE, Thomas M 66
MCKINSEY, Annie 58
MCLAUGHLIN, Wiliam 123
MCMULLENS, Minnie M 44
MEEK, William A 151
MEIGS
   James R 151
   Return R 151
MELTON, James 113
MERCER, Etta M 151
MILLER
   Beatrice 151
   Cornelius B 152
   Lizzie 58

Index

Ray F 134
William 70
Wm N 97
MILLS, Lizzie 58
MILO, Lizzie 86
MINEW, Rebecca 149
MOATS, Bertha 152
MOORE, Walter F 152
MULCARE, Mike 14
MULKEY
   James D 152
   Julia 152
MURPHY
   James L 152
   Jesse 152
   Lizzie 152
   Looney 152
   Sallie 152
   Thomas 152
   Thomas J 152
N TLU NO DO xii
NED, Nellie Josiah 57
NEE-DA-GUR-GAH 50
NEILSON, N L 40
NELSON, Roxie D 152
NEUGIN, Alice 6
NEWPORT, Jacob D 106
NIVENS, Helen Elizabeth 91
NUGIN, Alice 6
O'FIELD, Polly 77
OLDFIELD, Fannie 152
ORR, J W 33
PALONE
   Lacie R 152
   Nancy 110
   Nona B 152
PANN, Lewis 107
PANTHER, Josiah 138
PARCHMEAL, James 121
PARIS, Sirena 152
PARKS
   J T 107
   Jennie B 152
   Samuel F 152
PARNELL, Jesse 81
PARRIS, Mose 152
PARTIN
   Everett T 152

William T 152
PATTON, D M 151
PAYNE, Valzie E 152
PEAK
   Connell 90
   Lillie M 119
PENINGTON, Josephine 152
PENNINGTON, Malissa 111
PERDUE
   Ada E 152, 153
   William H 152
PHEASANT, Dick 69
PHILLIPS
   Archie 152
   Jessie D 152
   Macajah H, Jr 152
   Volney 152
   Willie L 5
POLAN, Ochelata 77
POLSON
   Charley 152
   Earl 152
   John W 152
   Kellie 152
   Martin 152
   Mattie 152
POTTS
   John 84
   Mary 84
   Richard 17
   Sallie 84
PRATHER
   Elizabeth 152
   George E 152
   John E 152
PRENTICE, Nevermore 104
PRICE
   Bunyon M 152
   David W 152
   Esther L 152
   Sarah L 25
PUMPKIN, Betsy 152
RAMSEY, Rebecca 152
RAPER
   Berry 152
   Harley 152
   Margaret 152
   Vida 152

RATCLIFF, Nannie 20
RATLIFF, Henry 18
RATTLER, Sar-da-gah 122
RATTLINGGOURD
    Jack 35
    Morgan 14
RATTLINGOURD, Judy 65
RAVEN
    Boney 64
    Mary 135,138
RECTOR, Eddie E 149
REED, Annie 48
RIDER
    Charlotte 148,152
    A J 97
    Sarah 148
RIDGE, Nellie 91
ROACH, Thomas 153
ROBBINS, William O 152,153
ROBINSON
    Etta 153
    Josie 3
    William H 153
RODGERS
    Bettie 153
    Nancy 148
ROGERS
    Camille 153
    Charley 153
    Cynthia 153
    Frederic E 153
    Iola 153
    Kenneth S 153
    Laura 153
    Lovely 153
    Missouri E 153
    Walter S 153
    William 153
ROOKER, Josie 153
ROOSTER, Maggie 73
ROSS
    Jess 153
    Maria 153
    Maud W 153
    Sarah 153
    William P 37
ROWE
    Alice 149,153

Felix 30
RUCKER, Josie 153
RUNYON
    Robert 153
    Robert C 153
    Thomas J 153
RUSH, Isabella 37
RUSHEN, Ella 46
RYAN
    Calvin 157
    Emmett 157
    William 157
SA LO LI
    Si qui tse xi
    U Cluh No Ta xiii
    U cluh no ta xiv
    U-cluh no ta xii
SAMUEL
    Carrie 66
    Charles F 66
SANDERS
    Elizabeth 79
    Harry L 61
    James M 153
    Jennie 67
    Jesse 72,81
    Mary 150
    Nellie 24
    Thomas D 153
SATTERWHITE, Elizabeth 18
SAUNDERS, Mary M 89
SAWNEY, Columbus 153
SCALES
    Ann L 157
    George 157
    Grover 157
    Joseph 157
    Lillie 157
    Louisa 157
    Mary E 157
    Mattie 157
SCOBEY, Floyd L 153
SCOTT
    Elizabeth F 153
    Nancy Tyner 155
SEABOLT
    James 153
    Sallie 153

Index

SEARS, Joel M 104
SIMERSON, John 116
SIMMS, Hannah 107
SIMPSON, George 65
SIMSON, John 116
SIX, John W 153
SLOAN, W R 25
SMILIN, Rachel 133
SMITH
   Annie 153
   Arch 157
   Charley 141
   Edwin B 153
   Elizabeth J 153
   Frank 153
   J E 155
   Jennie 153
   Jessie 157
   Jim 122
   Juliette 153
   Juliette T 153
   Junie 153
   Lee 157
   Love G 76
   Mae 153
   Mandy 157
   Mannie G 153
   Martha 157
   Mary 75
   Mattie 157
   Roach Young 153
   Robert 59
   Samuel 30,153
   Sarah M 58
   Susan 154
   Walter 154
   Wilson N 154
SNAKE, Betsy 27
SNELL, Youngbird 50
SPANIARD, Lizzie 24
SPANN
   G W 152
   Josphine 154
SPARROWHAWK, Maggie .. 152,154
SPEARS
   Mary J 48
   Walter 126
SPENCER, J J 154

SPLITLOG, Myrtle 154
SPRINGWATER
   Pollie 154
   Troy H 76
SPURLOCK
   Harden 1
   Louis 1
SQUIRREL, Sequichie .... xi,xv
STANDINGDEER
   Annie Stop 154
   Annie Stopp 152
   Nannie 40
STAR, Caleb 84
STARR
   Albert 22
   Lucinda 154
   Rena 68
   Saphronia 154
STEEL, Sarah 154
STELLE, Emma 22
STEWART
   Celina K 157
   George W 157
   James Austin 154
   John H 157
   John W 154
   Land 154
   Margaret A 154
   Max 157
   Nancy J 154
   William W 157
STILL
   Edward, Jr 154
   Elias 154
   Jane 154
STILWELL, Sarah E 154
STONE, Foster 154
STOUT, James R 127
STRANGE
   Ella 154
   Janie A 154
   John D 154
   Lula 154
   Mary B 154
   Mary E 154
STROUP, Edward L 154
STUDY, Polly 154
SUNDAY

Index

George 154
   Izora 154
   James 154
SUWAKE, Betsy 148
SUWAT, Margaret 154
SWEANEY, John T 157
SWIMMER, Louisa 157
TAFT
   Asa S 154
   Austin K 154
   Clarence A 154
   Daniel E 154
   Nellie H 154
   Sherman W 154
   Stanley B 154
TAGG, Soggie 21
TAHAY, Joe M 58
TALBERT, Arna 154
TANNER
   Nancy 154
   Peter 154
TAYLOR
   Clinton Roger 154
   John 154
   Lizzie 148, 154
   Sequoyah Gordon 154
TE-HEE, Charlie 58
TEHEE
   Elmira 114
   Susie 140
THOMASON, Wm H 97
THOMPSON
   Henry C 76
   Laura 154
   Lois 154
   William E 154
THORNTON, Polly 155
TIGER
   George 118
   Rachel 140
TILLEY, Oma 155
TITSWORTH, William E 105
TONEY
   Naency 149
   Nancy 155
TOOKAH 155
TOONIGE 155
TOWIE, Samuel 111

TUCKER, Mary 58
TYNER
   Amy E 155
   Daniel 155
   Jesse 155
U LI GV DA xii
U LV NE NV xiii
U LV NE NV xii
U TLU NO DA xiii
UNDERWOOD, Job 108
VANN
   Clem 108
   Leander 154
   William 155
VICTOR
   Delilah C 155
   Fred Samuel 155
   Gladys 155
   James Y 155
   Octa Lucile 155
   Sadoe 155
VICTORY
   Andrew 157
   Anna A 157
   Charles 157
   Donney 157
   Samuel 157
   Susan 157
   Tensy 157
WAKEFIELD, Iva May 155
WALDEN, Samuel 113
WALKABOUT
   Henry, Jr 155
   Joseph 155
   Levi 155
WALKER
   Bessie M 107
   Susannah 104
WALKINGSTICK
   Ezekiel 11
   Sallie 150
WARD, Annie 51
WATERS
   Albert 155
   Polly 157
WATSON, Homer 155
WATT
   Charley 155

Index

Edna 155
Jenie 155
Nannie 155
Rosa 155
WAYNE, John 155
WEBBER, Charlie 129
WEIR, Brack C 155
WELCH, Thomas S 120
WELLS
    Effie M 155
    Volnie E 155
WESSON
    Catherine 155
    George N 155
    Virginia 155
    Wiley A 155
WHALEN, Eliza 155
WHITEWATER, Geo 95
WHITMIRE
    Eli H 155
    Maud 115
    Ray C 155
    Reginald H 155
WHITNEY, Mack W 155
WICKLIFF, Sam 14
WILLIAMS
    Blanche 103
    Cornelia J 148
    Eli 117
    A J 125
    Louisa 157
    William P 87
WILLIS, Leander 41
WILLYARD, J H 116
WILSON
    Joe I 140
    John 52
    Watt 103
WINKELPLECK, Jane 32
WITT
    Dee 155
    William F 155
WOFFORD, Nona 9
WOLF, Ethel May 35
WOLFE, Eve 124
WOODALL, Beuna V 37
WOODS
    Amos R 155

Anna M 155
Cornelius M 155
Laura 155
WOODWARD
    Jennie 155
    Viola 155
WOOL, James 46
WRIGHT, Annie 155
YOUNG
    Amy 156
    Charles 136
    Lawrence 147
    Lydia 75
    Rufus 141
YOUNG DUCK, Mollie 49
YOUNGBLOOD, Annie B 156
YOUNGWOLF, Eliza 73

www.ingramcontent.com/pod-product-compliance
Lightning Source LLC
Chambersburg PA
CBHW020254030426
42336CB00010B/767